THE SNAKE, THE DRAGON AND THE TREE

Other books by John Layard

Stone Men of Malekula, London, Chatto & Windus, 1942

The Lady of the Hare, London, Faber and Faber, 1944

The Virgin Archetype: Two Essays (including *On Psychic Consciousness*), Zurich, Spring Publications, 1972

A Celtic Quest: Sexuality and Soul in Individuation. A depth-psychology study of *the Mabinogion* legend of Culhwch and Olwen, Zurich, Spring Publications, 1975

Selected articles

"Degree-Taking rites in South-West Bay, Malekula", *Journal of the Royal Anthropological Institute*, 58, London, 1928

"Der Mythos der Totenfahrt auf Malekula", *Eranos-Jahrbuch*, 5, Zurich. Rhein-Verlag, 1937. Revised and expanded version tr. Ralph Mannhein, *Spiritual Disciplines—Papers from the Eranos Yearbooks*, 4, "The Malekulan Journey of the Dead". London, Routledge; New York, Pantheon, 1960

"Incarnation and Instinct", *Guild of Pastoral Psychology*, Lecture No. 27, London, 1944

"Primitive Kinship as Mirrored in the Psychological Structure of Modern Man", *British Journal of Medical Psychology*, 20, London, 1944

"The Making of Man in Malekula", *Eranos-Jahrbuch*, 16, Zurich, Rhein-Verlag, 1945.

"The Role of the Sacrifice of Tusked Boars in Malekulan Religion and Social Organisation", *Actes du Congrès International des Sciences Anthropologiques et Ethnologiques*, II, Vienna, 1952. (Reprinted in *Harvest*, London, 1944, and *Ethnologica*, Vol. 2, 1955, pp.286-298)

"Boar Sacrifice (and Schizophrenia)", *Journal of Analytical Psychology*, 1/1, London, 195

"Identification with the Sacrificial Animal", *Eranos-Jahrbuch*, 24, Zurich, Rhein-Verlag, 1956

"Homo-Eroticism in Primitive Society as a Function of the Self", *The Journal of Analytical Psychology*, London IV/2, 1959; reprinted, Gerhard Adler, ed., *Current Trends in Analytical Psychology*, London, Tavistock, 1961

The Snake, the Dragon and the Tree:
An Analytical Case History
by
John Layard

Edited by Anne S. Bosch

Thanks and best wishes to you Shirley. Everyone is immediately impressed by your cover composition!

Anne S. Bosch

December 2009

Carisbrooke Press
2008

Order this book online at www.trafford.com
or email orders@trafford.com

Most Trafford titles are also available at major online book retailers.

Note for Librarians: A cataloguing record for this book is available from Library
and Archives Canada at www.collectionscanada.ca/amicus/index-e.html

Printed in Victoria, BC, Canada.

ISBN: 978-1-4251-8889-4

Library of Congress Control Number: 2009933630
Anne S. Bosch
    The snake, the dragon and the tree: an analytical case history / John Layard; editor: Anne S. Bosch
    Includes Biographical references and index.
        1. Jungian psychology -- Religious aspects --Christianity -- Case studies.
        2. Dream interpretation - Case studies.
        3. Jung, C.G.
        4. Dreams - Religious aspects - Case studies.
            BF175.5D74L39 2008
            154.6`3   2009 933630
        www.layardsmary.com

Cover Design: Shirley Chen

 www.trafford.com

North America & international
toll-free: 1 888 232 4444 (USA & Canada)
phone: 250 383 6864 ♦ fax: 812 355 0484

Table of Contents

List of Paintings

EARLY PAINTINGS

Illustrating visual hallucinations prior to analysis (between pages 14-15)

PAINTINGS

(between pages 42-43)

(between pages 134-135)

List of Figures

Foreword

In my encounter with John Layard's *Stone Men of Malekula*—some forty years ago—what first impressed itself upon me was a photograph (Plate VIII) picturing Layard recording in his notebook the tribal history narrated by an aged elder. This scene was the "intended" image—what Barthes calls the *studium* of a photograph. However, what stood out, what I was drawn to, what "punctured" my consciousness—and what Barthes calls the *punctum* of the photograph—was Layard's nose! It is a monumental nose. Here was a man of enormous intuition, a thought I dismissed as simple minded association of nose and intuition without significance, until, some 700 pages later, I came to the end of Layard's prodigious effort, and saw the last illustration (Figure 87). This picture shows Layard's informant scarifying her daughter's shoulder to preserve a memento of his visit with a mark the exact length of Layard's nose, his nose having been measured precisely with the aid of a dry pandanus leaf.

Scarified in my memory, Layard's nose became a permanent fixture in my psyche and came back vividly when Anne Bosch asked me to write a foreword to *The Snake, the Dragon and the Tree: An Analytical Psychology Case History*. I instantly agreed, partly because I have felt that Layard is one of the most undervalued and neglected voices in psychoanalytic history. Reading this "new" work—for it seems fresh and new even though written a half-century ago—has only strengthened my esteem for Layard. This is the story of his analysis of a young woman, "Mary," medically diagnosed as "mentally defective," a person one would not usually consider a candidate for depth psychological treatment. Yet, despite an impossibly impoverished childhood, raised in the confines of a rectory with a schizophrenic mother, several equally disturbed aunts, and a dysfunctional father, we witness Mary's dramatic recovery through the vehicle of her imaginal processes as expressed in dreams, fantasies, and paintings, all elucidated by Layard's penetrating understanding of the psyche and his capacity through "tough love" to engender the genuine healing of a deeply injured psyche. As a testament to the healing process, Mary went on to become a head nurse in a psychiatric hospital where she exhibited extraordinary sensitivity and relatedness to her charges.

This volume, like Layard's *The Lady of the Hare: Being A Study of the*

Healing Power of Dreams, is a significant contribution to the impoverished literature of case study in depth psychology. But more than this. This work truly is *interactive,* by which I mean not only the stunning richness of Layard's intended material, but the inevitable *puncta* the reader will experience in brooding on his profound text and gazing into Mary's primitively potent paintings. The reader will gain enormously by attending to and then tending the *unintended,* the numinous experiences this work has the power to engender. I encourage the reader, layman or professional, to go slow, to take time, to mull over the text, to gaze with agendaless vision into the paintings and the illustrations. Let the material in. Let it dwell within. I can't resist noting my memory of Layard's nose, because this volume's text and images are immensely psychoactive!

Layard is a fascinating figure in the history of psychoanalysis. Few, if any, have had the range of experience and passion he brings to his work. At the time when Jung was deep in his numinous encounters with psyche that formed the bedrock foundation of the analytical psychology to come, Layard was deep in the Islands of Melanesia, all alone with the Stone Age natives who had previously killed the missionary priest. There followed many bizarre twists and turns, analyses and trainings with Greer, Lane, Steckel, Wittles, Baynes, Adler and Jung; his writings (much still unpublished); his suicide attempts; his involvements with Auden and Isherwood and Ayerst; his training in child observation and development at the Davidson Clinic; marriage; deep affairs; a child who would become a famous economist and a British Lord. Layard aroused deep passions in everyone. He was greatly sought after as an analyst, and in this volume we can see why.

I can think of no one who combines the love of the work, the love of *all* the traditions of psychoanalysis, the love of patients in the manner we see laid out before us in this book. He is equally at home in all the psychoanalytic traditions and his work shows the fruit that such love of the opposites brings. He had an intuitive grasp of the essential aims of eros, to truly embody in the work, the spirit that animates the full potential of depth psychology.

This embodiment is evident in his analysis with Mary. He took her in to live and work in his household. When needed he gave her the physical contact she needed, including her sucking on his fingers, whereby he came to the realization that underneath Mary's incestuous wishes for her father lay the yearning for the mother's breast that had been so denied her. Layard argues that all pathology contains the cure and in explicating this, he distinguishes between "ego consciousness" and "psychic consciousness" and does not reduce the aim of development to a singular consciousness, but always consciousness as relationship between the two. This is a key idea and helps to make clear the meaning of Layard's most provocative assertions, many of which will turn some present day ideas upside down. Be prepared to be shaken not only by the visceral clarity of Layard's intuition, but by the extraordinary insights born in Mary's fantasies and stories, the progenitor being not Layard the external analyst, but Mary's internal analyst, the analyst of her psychic consciousness. Layard says that love without the critical faculty is blind, but the critical faculty without love to temper it is blinder still. Layard tells us that the truth will heal, however bad it is.

If you are new to what can be gleaned from the imagination through dreams and fantasies and paintings, then you are in for a treat. If you are a seasoned professional used to working in these ways, be prepared to learn something new on almost every page. Of particular value is the degree to which Layard's work reveals the spiral nature of the work through time, how later pictures reveal ever more fully what was inchoate in the earlier. This book truly is an education in psyche.

I would be remiss if I did not thank Anne Bosch for her most welcome invitation to write this foreword and for the opportunity to thank her for shepherding yet another of John Layard's masterpieces into print.

Russell Arthur Lockhart, Ph.D.
Everett, Washington
May 17, 2008

Preface

Terms and concepts extant in the body of knowledge known as Jungian psychology are used throughout, as well as personal intuitive insights of the author, Dr. John Layard (1891–1975). The glossary of Basic Jungian Terms will help those unfamiliar with these expressions.

Dr. Layard's fieldwork as an anthropologist took place in Vanuatu (formerly the New Hebrides, in the South Pacific), from 1914 to 1916. He witnessed first-hand the moiety system of community organisation in a band of Stone Age people. He was able to comprehend the significance of the incest taboo for the health of the community and for the human psyche. He understood that it was a development imprinted deep in human personality. Dr. Jung was appreciative of his scientific evidence in this respect.

Dr. Layard further prepared for his mission in life by training as a psychoanalyst in Zurich, London and Edinburgh. In the latter city he spent a year in the Davidson Clinic especially acquiring knowledge of the development of infants and children; in London this was rounded out through additional study and by discussions with colleagues who were child psychologists.

The Snake, the Dragon and the Tree is expressed in the unique language of the author. It contains information about the collective unconscious, and more specifically information about the personal unconscious. The latter amounts to all that is unknown to the individual's waking life——to her/his conscious awareness, ego consciousness, understanding of soul. This book deals, therefore, with one individual's non-ego energies, in this case Mary's complexes and their influence on her life—unaware as she had been of their existence. In such a situation where these energies are not consciously related to the Self, an individual may be one-sided or hardly able to function at all. She had been brought up in such an eccentric household that her psyche could not evolve normally.

Dr. Layard stresses that this does not amount to true human life. When such a situation happens in great numbers, society has ceased to be a nurturer of individuals; it is constricting and stunting them. In his *Introduction* Layard is concerned, therefore, with expansion of this young adult's ego consciousness and her understanding to a certain extent of operation of the Self.

Added to the accounts of her life and this series of dreams, are the author's expositions of allied symbols and councepts, which appear worldwide in various cultures and religions. Anthropological and theological material used this way in the methods of analytical psychology is termed amplication. [Jung, *The Structures and Dynamics of the Psyche*, gg 403, 404.] It is primarily concerned with archetypes, their nature, energies and significance.

Mary's Family Background and her Early Life

Mary was born circa 1925. She was the only child of the pastor of a small country parish in rural England and his invalid wife. The household consisted at its height of one male and seven females: Mary, her mother, her aunts Grace, Martha, Nellie and two more maiden aunts. These were from both sides of Mary's family. Aunt Martha took over the job of bringing up Mary, who was considered too delicate to go to school. Mary therefore became a sort of Cinderella in the household, running up and down stairs with trays of food for the two invalids, her mother and Aunt Grace, and emptying chamber pots. Mary was taught to read and write, however, by her father, Clarence, and spent time with him in the evenings in his study, including reading aloud to him.

At one time, in an abortive attempt to relieve the constriction of her surroundings, Mary decided to take up mediaeval exercises to encourage sainthood, such as wearing pebbles in her shoes to develop resistance to suffering. This practice was abandoned when she found that it did not improve her spirit.

Aunt Grace, sister to her father, played an important role in Mary's life. She had great imagination. Although confined to bed she was constantly inventing grand stories about living at a magnificent court and enjoying her life there. Mary engaged easily in these fantasies with her aunt and they were loving friends.

Mary's mother had been extremely attached to her own father, Frederick. Since he had expired and her own marriage had proved loveless, she wished above all for a male child. But her baby had been a girl and thus was largely unwanted. Although mostly bedridden, Mary's mother enjoyed playing her piano and was able to tend a standard-rose garden at the rectory. She was schizophrenic, however, and apparently suffered from chronic diarrhoea. Two of the aunts were also intermittently psychotic.

Clarence himself led a restricted life. He stayed mainly in the rectory, of which the front door was firmly locked. He preserved the illusion of a family clergyman but rarely received parishioners in his unusual household.

As well as being unschooled, Mary was not permitted to leave the rectory garden and thus developed no childhood friendships. When she was in her mid-teens, her father's sister Nellie, died of a heart attack. Mary had a waking vision of a "ghost man". This is shown in Paintings A, B and C. The positive, creative view of such a hallucination is that deeper, more natural psychic contents are attempting to communicate to ego consciousness—which is often restricted in its awareness—knowledge of a truth wider than what it at that point acknowledges. The vision at once fascinated and terrified her.

Mary subsequently developed tuberculosis and became confined to bed. At this period she experienced a vision of a "Death Woman" in blue who had come to carry her away (see Paintings D and E). In sketch E the Death Woman's robe is spangled with "diamonds" which turn out to be glistening ice flakes, symptomatic of the scatterings of coldness and death that were affecting Mary's spirit and body.

Fortunately her father, in an attempt to better care for her, moved his bed into Mary's room. His presence caused her to become intensely aware of her sexual interest in him, although no physical contact transpired. Dr. Layard points out that this awareness was a saving grace. Although psychologically and socially inappropriate, it banished the death urge — for Mary had been dying. The extreme interest or desire it involuntarily kindled in her body and psyche was sufficient to restore her to the life stream — however impermanently.

Several years later when both Mary's parents had died, she envisioned a face on a red curtain. This can be seen in Painting F: in the bottom left-hand corner is herself, lying on her bed, impotently bound and crucified. From Dr. Layard she was to learn that her release could come from more actively integrating the energy of the face and the red colour into her ego awareness.

Layard made a study running several generations back on both sides of Mary's family. They were country folk, many bearing Old Testament names. There were many instances of schizophrenia or tuberculosis, or both, among them. Mary herself contracted tuberculosis in her teens. The greater family ethos was continually struggling for physical and, more importantly, psychic health. Indeed, Dr. Layard points out that these illnesses were constantly calling attention to the imbalance of the family's psychic matrix.

Mary's family had been an elderly one. Her father passed away when Mary was 18 and her mother when she was 21. Mary had had to tend some of the aged aunts but was, essentially, a helpless, orphaned young woman. Fortunately, within a few years, she was taken in hand by John Layard. Medical authorities had classified her a "high-grade mental defective".

Mary lived in the Layard household for a time where she eventually acted as housekeeper. Dr. Layard knew the importance of body contact for one so undeveloped as she and professionally gave her physical contact appropriate for a very young child, encouraging a father-daughter relationship. This helped to form a psychological transference to fill the vacuum left after the deaths of her parents.

Dr. Layard apparently was able to follow to a certain extent Mary's life after she had completed the eight years of intermittent analysis which are chronicled here. We know that she became matron [head nurse] of a ward in a psychiatric hospital, indicating retrieval of at the very least a good deal of that natural intelligence and warm personality which her early years had failed to allow to unfold.

ASB

Acknowledgements

My greatest thanks are due to "Mary" for her generosity in allowing me to use the material incorporated in this book, a material so rich that many other volumes could have been written about it besides this one.

Thanks are due also to my wife for help in many practical ways at the beginning of Mary's analysis, and for help in getting the patient endless jobs, held down for a short time each, until she managed to fend for herself.

For help in the selection and arrangement of comparative material and in the discussion of some of Mary's dreams and fantasies I have to thank above all Dr. Lola Paulsen, who to my own female thinking has brought the maleness of a first class critical mind.

For secretarial work I have to thank John Millar for devoted patience in typing this and other manuscripts, and generally tidying things up.

The book could never have been written, however, without a generous grant from the Bollingen Foundation, and further financial assistance from Lord Marks.

I am grateful also to Professor C.G. Jung and others for permission to reproduce certain figures used in the amplification and explanation of the dreams and fantasies, as well as for theoretical considerations which are presented.

Finally, the genesis of the whole thing is the patient whose paintings form its background, who at first showed no interest in this writing, though she felt mildly flattered at being used, but in its latter stages has read it through to give her consent and to make sure that there are no factual mistakes.

JOHN LAYARD

Introduction

This book has a dual origin.

It began as part of a larger one dealing with the snake in mythology as symbolising a psychic function in men and women in its relation with the Tree of Life and the Tree of the Knowledge of Good and Evil in the familiar Genesis account. The two trees are one, seen from different angles, depending on what sort of knowledge one is seeking and how one uses it.

Its other origin is a case history of an unmarried woman whom we shall call "Mary". During treatment it was discovered quite by chance that Mary was able to express herself by painting in a simple but expressive way. The first painting she produced was of a dream (Painting 1) in which a green snake talked to her of food from underneath a fruit tree. This led to further paintings not only of dream scenes but also of what turned out to be a constant spate of fantasies which occupied most of her waking attention under a mask of extreme external vacancy.

Mary in her Garden of Eden

The parallel of her dream with the Genesis story could not be ignored. Although the setting and the conversation between Mary and the snake were both very different from what is recounted of Eve, the archetypal meaning was so similar that the individual differences could not disguise it. Even the garden was there. What in the Genesis story is called the Garden of Eden, which means paradise, was in her dream the walled rectory garden in which she had been brought up and, as only daughter of a father who doted on her and would not let her out of his sight, had almost never been allowed to leave. She had no friends, had never been to school, and had indeed thought of this garden as her paradise. Her parents had died by the time she was 21 and she was thrown out of it as a waif so unfitted for life that, by the time chance led her into analysis, she had already reached the stage of the drooping half-open mouth. The vagueness and vacancy of her look corresponded well to the vacancy of her mind with regard to most external happenings. She as so wrapped up in "father" who was "the perfect man", in fact the only man whom she had ever known, that this constituted an almost impenetrable bar-

1

rier to anything that went on outside. She was unable to keep the simplest jobs, which she had changed so constantly that she might soon have found herself in an institution of some kind, but for the chance that sent her into analysis—not having the faintest idea of what it would be.

Two things saved her: her fantasies, and the fact that these were recognized as having the importance that they had. After some eight years of hard but intermittent work, they were in the end joined to ego consciousness. So instead of draining her of psychic energy, which they were doing so long as she just thought of them as "fairy tales" having no connection with herself, they finally proved to be the most dynamic source of energy and self-knowledge. They were the chief contributors, along with the analytical transference, to her recovery. She is now a mental nurse with more than usual acumen and sympathy with other sufferers.

The dragon, snake and tree

The fantasies developed along many lines with unusually rich variety, but from the beginning both snakes and dragons had played their part, the dragons coming first and the snakes afterwards. The snake was usually connected with a tree or trees. These seemed somehow to be needed to balance the snake's activity with the tree's immovability, its being rooted to one spot. It took long years to find out what these various factors stood for in her psychology, which was by implication also their symbolic meaning in a more general sense.

By the time the stage was reached with which this book deals she had to her credit some 300 paintings of both dreams and fantasies, as well as some 1,000 recorded dreams. The latter had been dealt with together with the associations they brought up and the complex moods they reflected.

Mary's 40 paintings and images selected for reproduction in this book are some of those revolving around the theme of the snake, the dragon and the tree. Of these the first 14 were painted during the first seven years of alternately intensive and intermittent periods of analysis. This infrequency was owing to her incessant change of jobs and to her changing moods, in which she sometimes felt that she was not in need of analysis or was too occupied with coping with life to give the time or energy for it.

There came a time, however, when it was necessary to bring her back to earth by getting her to devote her next fortnight's holiday from the hospital where she worked to further work on her analysis. When the fortnight was over she said, "Now that's over. I'm analysed". Asked what she meant, she said, "You told me that I only needed another fortnight, and I should then be through, and well". I had of course said nothing of the kind, and it was a shock to her to realise how she had deceived herself by projecting her own thoughts so obviously onto me, who knew the contrary.

It was then that the fantasy "came" to her, seen in Painting 15, of the uprooted tree, uncertain in "its" mind whether it wanted to be rooted or whether it would not prefer to float up into a purple cloud that was conveniently above it. The purple cloud symbolised her own incestuous desires towards father and the idea that she was "analysed" and needed no further treatment: in fact had returned into "paradise". But the uprooted tree had seven green snakes spotted with red for roots, which wanted to "burrow into the ground" and so to re-root the tree. There was a scene of acute conflict about which of the two directions she herself wanted to take. In the end the conflict broke the illusion and she decided on further analysis on a more intensive and self-giving scale than she had hitherto been able to bring herself to risk. It was arranged that this should begin during another fortnight's holiday which she would apply for, during which time she painted Painting 16 of herself naked and red and slung up in mid-air by golden chains. This vision of herself brought home to her more than ever the need for more continuous analysis.

It was to this intensive period, which lasted for about five months, that Paintings 17 to 30 belong. It begins with the red-flecked green snake confined in a jar underground, accompanied by a small black tree, and with the mouth of the jar stopped by a huge black stone associated with father. It ended with a purple tree, now recognised as being herself, with an angry red snake issuing out of the tree-top and a purple snake growing in water from its roots—the red snake wanting "to meet the purple snake to relieve it of its loneliness".

Enough may have been said here to give a flavour of what is to come, and of the character of tree and snake as symbolising functions in her psychological make-up. For there are many clues indicating what they mean, not only for her personally but in world mythology. The tree symbolises that aspect of her that is indeed uprooted and needs rooting in mother earth. The snake symbolises the opposite dynamic principle of spirit and adventure, and "knows", for it also stands for the spirit of individuation as the growing point of her personality. Yet she must be rooted in something as an essential condition of growth if she is not to float back into the sky of unrelated fantasy.

The dragon, on the contrary, symbolises the principle of division that wishes to keep everything apart. It is the most complex of these three main aspects of her psychic structure. For while the snake has various characteristics it is basically a unity, as shown in Painting 29. Here the three snakes issuing from one side of her psychic body-image "instead of being three snakes with three separate sets of ideas . . . are three snakes all of one mind (her own words unwittingly describing the Trinity). The dragon on the contrary is always of two minds and is compulsively destructive (see Painting 24). Even the dragon, however, has the potentiality of becoming creative, not in a male way as the snake is but in a female way. Refer to Painting 14, in which it is seen to be pregnant of the philosophers' tree, or Painting 25, in which it is pregnant of two snakes.

Hysterical and schizoid symptoms complement one another.
Dragon and tree opposed. The snake reconciles.

In Painting 24 of the dragon overwhelming her the dragon is painted purple; at the same time it secretes a purple mist in which she is herself enveloped and paralysed. This mist symbolises one aspect of her inhibiting complex, the soft, female, helpless one which is hysterical. It is, or was, a constant feature in both dreams and fantasies. The other is symbolised by a thick layer of hard black "earth". In Painting 24 it is continuous, but is pierced in Paintings 19 and 23. The black earth represents the compensating hard, male fierce side of her, keeping her from contact with her own unconscious psychic forces, which are schizoid. Both opposite characteristics are to some extent always combined in the same personality. The stronger the one is externally, the stronger will be the other internally. The healing factor always lies on the side of hysteria, this being the womb-like aspect underlying the schizoid defence. Therefore it is that infantile side on which alone these defences can be resolved and the schizoid opposites reconciled.

4

In Mary's case the schizoid aspect was woven out of a tissue of compulsive lyings and evasions designed to conceal her real nature and to defend it from being seen, as she thought, by others. In effect, however, basically it concealed her split shadow from herself. The result was an enormous gap between her conscious thinking and her real feelings causing tremendous swings from one side to the other, each side concealing itself from the other and hating and fearing it. The hates and fears were naturally projected in paranoid suspicions and the certainty that the whole world was against her. Her schizoid aspect was symbolised by the dragon which, in her own personal mythology, was always cruel and destructive. It had the characteristic that it "leapt" from one place to another without any intermediate steps, ignoring all that lay between. This was her own description of its behaviour at a time when she was still unconscious of the fact that it described her own split attitude, lacking as she was a central consciousness of her ambivalence. The positive aspect of the dragon did not appear at this time in consciousness at all but was confined to painted fantasies of the pregnant dragon that have been mentioned. The snake and the tree, however, both symbolised what was directly opposite to the negative dragon, namely the tendency towards unity.

The main characteristic of the tree in this respect is that it cannot move. It can stay only where it is unless it gets uprooted, when it is lost and all possibility of security psychically dies. It does not act. It only *is*. It thus symbolises two aspects of infantility: its speechlessness, and its connection with the moist, mother earth from which it derives its sustenance. In other words the tree symbolises basic nature before the formation of a self-conscious ego.

The snake is like the tree in that it has a central trunk, but unlike it in that it is free-moving and also has no limbs. Limbs, like branches, project. In body imagery (the psyche symbolised by living matter, whether this is animal or vegetable) they literally symbolise psychological projections (see Paintings 21, 29, 30). The main symbolic characteristics of the snake in this respect are therefore, in an early stage of development, that it is free-moving and not imprisoned in earth (representing untransformed nature), though, crawling on its belly, it is in the closest touch with it. Having no limbs, it is symbolically also free from projections. It stands for the *principium individuationis*, the principle of individuation, of freedom from compulsions, and of the one-

5

pointedness of the individual. It is the liberator because it is uninfluenced by the illusions of ego consciousness, and it is not afraid. It can indeed divide itself up into two parts (as in Paintings 7 and 30), or into three-in-one (Painting 29), or into a multiplicity of snakes (Painting 6). It can fly (Paintings 7 and 28) as well as crawl. It can curl or rear upright (Paintings 8, 9, 17, 19, 20, 26 and 27). It can breathe air or water (Painting 30). It can be tortured (Paintings 22 and 27). It can be luminous (Painting 9). It can be gentle, and it can terrify, as Mary often avers. But, unlike the dragon which may be terrifying also but is "stupid", the snake is basically "wise", and symbolises psychic consciousness. It is the only animal that speaks. It is *logos*, and is of course phallic. At a later stage in this analysis, beyond the scope of this book, it gets attached to Mary's own body-image as a psychic phallus, giving it hermaphrodite characteristics.

It also rescues the uprooted tree from the destructive dragon (Paintings 24 and 28), and after almost perishing in its entanglement provides new roots for it in its own body by way of its mouth, symbolising another male-female union of opposites (Paintings 22 and 27).

Finally, it is the ultimate slayer of the dragon (the process starts in Paintings 26 and 27) and is also the impregnator for the birth of its own twin selves. An archetypal process of this kind which is produced in images is to some extent therapeutic by itself, the extent depending on the degree to which the mere perception of opposites can be linked up with real life experiences.

The tree and the dragon thus symbolise in Mary's psyche two opposite aspects of the feminine principle, the one static, rooted and growing, the other escapist. But the snake indicates the masculine principle. Of the two "movers", the dragon and the snake, the dragon is thus "female" and the snake "male". The dragon symbolises the maternal principle which gives birth but then tries to destroy by not letting go, lest the male principle assert itself to promote second birth. This the snake achieves by giving psychic value to the maternal, which, without the male, leads back only to death. For the male principle exists; however the female principle would deny it and claim "parthenogenesis". This means the power and right to destroy all males that the female has not itself engendered—and even its own unredeemed male progeny at times. It is a tenacious principle and requires persistent male energy to overcome it.

6

Ego consciousness and psychic consciousness

Psychological "masculinity" means psychic consciousness, "femininity" means psychic unconsciousness. Both terms refer to attitudes towards the dual nature of life; on the one hand there is the incest taboo instituted by the masculine principle for the sake of developing the psyche, on the other, femininity, symbolising unredeemed nature, which tries to ignore psychic development.

"Nature" refers to what comes "naturally", without effort and without any transforming frustration. Its catchword is what is "obvious" to any person concerned and indicates surface appearance and, to each individual, what comes to hand—namely the environment into which anyone is born. This may be in fact far from natural in terms of true nature, but it seems natural to one born in it; the infant has no criterion by which to judge its own development.

Mary had thus lived a living death in the illusory paradise of father's love. There she had replaced mother without knowing it, but this was "natural" to her. What thus "seems natural" lies at the root of what we are here calling any particular individual's ego consciousness. This varies with each individual and in different periods of each individual's life; it develops according to subsequent experiences and to the measure of understanding that has been acquired.

It may improve, or it may deteriorate. This depends on its relation to quite another factor, which has been called "the unconscious" (in opposition to what has been called "the conscious"). But these terms are most misleading. For, in the first place, what we call ego consciousness may, as we have seen, be far less conscious of reality than might be supposed. Much of it is compulsive, and in such circumstances as Mary was brought up in may be highly paranoid. It is composed partly of the individual's own psychic contents which struggle to break through the barrier of repression; but, since ego consciousness rejects them, these get projected on to other people, who are then thought to be persecutors or in other ways evil.

Even the most upright members of the community who uphold society and who may be its backbone are far less conscious than they think. They may be full of conventional assumptions which are a kind of rule-of-thumb

7

guide to everyday behaviour. These, however, often prove to be without any real validity in individual cases, and such guides may be really harmful. Those who hold them too rigidly may be quite unconscious of the harm they do. The term ego consciousness does not therefore in any way imply that what is thought or felt is true objectively. It may, in varying degree, be the contrary. What it does mean is what a person thinks he knows about himself, about others, and about the world around.

Secondly, the concept of "the unconscious" was evolved during the early days of depth psychology. It indicates such forces operating in us which clearly do not arise out of ego consciousness and by which the individual is driven as by forces stronger than itself. These were then little understood, so that the noncommittal term "unconscious" was used until such time as more might be known of them. Biologically some called them "drives", including instinctive urges such as those of hunger, sex, self-preservation and so on. Psychologically they were thought of as impulses, such as those for domination, love, etc. These were deemed allied to instincts in ways only vaguely understood.

What is undoubted is their power. It may be noted that the word "instinct" (from Latin *stinguere*, to prick; *instinguere*, to goad) is allied to "instigate", which indicates that the drives *instigate us*, not we them. From the point of view of ego consciousness alone we have to satisfy them as best we can and suffer insofar as we cannot. But ego consciousness by itself may not be a very reliable guide, for it is itself subject to all sorts of counter-drives.

Some of these seem to be under ego's control, as when we deliberately choose to inhibit some immediate desire so as to attain later some aim or satisfaction that may seem superior or more worthwhile. These help us to "distinguish" (another word allied to "instinct": Latin *distinguere*, to separate or mark out with pricks) between one kind of aim or satisfaction and another one. Thus we disidentify ourselves from the original drive to the extent that we imagine that we are no longer driven but that we drive ourselves—in fact are "masters of our fate". But some such inhibiting and so transforming mechanisms are certainly not under our control but on the contrary control us, and are our masters instead of we being theirs. These are what may be called "compulsions" or complexes of one kind or another. They have all the apparent force of instinct but are in fact directed not only against instinct but also against any satisfactory transformation of it. They leave us in fact more "driven" than by instinct itself, "tied up" in an entanglement of drives and counterdrives.

We then experience the original meaning of "instinct" as derived from "*stinguere*" with its meaning to stick, sting or prick—to goad in its most painful form, as being goaded by compulsions or "stung" by the "pricks" of a false conscience. Compulsions only too clearly operate against our own best interests and make us flounder all the more.

Such counterdrives were to the first investigators into the psychology of individuals so mysterious that they were classed as "unconscious" along with those very unconscious instincts which they at the same time combatted. There thus arose in Freud's mind the twin concepts of the id and the superego as two aspects of unconscious functioning. The id, a term covering all basic drives, was thought of as a kind of *prima materia* or basic principle from which all life-urges arise, with the superego as a secondary imposition on the id in human beings or social animals, whose instincts had been canalised and often reversed so as to serve society. (It is important to note that while the id or basic instincts appear unalterable and the force they represent is indestructible, the superego, tough and inflexible as it may sometimes be, is nevertheless subject to change, not only in societies but in individuals.)

Jung's terminology differs from Freud's in a useful way by distinguishing between what he calls the "collective unconscious", including what Freud calls the id, those instincts common to all humanity, and on the other hand the "personal unconscious", which is what each individual personally makes of these instincts as a result of the environment in which he is brought up. This is based on the infant's inevitable reactions to its environment at a time before the individual ego is formed and which, with modifications, are apt to last throughout its lifetime and form the basis of that individual's character.

But where Jung differs most profoundly from Freud (though not so profoundly as some make out) is in the concept of a third factor capable of reconciling these opposites: consciousness. Its development is believed to be the ultimate aim of life and of human existence in general. The solution of its "ills", if thus conceived, turns out to be not evils but opportunities.

This is what he has variously been called the "objective psyche" or the "autonomous psyche", which has the teleological function of transforming instinct (which drives) into spirit (which does not drive but leads).

As found in individuals we here propose to call this "psychic consciousness", so that the two main opposing forces in anyone's life may be thought of as follows: *ego consciousness*, including all that which ego is aware of or thinks it knows, and *psychic consciousness*, which is its opposite, comprising all that which ego consciousness does not perceive *directly*—and indeed often pits itself against. The indirect perceptions appear for example in images, dreams, visions, hunches and symptoms.

We need not choose here between Jung's view of the psyche and Freud's, since each has contributed to our knowledge of the structure of the psyche. Both are agreed that ego consciousness has somehow to be bypassed in order to arrive at some more basic truth. Freud uses the method of free association to bypass it and revive memories, in order to resolve complexes. This is a tool that no psychotherapist can neglect. But as all memories revolve around ego, however deeply they may go, there still remains a gap between ego consciousness and psychic consciousness—giving one-sided intellect too much play to feel itself superior and vaunt its own cleverness. Freud perceived this in his use of mythology in the formation of the Oedipus theory of unconscious incest, as envisaged from the male point of view. That Freud perceived this is borne out by his use of the Oedipus myth for his concept of unconscious incest. But he envisages the Oedipus complex only from the male point of view. He understood to some extent the meaning of the phallic snake, which will be investigated also in the following analysis, but the meaning of what is here symbolised by the dragon or the feminine principle remained in the background and not understood. This we know as he tells us with such candour in *Totem and Taboo* that he is at a loss to understand the meaning of the great maternal deities (Freud: *Totem and Taboo*, London, Kegan Paul, p. 247).

This is where Jung comes into the picture with his concept of the Dual Mother (see *Symbols of Transformation*, Chapter VII). Here duality is regarded not as an unfortunate or pathological ambivalence, as it is basically in the Freudian outlook, but as a fundamental characteristic of all human nature. This gives it not boundness but freedom, based on the incest taboo, which as Jung

10

emphasizes "created the self-conscious individual" (ibid. p.271). This theme is further elaborated in his later work *The Psychology of the Transference*[1] in which he quotes passages from my *The Incest Taboo and the Virgin Archetype*[2]. Both these works show how the kinship aspect of this phenomenon leads also to a psychic one and to the formation of the Self, the core of human existence. This is itself dual, containing in itself the opposites of *instinct* and of *instinct potentially transformed* as the *prima materia* of psychic life. By this is meant the distillation of basic instinctual emotions in the crucible of consciousness; no longer only ego consciousness, but ego consciousness joined to what we may now see is meant by psychic consciousness. This means ego's consciousness of its instinct, which thus ceases to be an unconscious drive compelling a person to do all sorts of acts and have feelings which may either overwhelm him or have to be repressed. The individual can then be at one with them because he understands them symbolically as well as actually. Ego can thus attain to a position in which it is neither "driven" nor "drives", but is a willing channel for the expression of the Self. It agrees with the Self and thus can serve it, as some hope they may serve God, or as an Easterner envisages some ultimate purpose, which he may only dimly understand but believes in and lives by.

It is this service which gives freedom, the only freedom that there is: freedom from compulsions and from the yet worse compulsion of having to repress. Beyond all these, and as a result of them, it confers freedom from judging either others or oneself in the negative sense of passionate disagreement. This latter is a passion quite as much as any sex passion can be, or the passion of hatred, or the passion to survive. For the battle for survival is over once this state is achieved—or even envisaged as a possibility—since there is no such thing as absolute achievement. The criterion for such things is never "what others do or think", which is the "dragon" aspect of compulsive life. It is rather what may be experienced in proportion as our understanding of the autonomous psyche increases. In Mary's mythology it is mediated by the "snake" symbolising a learning that can never cease, since what has to be learned is endless and immortal.

---

1. C.G. Jung, *The Practice of Psychotherapy*, CW Vol. 16, pp. 225 ff.
2. John Layard, 'The Incest Taboo and the Virgin Archetype', *Eranos-Jahrbuch* Vol. XII, 1945.

"Desolation" and its reward. Vocabulary of symbols

One of the indispensable predisposing conditions for the achievement of anything like the psychic balance or inner security that such learning brings, is its own opposite: the previous experience of desolation, which alone can teach that ego is not all. Ego can be all only if it allies itself to the greater "all", that psychic consciousness which understands duality. Otherwise it is a one-sided waif, wandering in unknown paths, uprooted and alone, without a guiding principle, disagreeing with its fate and thoroughly disgruntled. Ego then becomes a kind of "foreign body" in society; it becomes antisocial and hostile against itself. If psychic consciousness is denied expression, it will revenge itself by producing every kind of psychic or psychosomatic disorder. Such disorders are always symbolic and, if closely observed with the eye of faith that recognizes that psychic consciousness knows what it is doing, will teach us if we are teachable. If we are not, we shall succumb.

This book is an attempt to show at least one way of learning that worked. Mary found that a force quite unknown to her one-sided and torn ego consciousness took hold of her while she was painting. It had a symbolism of its own quite foreign to anything that she might think or even imagine in what she thought of as her "normal" moods—which were in fact highly abnormal. By giving herself up to this force while it gripped her, which, as she put it, "used her hands only to hold the brush and mix the paints" at its dictates, she gradually learned to give free play to the forms that came to her—that strange world of symbolic imagery whose own will was so different from her conscious one.

She would often start off with a blank sheet and "let the pictures come". To begin with, the three central motifs of the dragon, tree and snake (in that order) came to her simply as isolated and more or less unconnected fantasies. But as she gradually became more aware of what they symbolised and that they were expressions of her varying and (at first) chaotic emotions, there then grew up in her a whole personal mythology based on archetypal experience. By means of this she could begin to sort her reactions out to the extent that we could eventually refer to some given mood as a "dragon mood",

12

"snake mood" or a "tree mood". This gave us a vocabulary of symbols (there were others too) which were invaluable guides to discussion long before any formal psychological vocabulary could be used. They were of course much more dynamic for us to use.

Colours

As will be seen from this preliminary account, the colours that Mary sees and is compelled to paint are important. This is so much so that sometimes a fantasy-painting will begin only with a colour which "paints itself"; it uses her hand and brush as though they were its own, "in the shape it wants", and out of this the fantasy proceeds. The colours also symbolise psychic attitudes, such as the mood prevailing at the moment, so that we came to speak also of "purple moods" or "red moods" or "green moods" as the case might be. As the fantasy develops, other colours come, as different though cognate moods follow the first, giving the picture an emotional nucleus around which other emotions revolve. Sometimes these develop a scene originally envisaged, or sometimes contradict the first mood and its accompanying fantasy, always taking on shapes which help to clarify the meaning which psychic consciousness is trying to express. Thus both patient and analyst are assisted to understand the message it strives to convey. Consecutive fantasies sometimes use the same colours as previous ones but in quite different combinations, showing how her psyche moves in response to the last fantasy. She paints herself sometimes red and sometimes black, indicating in this way the point of view from which her psyche at that moment envisages things.

The parallels from alchemy and the worldwide individuation process

It has been said that this book has a dual origin. A third factor arose after the main analysis of these forty paintings had been made and typed out. It was the striking correspondence between the symbolical content of some of Mary's paintings and the alchemical representations of the philosopher's tree growing as a phallic extension out of Adam's body, and of the same tree growing out of Eve's head while she is contemplating a skull. Both these pictures are reproduced in Jung's book *Psychology and Alchemy*. During the course of

13

revision of my first manuscript, it became more and more apparent that there were many more correspondences between the alchemical opus and this modern girl's struggle to pierce and picture the obscurity of her psychic processes. Such parallels have now been inserted in the text.

JOHN LAYARD

14

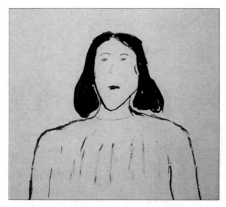

A. "Ghost Man": first attempt

B. "Ghost Man": second attempt

C. "Ghost Man": third attempt

I

D. "Death Woman"

F. "Life Woman"

E. "Death Woman": Second attempt

II

PAINTING 1 (DREAM) 14 OCTOBER 1951[3]

The Tree and the Speaking Snake

"Hands are too clean"

The first painting done during analysis was Painting 1 of an earlier dream scene (possibly c. 1948) in which Mary had found herself in the garden of the rectory in which for so many years she had been practically confined. This garden was partly enclosed by a wall. It was a high one built of red brick lengthened to the left by a lower extention of stone. In the dream she found herself facing this wall, but with the high and low parts the other way round, what had been on the right now being on the left, and what had been on the left now being on the right. This is a typical dream mechanism by means of which the autonomous psyche, or psychic consciousness, tries to show ego consciousness (the dreamer's waking self) that things are not what they seem, but may be the reverse.

There was in fact a plum tree at this spot in the rectory garden and she saw this plum tree in her dream, with at its base a snake rearing its head and very much alive, for it could speak. It had the form of a grass snake, though

---

3. The dates given with the paintings indicate the date of submission of each painting, not necessarily the date of the dream or fantasy itself.

15

very much bigger than any grass snake in external life, and it was green, in contrast to the brown tree-trunk, both colours being earthy ones.

Mary was trying to feed this snake with small cubes of white bread, but felt hurt and puzzled because the snake would not eat them. With the direct simplicity so typical of her, she asked the snake, "Why won't you eat my bread?" and he replied, "Because your hands have touched it".

This was a cryptic saying, like that of any oracle. Fears crossed my mind that this might mirror some notion that the host in the communion rite, which she was familiar with in its low church aspect as cubes of bread, might be too holy to be touched by sinful hands, with the corollary that sinners should not communicate and should be denied the means of salvation. Psychotics often "stick" at points like this, using them to block further analysis. But these fears were allayed by her reply to my question about what she thought it meant, when, after a long inward-looking pause, she asked,"Do you think it could be because my hands were too clean?"

Insight like this reached her at that early stage in the analysis only in connection with her dreams and fantasies. Some might think that this was directed against a conscious fear of masturbation or of touching herself. This does not seem to have been the case, however, for the effect of her Aunt Eileen's strictures on Mary viewing herself naked in the looking-glass at the age of about 10 or earlier was that of stimulating her natural and healthy interest in her own body in the form of secret masturbation. This she believes started at about that time, and of which she says that she was not personally ashamed. There may have been traces of unconscious guilt in that she did not stimulate herself by hand, which she had probably been told not to do, but found that wriggling her legs gave her the physical sensation and bodily awareness that she otherwise lacked. This was supplemented by manual rubbing at about the period of the ghost man, at the age of 16, but it did not continue long, as the leg wriggling gave her greater satisfaction. She went on with this up to the time of coming into analysis with no conscious guilt feelings so long as she was "not found out".

What the snake, symbolising psychic consciousness, meant by her hands being "too clean" cannot therefore be taken as indicating lack of consciousness of sex, which was highly developed in her almost agonizing awareness of her father's physical masculinity and her frustrated sexual desire for him.

It symbolised something much more subtly dangerous. For on the one hand even primitive peoples with ample opportunities for sexual intercourse may masturbate as a reaction against the incest taboo, this being a necessary evil of even the most elementary civilization. On the other hand, in our own civilization, a too great physical control based only upon fear sooner or later breaks down.

Parallel from *The Book of Job*

Rather, Mary's fault was, in her obscure way, more of the order of Job's who, over-confident in his own righteousness, used the same imagery when he cried to the Lord, "If I wash myself with snow water, and make my hands never so clean; yet shalt thou plunge me in the ditch" (Job 9:30-1). We may be reminded of Pilate who similarly "washed his hands" while protesting his innocence (Matt. 27:24), and of the Pharisees to whom Christ said "Now do ye Pharisees make clean the outside of the cup ... but your inward heart is full of ravening and wickedness" (Luke 11:39).

Job's sin is described in the beginning of the Book of Job as being that he "was perfect and upright ... and eschewed evil". Apart from the fact that no man is perfect, this sounds an excellent recommendation until we realize that the real evil was precisely that he was so righteous in his own eyes that he could not admit human weaknesses. Job is an archetypal figure whose name, according to Cruden [the 18th century biblical scholar[4]], means "he that weeps" or "cries" or "speaks out of an hollow place". Such hollow places are apt to be filled with secret pride. But Job had the good fortune to he visited by God's emissary, his initiating or "shadow" side, Satan, who deprived Job of all his goods, his cattle and his sons, and finally his health. This was so that he might at last look inward and find himself, and in the end be "doubled" by this self knowledge, symbolically expressed by his being given twice as many livestock as he had before (Job 1:3; 42:12).

Mary's sin was similar to Job's. She had "eschewed evil" in two ways: by

---

4. Alexander Cruden (1699-1770), *Complete Concordance to the Holy Scriptures of the Old and New Testament*, 1737.

17

in the first place ignoring her mother problem, and putting her trust only in father, so that she became mother's successful rival in her own eyes as well as mistress of his affections; and in the second place by hiding her sex desire from him in such a way that it proliferated quite unchecked, deprived of any overt expression, and gave rise to hidden hatreds that had become like cankers in her life.

Her concealments had led to a compulsive habit of telling such complicated lies that, often not able to remember what they had been and being too ashamed to own up to them, she found they made almost any relationship impossible. This was the case also with Job. One of his friends, bored by his evasions, burst out, "Should thy lies make men hold their peace? and when thou mockest, shall no man make thee ashamed? For thou hast said, My doctrine is pure, and I am clean in thine eyes. But oh that God would speak, and open his lips against thee; and that he would show thee the secrets of wisdom, that they are double to that which is!" (Job 11: 3-6). This refers to the solution which was in fact in store for Job, the adding of psychic consciousness to ego consciousness resulting from accepted suffering and the abandonment of self-regard—a boon granted at the end of Job's life when "the Lord gave Job twice as much as he had before" (Job 42:10).

It is the solution hoped for Mary too, and for any who have been so split as to be forced either to become stultified through a too great rigidity based on fear of self-knowledge, or to achieve that second awareness that comes of bringing hidden matter into the open and examining it rather than hiding it. One of Job's friends, exclaims, "What is man, that he should be clean? And he which is born of a woman, that he should be righteous? ... In prosperity the destroyer shall come upon him ... because he covereth his face with his fatness", in other words with incestuous self-satisfaction, "and he dwelleth in desolate cities, and in houses which no man inhabiteth, which are ready to become heaps". This accurately describes Mary's own state of desolation and homelessness, both inwardly and outwardly, when the enfolding but destructive anima of her father, whom she thought so perfect, was no longer there to rely on and be devoured by. For "he shall not be rich, neither shall his substance continue, neither shall he prolong the perfection thereof upon the earth" (Job 15: 14-29).

All this confirms what the snake was trying to convey to Mary about her "hands" being "too clean", referring to her view of herself as being too perfect an imitation of her father's "perfection". After the painting and interpretation of Painting 1 Mary slowly began to change, to become more human, less schizoidly self-centred. She now began to join her dreams and fantasies with new awakening powers of perception which had hitherto been locked up in fantasies for want of relationship, to think of them no longer as quite such unrelated "fairy tales", and to take some very small part in social life.

The plum tree as a symbol of psychic structure

One of the striking things about the tree in this painting is its peculiar shape, having two thick branches and almost no main trunk. If we envisage this as a genealogical tree, the two branches symbolise her own two origins in mother and father, but psychically they derive on the one hand from the mother's unrelated and thus unintegrated animus, and on the other hand from the father's equally unrelated and unintegrated anima, splitting her into two quite different and opposed ambivalent parts - the one which consciously hated her mother but secretly admired and copied her, the other which consciously loved her father but secretly defended herself against him.

The almost total lack of central trunk suggests that lack of centrally integrated personality resulting from such a schizoid make-up. But mother's animus and father's anima were in the case of Mary's parents both matriarchally possessive, so each of the two branches is thus symbolically feminine. The only male element tending towards consciousness is the snake at the base of the tree, introducing the self-critical element.

This view of Mary's schizoid psychic structure, bound as she was in two divergent directions, both matriarchally conditioned, is strongly reinforced by the choice of this particular tree by means of which the dream-world sought to enlighten her. For it was not a tree standing by itself like the cedar tree in the middle of the lawn of the rectory garden, which was her father's favourite and which she consciously identified with him. It was a plum tree bearing fruit, thus symbolising the archetypal mother with her potential breast-offerings, as all fruit trees and other food-bearing objects do. Fig. 1, published by Neumann, illustrates a limestone stele from the XVIII Dynasty of matrilineal

19

Figure 1. "Veneration of the Tree Goddess, Limestone stele, Egypt, XVIII Dynasty".

Egypt, in which the Tree as Mother offers a tray full of fruits and other foods in jars to two of her male and female devotees and at the same time blesses them with emanations from a jar held in her other hand, "the goddess as the tree that confers nourishment on souls"[5].

Mary had rejected her actual mother, as her mother had previously rejected her. Regarding her mother with distaste mixed with contempt, she thus cast motherhood away, suspecting it, and the dream tries to redeem the image of the good mother she had lacked. It is notable that, in the dialectic between psychic consciousness and ego consciousness which all dreams portray, while in this case psychic consciousness brings up the archetypal image of the tree, the dream presents to her a fruit tree that is in no way a special one. On the contrary it was rather despised, as being one of too many plum trees growing in the garden, the fruit of which Mary did not particularly like. She was in fact bored with plums because they had to be made into jam, an occupation she disliked, and there were so many of them that a great number had to be given away to villagers whom she also disliked. Further, this plum tree turned out on enquiry to be trained to the wall, thus symbolising her own lack of free will.

---

5. Egyptian Collection, August Kestner Museum, Hannover, Germany

All this was symbolic of her acknowledged attitude towards her mother. It was also her quite unconscious attitude towards her father's anima which, while adoring him, she at the same time trusted so little that she not only concealed her sex desire from him but also despised him in many ways which she never expressed but hid from him. For, if he mothered her, she also mothered him with a love based on shielding both herself and him from anything that might upset the false heaven in which she lived with him.

Plums were for Mary thus "rejected fruit", symbolising the rejected breast. For if the mother withholds in physical and emotional giving, the child reacts by not being able to receive, rejecting even what may be offered afterwards, or by others in compensation for the mother's withholding.

The serpent as symbol for incest and the incest taboo.

Split as Mary's psyche was into the two conflicting matriarchal "branches" of the mother-image and the father's anima, both of which lacked the necessary counterbalancing image of a good father, brother or husband, her psychic consciousness nevertheless threw up, under the influence of the analysis, the image of the snake as a possible integrating factor.

The serpent is a worldwide symbol for psychic unity, on the very deepest (lowest) and highest levels. It is phallic, but in its lack of differentiated features it is also symbolically feminine. This snake thus had in it the potentiality of uniting Mary's conflicting parental images, as well as ego with psychic consciousness. Being too good in her own eyes ever to acknowledge her lack of adult femininity, however, she did not like the common plums growing in the rectory garden, which actually symbolised "the garden of her soul".

Mary might not have recovered from her hidden physical obsession with her father if she had not had the good fortune to have a strong though equally hidden fantasy life. This the analysis stimulated her to foster rather than to repress, with a view to making it available for the purposes of transformation which the father had failed to serve. It was through this kind of encouragement that her psychic consciousness was able to pierce the thick hide of her self-deception and appear to her as the subtly speaking snake.

Mary in fact loved worms and snakes and all such creeping things, and slugs, which she would tenderly pick out from the cabbage leaves she was

Figure 2. Headless snake picked up by Mary on a path

preparing for dinner. One day she brought to me the headless body of a small snake which she had picked up on a path. Its head had been knocked off, and in one place the skin was torn off exposing the skeleton. It was no 'sloughed skin, but was the whole body of a snake minus its head. It was contorted in a way not usually seen in a live snake, and may explain certain Greek images of snakes being worshipped that are similarly twisted into strange shapes, such as the reliefs from the 4th century BC of Zeus as a snake.

This may help us to understand Mary's fascination for the dead snake picked up on the path, which she took home as a trophy to be put on her mantelpiece, where it remained for over a year.

The painting as a whole

Taking the painting as a whole, we may now be in a position better to appreciate Mary's psychic structure. Not only has the tree two main branches, but the whole picture is divided into two, the one side having a background of red brick, the other of grey stone. Thus dreams use objects in the material world as symbols for what they wish to convey.

The left-hand part symbolises her emotional life, which we have been here considering, the life of the senses and of conflict, that part of her which can grow and has the possibilities in it of change. All the colours in it are earth and vegetation colours, brick-red, brown, bluey-black for ripe fruit and grass-green for the snake, with the exception of the very cold green for the leaves which looks somewhat artificial, possibly symbolising the artificiality of her conscious thoughts, or at least those which she thought fit to utter, which were often of the most superficial and hidebound kind. Her tree of life is split. Its roots are not rooted in earth. She has forgotten to paint in the ground. But at the base of it the snake symbolises that living thing, the possible third function that has been stimulated by the analyst and by the analytical process, so that what was but "two" may become "three", with the third function acting as the integrating one.

The right-hand part of the painting symbolises, on the contrary, all that was "grey" and theoretical and barren connected with her father's restricted thinking and theological background, and with his abortive attempts at educating her, which had resulted only in the greatest inhibitions. So here there is a perfectly formal and lifeless trinitarian design shown in the stiff threefold flowering plant which was not even in the dream; nor did she mention it in her explanation about the painting, till, asked what it represented, she simply said that she had put it in as "decoration". This side of her, the ego conscious or the overt side, was so empty that in this painting it contained only matter about the Trinity that was as worthless as all the formal dogma and religious practices she had picked up, without having any idea of what they meant.

The dream thus painted was a deep initiating dream, the first notable one of many dreams in which the snake played a vital and illuminating role. But it was on such a deep level and in such general terms that, while it gave the analyst some picture of her psychic make-up and of her need, she had but little power at that time of linking it with ego consciousness. She did not dream of snakes again till she had had many further dreams and fantasies about the "tree" which is so often mythologically coupled with the snake, but does not speak and is less challenging.

Figure 3. Zeus as a snake. "The sacrifice to the snake deity. Bas relief from Boeotia. Attic, 4th cent. BC, Berlin." Jung, *Symbols of Transformation*, Pl. LVII

23

PAINTING 2 (WAKING FANTASY) 26 JANUARY 1952

The Girl, the Thistle and the Tree

1. Formation of an autonomous complex

More than a year after the dream about her conversation with the snake, during which time contact was being made with her by slow degrees, Mary had a waking fantasy which is included here as being one of two that were a revelation of the way in which an autonomous complex may arise, though at the time Mary herself was quite unaware of this. (The fantasy may have occurred c. 1949.)

She was so unaware that, even though this fantasy was all about herself, she had no notion that the unknown "girl" in it was her. The picture that she painted was of a girl sitting up in the air upon a giant thistle and holding in her hand a small leafy tree which she was looking at. To the right side of the thistle was an old dead tree while on the left there was a scythe and her description was:

"The tree is a very old one, and dead. But before it died it had dropped an acorn, which the girl had picked up, and it had grown into a small tree which she had in her hand. But she was so fascinated watching it grow that she was quite unaware that she had been sitting on a thistle which had grown up beneath her and had pushed her up into the air. But there is a scythe coming, which is going to cut the thistle down. The tree has fungi on it to show how old and dead it is. The bat is there just because I thought I'd like to put it in."

If we compare this painting with the left-hand side of Painting 1, which

24

symbolises the potentiality of "growth", we may observe that the central factor is here not the wise snake, but the thistle which has grown up without "the girl" noticing it, so that it "pushed her up into the air", into the realm of unrelated fantasy. In terms of parenthood, just as the snake symbolised psychic consciousness based on the father-principle, such as the father himself was so lacking in, so now in Painting 2 the thistle symbolises the very negative experience which Mary must have had of her actual mother, and of the mother-principle as she alas envisaged it.

She had sat on the thistle as on a mother's lap, so trustingly (as every child must begin with trust), but from her earliest infancy it had turned out to be the reverse of motherly, reflecting the mother's animus in its most negative aspect, having the quality of a hostile male. Like an instinct the consequent anti-instinct fear of life grew up in her, replacing the breast that should have suckled her by a kind of phallic monstrosity, which she inevitably reproduced in her own psyche, being propelled by it upward and away from her own feminine instinct with all the force borrowed from that instinct, which it thus counterfeited and almost destroyed. This "thistle" or prickly animus operated in opposition to the real instincts of her own life-force, making her so bitter inwardly that her attitude towards life had become largely negative, fearful and hostilely defensive. This was under a cloak of innocent mildness that would not hurt a fly—though internally she was a mass of self-destruction and of paranoid suspicion of the world.

The first thing to be noted therefore is the unconscious nature of the growth of the complex, showing how, if the fear of life sets in early enough during infancy before ego consciousness has developed sufficiently to cope with it, it joins itself to the collective unconscious. It thus grows up with all the qualities of instinct, so that the desire for life and the fear of it are almost indistinguishable.

THREEFOLD STRUCTURE

The thistle and the snake. The mother problem.

Negative as the thistle at first sight seems, nevertheless it has in it all the potentialities of a revelation if we can understand the message which its structure conveys. For the thistle in this painting is structurally composed of three

25

parts, which correspond to the barren right-hand three-fold flowering plant in Painting 1. That trinitarian plant was unrelated to the dream and put in only as an afterthought. But the thistle in Painting 2 is a vital feature of the fantasy. Its three-ness is here differentiated into two huge prickly leaves, having between them an equally prickly central stem, leading to the purple flower on which the girl sits, contemplating the small tree in her hand.

This small tree is held in her left hand, which is symbolically by no means so "clean" as her right hand which fed the snake, since it includes the knowledge of her incestuous desires as well as of the "fairy tales" she told herself (but hid from her father, fearing that he would disapprove of them). These fantasies, including the sexual ones, were now coming into the open in the analysis, which had robbed them of their total secrecy and of the shame that went with it.

The thistle contrasts with the snake in that Mary likes snakes and worms and slugs and all manner of creepy-crawly things, which are all phallic symbols in her fantasy, but dislikes thistles which have no "love" in them. This thistle symbolises not only the mother but the whole frustration of her life, including her own self-frustration which had grown up in automatic response to her mother's hatred and neglect of her. But the acceptance of aridity was the precursor of her subsequent fecundity.

From this point of view, the whole painting can be envisaged as a kind of prophetic vision symbolising both past and future events, beginning with the thistle itself on which she sits, representing the negative experiences she had as an infant with her mother. In the dream illustrated in Painting 1, the snake was vocal and it spoke, because it stood for the word as representing psychic consciousness connected with the father-principle. But, in terms of the dragons later infesting her fantasies, the whole thistle might be thought of as a dragon's mouth with its two jaws. The two "jaws" are the toothed leaves, representing the *vagina dentata*, ready at any moment to close in and to devour her.

These show the mother in her most destructive aspect, and at the same time the split in Mary herself, unconsciously identified with the mother's schizoid personality, at one time feeling superior and at another inferior.

The stiff central stem may be thought of as the mother's negative animus, and thus also the daughter's animus, which could deceive but also could

26

illuminate. For it will be noted that the hostile phallic thistle stem adumbrating her superego unrelatedness and the small tree indicating her psychic perception (though it is still wrapped up in fantasy) are directly in line.

The colour purple symbolises incestuous desire

But the small tree here is too high up, indicating how unrelated Mary's rich fantasy life was to the realities of her drab external life. The clue both to the reason for this divorce and to the means of its eventual healing lies in the purple colour of the thistle-head and of the unknown "girl" symbolising the unknown part of Mary herself. The colour purple is a disturbing one. When it appears in dreams it is always a warning colour which the dreamer or the psychotherapist should not ignore. It invariably indicates the presence of a hidden and basically incestuous complex which may give rise to a psychosis if it is not made conscious and then understood.

Psychosis indicates a truth which has been totally repressed, expressed in this painting by the fact that Mary did not so much as suspect that the girl clothed in purple sitting on the purple flower was really herself appearing as the potentially psychotic part of her of which she as quite unaware. The basis of psychosis is lack of psychic separation between the parent and the child.

To illustrate this briefly from another angle we may here cite the instance of a wealthy mother with a so-called "perfect" daughter who was said to be highly intelligent and to "tell her mother everything". One day a young woman acquaintance confided bitterly to the mother how her own mother had insisted on her confiding everything to her and had thus stultified her life. The mother of the girl had an internal crisis in which she had the momentary insight to ask herself "Am I doing the same to my daughter?" But she immediately repressed this insight and said "No!" Soon afterwards the daughter died of a mysterious disease which the doctors were unable to diagnose. The mother felt desperate, and went for comfort to see a friend. The friend was out, but in her room the mother saw a purple scarf which she felt compelled to steal, and then when she got home to tear to bits. She had no idea why she did this, knowing only that she first was fascinated by it and then loathed it. This was the beginning of a severe nervous breakdown.

A man once saw in a dream two purple patches on a lake. Not knowing what these meant, he plunged enthusiastically into a relationship with the girl-friend of a man whom he admired and also depended on. The result for him was a temporary but disastrous loss of soul and of the friendship of them both.

But the deep upheaval indicated by the colour purple may equally lead to the reverse of potential disaster: the transformation of a pathological situation into a healthy one. Such is the story of this book, in which the colour purple, occurring frequently in Mary's fantasies, gradually changes its significance.

Purple thistle

The toughness of the problem is well illustrated by a vivid story of Tolstoy's in which the motif of psychological incest is typified by the fierce cohesion of a primitive Caucasian tribe with all its heroism and its feuds resisting more civilised advance. The hero, one of the tribesmen, is likened to a purple thistle in full bloom of a kind called "Tartar" which is never scythed, or if it is accidentally cut the mowers throw it out of the hay to save pricking their hands on it. Tolstoy symbolically describes how he once tried to pick such a thistle, in which a bumble-bee was fast asleep in the heart of the purple flower. "But it proved obdurate; the stem was surrounded with prickles, ... it was so frightfully strong that I struggled with it for a good five minutes, breaking the fibres one by one. When I finally plucked the flower ... I regretted that I had foolishly spoilt a flower that looked fine where it stood.... How desperately it defended its life."[6]

The prickliness of the thistle, its wildness and beauty but its enmity to men as tillers of the soil and its determination not to die but to defend itself, the mention of the scythe, and of the bumble-bee drunk with the nectar of the purple flower, nestling in it and so almost identified with it as was the girl in Mary's fantasy, may all remind us of the self-defensiveness of the complex which it revealed. The similarity to Mary's fantasy does not end here, for he describes another purple thistle which "had three branches. One was broken off, and the surviving part stuck up like the stump of a severed arm.... The whole plant had

---

6. Leo Tolstoy: *Hadji Murata; A Tale of the Caucasus.* Tr. W.G. Carey. London, Heinemann, 1962, pp. 7-9.

evidently been crushed by the plough-wheel and it had sprung up again crooked but standing …, it still looked defiant…." Tolstoy exclaims, "What energy". But it was an energy doomed to defeat like the Caucasian hero: for "the doomed tribesman, encircled and at last mortally wounded, … fell full length, *like a scythed thistle*, onto his face…."[7] (my italics).

In this example the purple of the thistle symbolises almost unconquerable and "prickly" pride: the pride of a primitive force (like Mary's incestuous desire) battling against a more civilised and conscious form of life to which, however, it must in the end be sacrificed.

Conscious and unconscious sacrifice.

Sacrifice is an important aspect of the meaning of "purple". When the soldiers scourged and mocked Jesus before his crucifixion they dressed him in a purple robe. Elsewhere in the Bible purple is associated with suffering symbolised by the purple grapes that are crushed to make wine as in the Messianic prophecy: "I have trodden the winepress alone; and of the people there was none with me" (Isaiah 63:3).

Purple can thus symbolise pride and power, or exactly the opposite, suffering and humiliation; for colours, like other things when they are used as archetypal images, combine opposites in their meanings. As a pigment purple is a mixture of red and blue, standing for another pair of opposites: on one level red for passion and blue (the colour of the sky) for unattainability; or alternatively red for instinct and blue for spirit. Purple can symbolise on the one hand, as it did in Mary's case at the beginning of analysis, a state of psychological incest in the sense of a frustrated infantile incestuous desire of an undifferentiated and chaotic kind, based on unconsciousness and shame and fear. Instinct and spirit had merged and been unable to crystallize out into two streams.

(Again, there is another somewhat tangential use of the two colours red and blue as separated out in the traditional colours of the Virgin Mary's robes. The outer one is painted blue representing her symbolic virginity, but the inner is red stressing the warmth of love, self-giving and of all-protecting

---

7. Ibid, p. 195.

motherhood. The combination of these two separated colours indicates renunciation of personal desire for the sake of the resulting spiritual benefit.)

This is the opposite of what Mary up to that time had done, being consumed by desires, which she did not know how to satisfy, and so became a prey to them. Pebbles put in her shoes had not transformed these earthly longings but simply repressed them and caused inner fury, so that the psychic "garment" which she wore had just the opposite effectæthe red turning to anger and the blue to impotence, lack of relatedness, and a frustrated hiding from the world. The two reactions, mixed, not separated out, gave rise in Mary's colour symbolism not only to the purple in her fantasy paintings but also to her predilection for purple in such things as the scarves she wore. This could perhaps be traced back to the purple velvet chiffons which in Aunt Grace's world of fantasy her princesses and duchesses wore streaming from their hair.

Just as there are two opposite meanings for red and blue, so are there two opposite meanings inherent in the purple in which both are mixed. There are the grapes and the crushed grapes. There is the body and the soul. In the bisexuality of the human psyche, soul is feminine, and femininity has to be pierced if it is to become pregnant. Matriarchal possessiveness must be exposed for what it is, inimical to psychic growth. It must therefore be crushed like the grape, for the inner truth to be allowed to flow from it in the form of saving grace, the purple wine, the blood of sacrifice. And so liturgically purple becomes the penitential colour, used during Advent and the forty days of Lent (except for Maundy Thursday) which culminate in Good Friday (for which the colour used to be purple but is now black). During Passion Week all images are draped in purple, and it is the colour also for vestments.

In imitation of (or in identification with) the purple garment put upon Jesus before being crucified, purple is the colour worn discreetly by bishops, and less discreetly by archbishops whose whole cassocks may be of this purple colour. This has now become a mark of distinction, but it is only so because it was originally an indication of self-sacrifice. Its use as a symbol for magnificence when worn by royalty, though it has now become purely secular, is derived from the era of priest-kings when the king was the supreme sacrificial personage. And this in turn means that he was regarded as divine, in this respect above the law. This was exemplified perhaps above all by the

30

fact that such divine kings often (as in ancient Egypt) married their sisters, which was forbidden to more ordinary folk. Marriages of this kind were "sacred marriages", so that the incest motive is here sanctified.

The paradox is thus a flagrant one. As the divine king unites himself with his sister, so the saint does with his anima or soul in a symbolic marriage (*hierosgamos*) which in the physical analogy involves the breaking of the hymen and the flowing of the blood, the blood of sacrifice which in this case has the meaning of self-sacrifice: the "giving up" or yielding of the soul to higher influence through the abandonment of its hidden possessiveness commonly called its "pride" (which necessarily includes the "fear" of losing it). The inner virginity thus pierced becomes the mother of a new release of psychic energy. The nun becomes the bride of Christ. The man's anima is fertilised. Possessive love turns into unpossessive love.

But there are many dangers on this path, the greatest of which is unconsciousness. Unconsciousness of sexuality means being negatively bound to it, in bitterness or in self-righteousness. Mary's paintings have so much purple in them in the first place because she was still so incestuously inclined, and in the second place because her psychic consciousness was striving to bring the incestuousness to the attention of her ego consciousness by means of her fantasies which, like dreams, convey their own message and thus can be interpreted.

Purple in Goethe's Theory of Colours

The meaning of purple is further illustrated by "Goethe's Theory of Colours"[8], written in opposition to Newton's theory that colour is only split-up white light. Goethe's experiments proved to his satisfaction that colour is, on the contrary, formed by a mingling of darkness and of light. He takes as his analogy what he refers to as the "semi-transparent" composition of the atmosphere surrounding the earth from which the sky at night looks black. The opposite to the blackness of the sky is the intense white light emanating from the sun. These are the basic principles of darkness and of light, which

---

8. *Goethe's Theory of Colours*. Tr. from the German with notes by Charles Lock Eastlake, London, John Murray, 1840.

interact in such a way that during the daytime the white light reflected by the atmospheric particles makes the black sky look blue, while the same atmospheric particles interposed between us and the sun make the white light of the sun look yellow, deepening to orange and to red. The thicker the atmospheric layer (as at dawn and dusk), the redder the sun appears to be. The sun appears as red also at noon to divers at the bottom of the sea, owing to the opaqueness of the water it shines through. These colours in Goethe's view are thus due to what he refers to as the imperfectly transparent nature of the atmosphere, or its "impurities". The colour blue which is so beautiful may thus be thought of as a lighter form of black, while the yellow colour of the sun as we see it might equally be thought of as a "dirty white".

The nature of the atmosphere of this our earth thus modifies the archetypal opposites of black and white to produce the colours that delight the eye and give such infinite variety to life. So human nature also modifies the opposites of light (or white) and darkness (black) which are used so constantly to symbolise consciousness and unconsciousness, male and female, good and evil and so on.

In Goethe's theory there are two series of colours, the one starting from light, the other starting from black. The white series goes through the transformation from yellow (usually an "innocent" colour) and orange, which is a bit more disturbing, to scarlet which is more disturbing still, as in the symbolism of the "scarlet woman" or "red rag to a bull". This is the extravert series. The introvert series starting with black proceeds through blue (another "innocent" or idealistic colour) to mauve, which is already slightly disturbing, and then to purple which is more disturbing still. In colour symbolism it indicates either an approaching psychosis or, as its opposite, the self-realisation resulting from the understanding of the threatened psychosis. In this way it can be transformed into enlightenment. In Painting 2 the colour purple both *cuts off* and *mediates*.

One of the products of this contrast between the extravert and introvert series of colours is to be seen in Mary's Painting 30. It is a fantasy she had six and a half years later, when her treatment was further advanced, in which a bright red snake symbolising her thwarted anger, passion and desire is striving to meet a purple snake standing for the greater awareness she had by then achieved.

32

Although, as we have seen, Mary's incestuous desire was towards her father, it is in all cases originally directed towards the mother, as the inevitable longing and need of the child for its mother's breast and for her psychic mothering. Its origin is in the identification between the mother and the child shown by the fact that what is here painted purple is not only the girl but is the thistle flower itself, the mother's lap in fantasy or in desire, so different from her rejecting lap in actuality. It is a fantasy of identification between the mother and the child, which is normal and life-giving in early infancy but becomes negative if the mother does not co-operate. Later transferred in Mary's case to the father, this fantasy of oneness with him had the result we know. It cut her off almost completely from herself.

But there is also the possibility that this same purple indicating incest desire may act not as a divider but as a mediator between the two aspects of the woman's animus: the bitter and self-defensive thoughts here symbolised by the hostile prickly thistle stem, and the secret fascination that Mary had for her own inner life and its potential growth as indicated by the small tree which she holds in her hand and gazes at.

Figure 4. "Dragon with tree of the Hesperides, reprod. fm. Boschius, *Symbolographia* (1702)". Jung, *Psychology and Alchemy*, Fig. 189

2. The Philosophical Tree

An ex-schizoid and quite uneducated woman with deep understanding to whom I showed these paintings for the first time without trying to interpret them and simply waiting for her reaction, astonished me by immediately singling out the small tree in this and subsequent paintings, saying, "That is *new life*". It is in fact the *arbor philosophica*, the tree of the philosophers, known to the alchemists, as illustrated by Jung in *Psychology and Alchemy*

(reproduced here as Figure 4, which he entitles "Dragon with Tree of the Hesperides"). That this is not confined to alchemy can be seen from Figure 5, taken from his *Symbols of Transformation*, a tattoo pattern from northwest Canada showing the woman in the moon, likewise gazing at a tree. In Figure 4 the dragon is threatening the tree as will be seen also in Mary's Painting 24.

Figure 5. "The woman in the moon, tatoo pattern, Haida Indians, Northwest America." Jung, *Symbols of Transformation*, Fig. 32

What is the meaning of this tree in Mary's fantasies? In Mary's account of Painting 2 she said about the big dead tree, "... *before it died it had dropped an acorn, which the girl had picked up, and it had grown into a small tree which she had in her hand*". If the dead tree represents the Father, which in this case it does (since for her the father took the place of the mother whom the Tree more usually represents), the acorn symbolises the "semen" or the seed, in other words the Spirit deeply hidden in Mary's psyche. It expresses itself in the form of the fantasies which were the main form of vital life she had, though she was still not conscious that "the girl" was herself.

This all sounds very theoretical but may be brought right down to earth when we consider Figures 6 and 7. Of Figure 6[9] Jung says that it symbolises "Adam as *prima materia*, pierced by the arrow of Mercurius. The *arbor philosophica* is growing out of him". This shows the transformation of the incestuous component of Adam's sexual libido into psychic power as cultur-

---

9. Jung, *Psychology and Alchemy*, Fig. 131; from "*Miscellanea d'Alchimia*" (MS 14th cent.).

Figure 6. "Adam as prima materia, pierced by the arrow of Mercurius. The arbor philosophica is growing out of him, reproducing *Miscellanea d'alchimia* (MS 14h Cent.)". Jung, *Psychology and Alchemy*, Fig. 131.

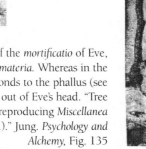

Figure 7. The skull, symbol of the *mortificatio* of Eve, the feminie aspect of the *prima materia*. Whereas in the case of Adam the tree corresponds to the phallus (see Fig. 131), here the tree grows out of Eve's head. "Tree growing out of Eve's skull. reproducing *Miscellanea d'alchimia* (MS 14th cent.)." Jung. *Psychology and Alchemy*, Fig. 135

al force, forming the foundation of human society. The arrow pierces his breast which is the seat of the emotions in which the transformation takes place. The bursting of the tree into leaf and fruit is like an orgasm of psychic activity. This is the first stage in the phallic transformation which takes place in the man.

Figure 7[10] shows the effect on Eve from whom the tree arises not out of her genitals, which she covers with her hand, but out of her head–in other words out of her dreams and fantasies in relation to Adam her man. What is it that Eve sees when she and Adam are naked, and that fascinates her so? What is the tree of the knowledge of good and evil *in the midst of the garden*, which God planted there?

What then is Eve's "garden", if it is not Adam himself? And what is "in the midst" of it if it is not Adam's phallic power? If Adam is made in the image

10. Ibid, Fig.135; from *"Miscellanea d'alchimia"*.

of God, the phallic tree symbolises also God's creative power. And the serpent knows that this is so. Does he not say "in the day ye eat hereof, then your eyes shall be opened, and ye shall be as gods"? And Eve perceived that it was "a tree to be desired to make one wise" (Gen. 1:5-7). It is no ordinary tree, since it is sex somehow transformed. So in Figure 7 Eve is at the same time pointing to a skull. Jung calls this skull a "symbol of the *mortificatio* of Eve, who is the feminine aspect of the *prima materia*". The skull symbolises a death, which in its turn is a transformation of the incestuous component of sexual desire (Adam and Eve being traditionally brother and sister and Eve being the mother of mankind) into psychic relationship.

The composition of this Figure is strikingly similar to that of Mary's Painting 2, with the skull corresponding to the big dead tree, and the tree growing out of Eve's head to the small tree, which Mary holds in her hand and contemplates. This is the living tree blossoming in Mary's world of fantasy, founded on her frustrated longing for the breast and sexual desire for the father. It was hitherto going to seed because, as in her painting, it is as yet so cut off from the earth on account of the dragon-like thistle that she sits upon.

Among the many medieval paintings of Adam and Eve and the tree and the serpent there is one dated 1481, in which Adam is depicted as being asleep with his genitals covered by the dual symbol of the tree-trunk with the serpent coiled round it. [See pp. 60, 61.] The tree is full of pale-coloured fruit, round like the Host, and has two sides to it. To the right there is a skull, and it is on this side that the serpent hands to Eve the fruit of concupiscence, which she then hands on to men. To the left is the Christ crucified as yet another fruit, and it is on this side that the Virgin Mary dispenses the Host, symbolising transformed desire. The connection between the phallus, the tree-trunk and the serpent is here obvious, as it is not in Mary's case owing to the thistle on which she sits.

Two trees, dead and living. Breast and phallus.

If Mary could not yet acknowledge the deep mother-longing which underlay her complex fantasies, it was because of her fear of her mother, so that such a desire was the last thing that she could envisage. To understand therefore the meaning of this small but living tree, as it was mediated to her by her father-love, we have to compare it with the big dead tree on the right. The small tree symbolised, in contrast to the thistle, the potentially creative part of Mary's psychic life, including all that wealth of fantasy, which she kept hidden from the outside world.

All this went on in her, however, as a kind of autonomous complex, secretively and without her relating it to the external facts of her own life. This was owing to fear of the two hostile forces which threatened her, one of which was the "thistle" of her mother's neglect and scorn, the other symbolised by the old tree that dominates the picture from the right, and overshadows her. This tree might have been thought to be an archetypal symbol for the mother, but we have seen how, in Mary's case, the father had taken over the mother-role, thinking to protect her from the schizoid mother. He ignored, however, the fact of his possessiveness, which counteracted much of the good he tried to do for her. If we are to understand properly how such a transfer of basic libido from mother to father takes place, we must examine the foundation of the infant's imaginative life. This is its biological need to survive, not caring what channels may be used to ensure its survival.

Basic libido starts in the infant by being directed towards the breast. A bottle-fed child may well resent the substitution of a rubber teat for the mother's nipple, but the need for survival overcomes this, and the rubber teat itself becomes an object of desire. In some extreme cases all rubber objects become fetishes so that, in later life, some individuals can get not even masturbatory pleasure without handling for instance a mackintosh [rubber raincoat] as a symbol for the withholding mother. The adult nevertheless unconsciously believes she could still breast-feed him if she would.

To such length can the psyche go in substituting one object for another one. A much more common form of transference is onto the father, in the belief that if the mother has no nipple the father must have one. This is not too difficult even for the adult to understand, once it is realized that the nipple indeed protrudes and gets erect as the male member does, penetrating into the infant's mouth and ejaculating into it just as the male member ejaculates into the receptive womb.

This symbolism may seem far-fetched to those not familiar with infant psychology, and with much archetypal symbolism which may sound even more strange. For if the mouths of infants of both sexes are likened to the female receptive organ, which is a common primitive image expressed in the saying that all infants until they are initiated are "like women", what of certain mediaeval paintings? In some of these even the ear is likened to a vagina receiving the Word in the form of a small babe, sliding down a long tube issuing from the Father's mouth and entering the Virgin Mary's ear as the Seed of Truth.

Dreams afford much information about the "male" nature not only of the nipple but even, and very frequently, of milk. For instance, a normal, well-developed woman found after giving birth to her first child, to her distress, that her milk did not flow. She dreamt that she found herself in a field outside a ring of tough-looking characters, surrounding a man whom they appeared to be holding prisoner. This man was struggling to get out, but could not break the ring until he caught sight of the dreamer (her dream ego) outside the ring, whereon he made a dash for her, broke through the ring, and thus got free. The dreamer woke up from this dream in bed with her nightgown wet with milk. The infant came to the breast, and there was no more feeding trouble.

I give this instance out of many similar ones to illustrate the symbolic "maleness" of milk, which might otherwise seem somewhat paradoxical. The maleness of milk supports the symbolic maleness of the nipple from which it issues, and thus is the first phallic emblem which we all encounter in infancy.

As time goes on, the infant's fantasies about the father invest him also with the attribute of being able to give "milk", not connected with his male breasts, but with the virile organ that has life-giving fluid, symbolically "male milk". This happens in the case of both boys and girls. The fantasy is usually repressed. If it is not, the boy, if sexually repressed enough, may become homosexual, by means of a double projection of mother's breast and of his own unacknowledged psychic maleness onto other males, while the girl may, as in Mary's case, become abnormally attached to the father while being on another level lesbian.

This would account for Mary's double fixation: on the one hand onto a father with whose moods and repressed masculinity she was identified, and on the other onto women. These could be anyone who could in any way be fantasied as fulfilling the role of the "good mother" she had not had, or a younger girl, such as the one she was attracted by at a school in which she worked. The same ambivalence is seen in the shape of her fantasy tree, with its straight single phallic stem and the round breast-like circle of its foliage.

The phallus thus carries with it the image of the breast but at the same time prevents contact with the breast: in the image of *her* small fantasy-tree, the trunk comes between her hand and the breast foliage, so that she does not actually touch the breast image but only the phallic trunk. This is precisely what in her fantasy of father-incest she wanted to do.

Imagery of this kind ran through all her fantasy life, and dream life too. One instance is a fantasy painting she made much earlier in the analysis of a cave with a treasure somehow vaguely inside it. The cave is a well-known symbol for the mother or the mother's womb. In front of the cave, barring her way to it, there stood a tree, which, as she painted it, "caught fire", so that she painted it with flames consuming it. This was a symbol for Mary's love for her father, which so disguised the need for the loving mother.

In Mary's case the problem of the mother had been so shelved, that she at this time hardly thought of her as a mother but simply as a nuisance, and that all the love and dependence normally attached to both parents had become concentrated on the father only, whose image in her mind was that of a combined father and mother, comprising good and bad aspects of each. It thus came about that the tree, usually a mother-symbol, became for her a symbol for the father.

Transference of libido from mother to father is, up to a point, a normal process in childhood, but when it carries such extreme displacement as in Mary's case it fosters a schizoid attitude. This complex set of facts is recognized as being abnormal by Jung, who cites an isolated case recorded by [the psychiatrist] Nelken of a schizophrenic patient "in whose cosmic system the All-Father (*Urvater*) of the world wore the image of the Tree of Life upon his breast"[11]. The image is similar to Mary's in that the phallus takes over the function of the woman's breast, which leads to great psychological disturbance.

---

11. Jung, *Von den Wurzeln des Bewusstseins*, p. 480

It is important here to understand the potentially opposite effects of such transpositions from mother to father. They may on the one hand be schizoid. But on the other hand, if handled with success, they may be the means of self-realisation once the barriers of fear have been removed so that the repressed knowledge which lies potentially behind all psychoid phenomena may come through, replacing autonomous complexes by conscious understanding.

In this context we may recall the accusation levelled against St. Paul: "Thou art beside thyself", to which he replied, "I am not mad ... but speak forth the words of truth and soberness" (Acts 26:24-5). Being "beside one-self" may well include such misconceptions as mistaking father for mother. But rebirth comes through the father or the father principle, as in the account of Lazarus being "carried by the angels into Abraham's bosom" (Luke 16:22), or Christ himself being "in the bosom of the Father" whence "he hath declared him" unto man (John 1:18). This latter image is of Christ functioning as the fruit of the male breast, as seen in Figure 12,[12] to which the parallel in Mary's Painting 2 is the acorn dropped by the old dead tree, now grown into the small living tree which she held in her hand symbolis-ing "new life". This is a symbol for psychic fertilisation. For though Mary's father had died, his influence persisted in the form of the great and power-ful tree still overshadowing her, of which she gathered up the seeds, incubating them secretly in the form of these fantasies. They still remained, however, to be "made real" to her.

Highest and lowest here combine, for on the one hand Mary loved her father, as indicated by the fungi she painted on her tree trunk to show not only how old and dead it was but because fungi are one of the forms of growth she loves, as she loves all primitive living things. But at the same time she painted a bat on its upper branch, which she characteristically said "is just there because I thought I'd like to put it in". But none of her decorations were there by chance. Unerringly her psychic consciousness prompted her to include such a symbol indicating "bats in the belfry" or "battiness", a word she often used, well suit-ed to her own condition, blindly clinging to her father or "flapping around" as she so often did, in what she called her "scattiness".

---

12. See footnote 18 re Fig. 12, p.60

The scythe

The "making real", however, lay in the future. At the time when she produced Painting 2, her fantasy life symbolised by the small tree, although no longer hidden from the analyst (though no one else was yet allowed to know anything about it), was still hardly related by her to practical life. She was still up in the air, quite literally supported by such "prickly" thoughts and cynical assumptions as the thistle symbolised, so that to most people she was still almost unapproachable. She was in her view, that is to say in ego consciousness, still "innocent", believing her own rejecting thoughts so utterly that she had no suspicion of the extent of her hostility to life in general, and in particular to her own life.

But psychic consciousness stepped in to show her one further factor in the situation. For, as she says, there is another influence "coming" which "*is going to cut the thistle down*". It will bring her down to earth so that the small tree of her potential life should not go on being wasted in unrelated fantasy but should take root, as it is later seen trying to do in Painting 15. This was the first painting in which she thought of the tree as having feelings like her own and therefore furnished it with eyes and mouth.

The scythe is a well-known symbol of Father Time in his role of death-dealer to cut down that which has already lived too long. False spirit is also dealt with in this way in the Bible when the Pharisees and Sadducees were warned to flee from the wrath to come with the words, "And now the axe is laid to the root of the trees: therefore every tree which bringeth not forth good fruit is hewn down" (Matt. 3:10; Luke 3:9).

One of the paradoxes of Mary's life was that, in rejecting her mother and putting all her trust in father, she had in no way freed herself from mother-influence, since father had become "mother" too. There had been no real masculine influence to sever her psychic umbilical cord to the whole world of mother-possession, resulting in the fact that she became increasingly like that very mother whom she consciously so abhorred. Cutting instruments of all kinds, such as the scythe or axe, or the scissors which cut the umbilical cord in infancy, or the circumcising knife, are all symbolic of the severance of incestuous connections, which in her case had psychically never come about. In this painting the old

41

tree and the scythe form a pair of opposites, the scythe "coming" to do that which the father had not done, thus symbolising on the one hand the action of the analyst who was a substitute father having to take his place, but playing the contrary role of supporting her individuality rather than trying to dominate it, and on the other hand the response to this called forth within herself. The scythe "cuts down" so that the old false structure may gradually disappear and so stop hindering new life from being rooted in reality.

The releasing force comes, to begin with, from without, in this case through relationship with the analyst, as the repressions had also come originally from without, from the parental influence. The analyst, to the best of his ability, joins in the play between the patient's ego consciousness and psychic consciousness, allying himself with neither to the exclusion of the other but playing the role of the "mediating third factor". He takes his cue from the patient's own unrecognised mediating function within, so as to reinforce wherever possible the patient's own inner knowledge brought forth in free association leading to the release of repressed memories, and stimulated by fantasies and dreams. In terms of Painting 2, he "mothers" as the big tree archetypally does, but at the same time cuts down like the scythe, not being afraid to attack illusions through appreciating how they arose; seeking, as a basic principle, the good lying at the root of what may seem at first sight to be evil; and never losing sight of it in the welter of twists and turns that tie the patient's psyche up. This is released eventually by persistent faith in that which wells up from below, ceaselessly trying to express itself and, like a child, longing to be understood.

Mary's small tree of new life is right in the middle of this painting. It took a long time to burgeon, but in the next painting we catch a glimpse of its first fruits.

1. The tree and speaking snake

2. The girl, the thistle and the tree

III

3. Hanging boy

4. Grafting onto the tree

IV

5. Tree and black rotting corpse

6. Ghost man piping in the snakes

v

7. Dragon waiting to be born

8. The poor narrow street

9. The luminous snake

10. The lonely island and the great fish

VII

11. The sleeper awakes

12. Two-headed serpent issuing from the boiling cauldron

VIII

The Hanging Boy. Closed Garden of the Soul.

Dream-boy and real-life girl

Two years after the waking fantasy of Painting 2 [that is, c.1951), Mary had a dream showing the first fruits of her tree. For that moment it was planted in the ground, though only to be lost again as the autonomous complex of forgetfulness re-formed.

She was by now beginning to have some glimmerings of self-knowledge, mostly revealed in dreams, though still so deeply buried that it was attained but fleetingly. It was all too apt to disappear again under mountains of fear and disbelief and of compulsive clingings to her incest fantasies and consequent terrified defences.

During the first years of her analysis she never wrote down her dreams or fantasies. By now, however, she had started very briefly to write down the barest outlines of her dreams. Her account of this dream was:

"I was in an open field seeing some children go away in a plane.

"As soon as they had gone it got rather dark and I was alone in a neglected garden with high walls. I watched a young boy playing there. He seemed sad and lonely, and I watched for a long time.

"Then I saw that he was hanging dead from the branch of a tree with a heavy

43

chain round his neck. As I looked, a wall grew up from the ground and hid him. A voice told me to pull down the wall and I should find him alive again, but I did not really believe it."

When questioned afterwards, she added: *"The boy was wandering aimlessly about, just as I do myself. It didn't occur to me to do anything about him.*

This was dreamt at a time when, for the first time since her father's death about five years before, she had become conscious once more of sex desire, though it was now directed towards a young girl whom she had partly under her care, as she now had a very junior job in a school. It was a delicate situation, as it was absolutely necessary that Mary should not be made ashamed of her desire; while it also was to be hoped that she could somehow maintain the position of some small responsibility she had towards this girl and to the other children in the group, and not do anything too overtly scandalous. Psychologically she was seeking the mother in a mutually loving situation. In this case, however, it did not turn out to be possible as the girl did not respond to the extent which she desired. She was lucky in the headmistress of the school who, when the matter was explained to her, behaved with rare and truly tolerant insight.

Paradoxical meaning of "going away"

With this brief introduction we may now understand something of what the dream-work is trying to convey. The dream was in three scenes, of which the first is a kind of introduction dealing with her loneliness. This was symbolised by the "open field" from which the children were flying away in an aeroplane up into the air corresponding to the position of "the girl" in Painting 2, who was also "up in the air". The feeling in the dream was one of disappointment that childhood had fled, corresponding to the fact that Mary never had had childhood friends, confined as she had been in the rectory garden which was for her an emotional desert. But the possibility of recovery from even the severest deprivation need never be despaired of, if we can but take note of the efforts of psychic consciousness to make good that loss. It cannot indeed alter the past, but it can recall it so that that can transform its results.

Whenever things appear to be "going away" in dreams it means two things: firstly, that the psyche is mercifully relieving the dreamer of the illusion that what is lost (in this case a satisfactory childhood) can be recaptured exter-nally, and it is asserting that it is a waste of time and psychic energy living in vain regrets. Sometimes, however, the dreamer may have become so repressed that he or she is not even aware that anything has been lost. What is not missed consciously is not looked for. Unless some memory of the loss comes back, the dynamic energy connected with what has been lost works, all uncon-sciously to the person concerned, to drain that person of life force and leave him or her listless or ineffectual. Anything seen to "go away" in dreams func-tions as a kind of fleeting glimpse of something that had not consciously been missed, or as an intuition that comes and then goes away again, till by some effort of concentration we may recapture it. In such a case "going away" in fact means that memory, or the affect attached to it, is "coming back".

What comes back is never the same. The psyche offers on the contrary something better, a new and deeper inner life that the externally self-satisfied may never get. It offers to show, not the mistakes of others in having brought one up so badly, but the mistakes that oneself as a child inevitably made in reacting autonomously but mistakenly to unfavourable circumstances. And at the same time it provides the answer, and the reward for looking inward. There, if one can but receive what is offered, one gets doubly repaid for the external deprivation by the intense joy and much deeper experience of one's own reborn inner life.

In the immediate situation her loneliness had been reactivated by her disappointment at the failure of her first love impulse outside the parental sphere, towards the schoolgirl she had in her care. This impulse would natu-rally have shocked her possessive father beyond words. But although this love impulse had not yet found an appropriate object and had been repulsed by the girl, the experience itself had been a healing one because it had been accepted without criticism by a non-possessive father-image. This was the sympathetic analyst, and the problem then did not need to be wholly repressed and could be dealt with in the dream.

Meaning of "getting dark"

There is thus a great contrast in this dream between the opening scene in full daylight (indicating the external life) in which the children "go away"

45

and the next scene which is introduced by her remark that it *"got rather dark"*. This, in dream language, is an invariable indication of turning inwards, of the withdrawal of projections and looking inside into the recesses of the soul. It means not being blinded by or caught up in external happenings which are beyond one's own control but being mercifully drawn back into oneself. There the inner healing powers may operate.

It is a feature of such "darkness" that usually (though not always) the dream images are as clear and visible as in the "light". Thus what darkness in dreams means is that what is now going to be revealed is inner and not outer truth. It is therefore "more true" than what is seen outside in the "light" of external experience which is often but a half-truth and may be misleading if taken as a whole one.

Mary's neglected "closed garden of the soul". Square wall. Wandering boy.

Thus, in this dream, the darkness revealed many things. To begin with, it revealed the walled garden which, in contrast to the open field, is similar to what in mystical language is called the *hortus inclusus* or closed garden of the soul. The high wall kept out not only the external world but, more important still, Mary's own self-hostile superego formed by her terrible experience during infancy and childhood in a home from which the world had been shut out. It also reflected, coming at this time, the analytical situation of non-criticising acceptance of "whatever was" in Mary's psyche as the most precious possession which she had. In the "closed garden" of the consulting room inner conflicts could safely be brought to consciousness and openly talked about, and the rejection by the world could be turned into her own personal acceptance of whatever went on internally.

That the dream should take this form at all showed that the analysis was on the right lines. Otherwise she would not have dreamt it, for she would not have been able to face, even in a dream, what it revealed of self-murder in the form of the hanging boy.

It turned out on enquiry that the enclosed garden was square and thus a form of mandala with a central point—the tree on which the boy was hanged. A square differs from a circle in that a circle is featureless and symbolises something too perfect to be human. A square may be regarded as a circle differentiated into four, the four sides (points of view) changing direction at each of the four angles where two points of view meet. The square is thus the simplest geometric symbol for the human psyche, such as will be seen in still more differentiated and dynamic form from Painting 8 onward. It will be in the shape of the snake's square head which then became a symbol for Mary's own dynamic psychic consciousness.

But Mary's garden of the soul was a "neglected garden", as she said in her description of the dream, in that she had not tended it. This neglect showed itself also in the fact, that as in Painting 2 she did not recognise the girl sitting on the thistle as being herself, she in this dream could only see her own "aimless wandering" in the form of the boy who was at first *wandering aimlessly about, just as I do myself*". This was an animus figure symbolising her own aimlessness at puberty, which had continued into later life in the form of mooning around absorbed in fantasy or "telling herself fairy tales"—a practice she would indulge in when she was expected to be doing other things. Not tending her own garden, expressed in the words, *"It didn't occur to me to do anything about him"*, means that, caught between the two powers of her hatred of her mother and her adoration of her father as "the only man", she had failed to develop ordinary teen-age desires—not even speaking to the butcher's boy who came to the back door. So had she murdered her own animus, here symbolised by the dream boy later seen hanging on the tree.

Painting 3a. Circular wall autonomously growing up to hide the hanging boy. A symbol for amnesia.

The central tree, the hanging boy. Circular wall symbolising amnesia. Circle and square.

This tree is in the centre of the garden, just like the Tree of Life in Genesis. It is the central feature of the dream, just as in Painting 1 the central features were the tree and speaking snake, and in Painting 2 were the thistle with Mary sitting on it "up in the air" in contemplation of her fantasy-tree. Here too we have the boy "up in the air".

Now comes the most revealing feature of the dream. A circular wall grows up to hide the hanging boy from her. Painting 3a, a brush drawing, which Mary made later to illustrate this book, shows the wall growing up. It grows up of its own volition just as the thistle did in Painting 2 without any action on the part of Mary's ego consciousness. What grows up in each of these cases is the most striking symbol of amnesia, showing the power of forgetfulness as an autonomous complex designed by an unconscious superego to conceal the truth.

There is a difference, however, between the two forms of amnesia. Two years before the present dream occurred, the thistle of her fantasy had grown up without "the girl" noticing it. This time she *sees* the wall autonomously growing up and a voice tells her that if she pulls it down she will find the boy alive again. This means that he once lived, and that the living psychic force he represents can be recaptured. That Mary does not believe this is yet another form of the strength of the amnesia which Mary feels herself, in loyalty to her dead father, still bound to maintain. But there is a clear advance in that she can now see it happening. We may regard the autonomous growth of this wall as being one of the most important features in Mary's dream life and of this book.

It is a most vivid example of how, even if some new insight has been momentarily achieved, old complexes of almost instantaneous rejection have the power to re-form themselves. We may here quote the phrase, "They will build up walls a thousand feet high to veil the sun," referring to the rejection by the church (both Catholic and Protestant) of Copernicus' revealing discovery that the earth was round (not flat) and moved.[13]

This forces us to note the difference between the two walls in Mary's dream. The outer wall enclosing the garden is square and is a necessary one, the square wall being a symbol for human consciousness and, as has been pointed out, for the humanly acquired psyche as opposed to untransformed nature. Square forms rarely appear in nature but are abundant in man-made structures like houses or rooms. But on the contrary circular forms are natural and can be seen by day and night in those of the sun and moon, in many

---

13. Hermann Keston, *Copernicus and his World*. London, Secker and Warburg, 1945, p. 283.

seeds and fruits and flowers, in stems and in circular trunks of trees. Through force of gravity the earth is spherical. Circular forms are autonomous in a way that square ones rarely are.

This fact gives us a clue regarding the autonomous growth of the circular wall in Mary's dream indicating amnesia. The outer square wall enclosing the neglected garden of the soul had come into being as a result of about three years of intermittent analysis, during the course of which some of her numerous projections had been withdrawn, enough at least for Mary to see the "hanging boy" as something that was within and not without. But now the second, inner, circular wall grew up between herself and that was to reveal itself as her own animus, strung up so that to all intents and purposes it seemed as dead.

Why should the wall thus grow up? It is important for us to realise that any kind of defensive mechanism such as this has in the first place a positive purpose, being created by the child in order to protect itself from adverse influence. If established early enough in infancy it acquires something very like the quality of instinct. It represents an instinctive defence against unfavourable influence. The trouble is, however, that once such a defensive attitude has taken root it may continue automatically although the adverse circumstances are no longer there. The defensive mechanism then persists not only against what may be harmful to the child, but also against whatever other influences may be operative for good.

It functions as a kind of wall surrounding the individual and isolating him. This was the case in Mary's life as when she had refused the help of certain relatives seeking to free her from parental dominance and get her out into the world. But inner and outer are alike, so that the wall also conceals the truth of a person's own real nature and desires. And so this inner wall thus growing up to hide the truth behaved in just the same way as her father had in "protecting" her from life, from self-knowledge and from the object of her real desire—in other words from what he thought was evil but was in fact good. In sum it amounts to the truth that heals, however unpalatable it may be to ego consciousness in its sad battle against psychic consciousness.

It is not easy to pull down such a wall. It needs much time, extreme patience, and a mixture of love and perception on the part of anyone trying to help. Before she came into analysis Mary had been almost completely with-drawn into her world of fantasy. She had been "unapproachable", surrounded by a kind of circular fence without features. Analysis had altered this to the extent of making her more conscious of herself and less ashamed of her most primitive desire. Six years later in Painting 28 Mary fantasied that she was herself taking refuge inside such a fence which was then threatened by a flam-ing "dragon-man" coming to burn it down—and possibly burn Mary too, that is to say transform her fears into something more positive.

The meaning of the hanging boy, and archetypal parallels

The boy may be thought of as a kind of Eros figure. He symbolises the power of relationship and normal erotic development; this had been so maimed in Mary's case that he was here seen as strung up on the tree in the same way that she herself felt "strung up" because of the frustration of her love-life. She dreams of a boy at the age of puberty because, though she is now almost thirty, that was the age at which her vital life was finally impris-oned, and was the age of the girl she now desired. But the image was that of a boy, symbolising her active (symbolically "male") desire, which can for a woman operate as the function of relatedness.

The boy was thus another aspect of the ghost man whom she had seen when she was sixteen, but had not understood the meaning of. So he was a kind of *revenant* symbolising "the return of the repressed". But Mary's fear of love, based on her earlier experience with both parents, was so great that the wall of her resistances grew up again. However, psychic consciousness is not so easily put off. A voice, "the Word", told her that if she pulled it down she would find him alive again. But even then the cynicism which had so warped her psychic life reasserted itself, and she did not believe.

Figure 8. "Crucifixion, and the serpent lifted up. Thaler [coin] struck by the goldsmith Hieronymus Magdeburger of Annaberg." Jung, *Symbols of Transformation*, Pl. IX b

This is a reference to the resurrec-tion, which is what all psychotherapy is concerned with, namely the resurrection of lost powers, or affects that have been

50

denied. The crucifixion is referred to by St. Paul as "Christ hanged on a tree" (Acts 5:30). This is indeed the Tree of the Philosophers which incorporates good and evil in one, the death of outward appearances leading to the revelation of inner truth. In this way Christ is sometimes mystically equated with the serpent hanging on the tree in the form of the brazen serpent which God caused Moses to set up in the wilderness for the healing of the people who had gone astray. This links the hanging boy of Mary's Painting 3 with the green snake of Painting 1.

Judas, too, hanged himself as a prelude to Christ's death and resurrection, as may be seen in their simultaneous representation in Figure 11. Judas himself was reckoned in early times as a saint owing to the necessary part he played in this universal transformation process.

Figure 9. Ivory panel from an early Christian casket, with scenes from the Passion. Here, the Crucifixion of Christ. About AD 400. The hanged Judas, Mary, John, the vigorous Christ on the Cross, and Longinus. "In the branch of the tree which bends towards Christ, a bird feeds her chicks—a symbol of the life-giving power of His death." British Museum

Figure 10. The Lily Window: Christ as the flowering plant. Church of St. Michael at the North Gate, Oxford. Old glass dating from the XVth or early XVIth century.

A third illustration, Figure 10, shows Christ identified with the tree in the form of a lily in a peculiarly English type of stained glass window called a "Lily Crucifix". These were always connected with glass windows depicting the Annunciation—glad tidings of new birth.

Fruit of the tree

The symbol of human beings as fruit of the tree is a worldwide one, as in an illustration reproduced by Jung in connection with "the Battle for Deliverance from the Mother" of the West Indian "wak-wak tree with its human fruit" (see Figure 11). Other instances are Plate XLV in Jung's *Symbols of Transformation* of "Death the archer" shooting down human figures hanging on a tree, or the tree hung with Bacchus masks used as an illustration by Neumann in *The Great Mother* (Figure 60). We have already referred to Figure 14 where the crucified Christ is depicted as the fruit of the tree of Life and Death. In the same way the boy hanging from the tree in Mary's Painting 3 may be regarded as the first fruit of the tree of her new life. This tree "grew out of " the acorn in Painting 2, and she, now come to earth, here gazes at it with the same intensity as formerly at the small tree in her hand.

This boy is an archetypal, therefore godlike, figure whom we have referred to as Eros, the god of love, and reflecting Mary's tenseness and feeling of being so "strung up".

But there are two aspects to this. Internally Mary had to relinquish the love projected on to her father usurping her mother's place with him. It was *this* "god" that had to die. So we may here not be far

52

Figure 11. "The wak-wak tree with its human fruit." Jung, *Symbols of Transformation*, Pl XXXIX

off the mark in quoting Jung saying that, "The hanging up of the god has an unmistakable symbolic value, since suspension is a symbol of unfulfilled longing or tense expectation [suspense]. Christ, Odin, Attis, and others all hung upon trees".[14] The gods were all lovers by whose death love was transformed.

Thus we have Odin, who as a soul-leader was called "The Hanging God", "Lord of the Gallows", "God of the Hanged" and "The Hanged One". This was because he hanged himself on the World Ash Tree, Yggdrasill, so that he might "learn the secrets of the runes of wisdom there". Men were sacrificed to him by hanging. He sings:

Myself an offering to myself
knotted to that tree
no man knows
    whither the root of it runs.
None gave me bread,
none gave me drink,
    down to the depths I peered...
Well-being I won
and wisdom too,
    I grew and joyed in my growth...[15]

Neumann points out with reference to Golgotha, which is the "place of a skull" (Matt.27: 33), how the Goths and Anglo-Saxons rendered the word "cross" in their language as "gallows" (Gothic. *galga*, Old English *gealga*). He goes on, "Here, it is evident, sacrifice, death, rebirth and wisdom are intertwined on a new plane. Thus tree of life, cross and gallows tree are ambivalent forms of the maternal tree. What hangs on the tree, the child of the tree-

---

14. Jung, *Symbols of Transformation*, p. 383.
15. Brian Branston, *Gods of the North*. London, Thames and Hudson, 1955, pp. 79 and 114-15.

mother, suffers death but receives immortality from her" as "giver of wisdom". "Christ, hanging from the tree of death, is the fruit of suffering and hence the pledge of the promised land.... According to the Christian myth, the Cross was set up on the site where the tree of knowledge had stood" as its "mystical fruit".[16] The seed that grows upon the tree must fall so that new life may spring from it. It is a heresy to suppose that Christ ascended into heaven directly off the cross. His body had to be taken down from it, and his spirit had for three days to go down into hell before it could arise, having experienced the depths and rescuing souls out of it. So also Odin attains wisdom only in "falling from the tree".[17]

To be hung on the tree means acceptance of fate. It does not mean, however, clinging to it in impotent suspension but fulfilling one's fate by coming down to earth—the "earth" of one's own psyche with all its highest and lowest potentialities. This is equivalent to knowing oneself, and to the realization that, whatever fate has had in store for one, it is one's own peculiar destiny not just to "put up with" but to fulfil. It is the message of this whole book that the lowest is as important as the highest.

The most shut in are the most proud in the isolation of their concealments. If the shell can be pierced and the ground watered with knowledgeable sympathy, then the seed, previously fearful of falling on to barren ground, may drop and fructify, leading to the next phase of development, whatever that may be.

Purple and rotting flesh

Mary's body-feeling had been starved, so that in her vision of the tree the hanging boy seems dead. She sees a male animus figure symbolising her desire, but it is not yet "animated". She is almost without a soul. The adumbrated *hierosgamos* (marriage) between the body and the soul is still a long way off. An indication of this may be found in the purple colour of "clothes" which the boy appears to be wearing. We have already noted what this colour means as a symbol for incest.

---

16. Neumann, *The Great Mother.* Pp. 251-2.
17. Ibid, p. 252, note 36.

The boy's body is painted red, which Mary described as representing "natural flesh"—indicating natural emotion—but part of the red has been mixed with blue to produce purple. Mary said this was not the colour of his clothes as it appears to be, but of his "rotting flesh". The boy has been strung up so long that his flesh has begun to rot. Like all symbols this has a double significance. On the one hand Mary's own psyche is "clothed" in incest, that is to say is still within the womb, for "purple" also means the womb. Her animus is still unborn, therefore suspended on the mother-tree which has for her become the father-tree owing to the transposition of mother-longing on to him. And he all too readily accepted this while projecting his anima onto her and thus "clothing" her animus with it.

On the other hand, symbolically "to rot" means "to transform". As rotting dung brings forth new life, so also does anything that has been "let go" and allowed to fall and re-enter the earth. The word "rot" is thus not only passive, but active too. There is another form of this word, to "ret", which means to rot down purposely such things as raw (natural) hemp for human use by steeping it in water and thus softening it, at the same time removing the hard skin which covers it. Used as a symbol, it is one of the first operations of the *opus* or "work" of transmutation from what is hard and resisting to what is more malleable or receptive to psychic consciousness. Transformation never is the work of ego consciousness alone, which can only consent, co-operate, and refrain from hindering. Such are the concepts underlying "the rotting of the boy". Many of the paintings in this series show the process at work, notably Painting 5. Here Mary's Tree of Life draws sustenance from her father's rotting corpse.

Another such instance is Painting 11 in which a purple dragon bursts open a black coffin of the same shape and colour as the father's cassock, releasing the body of a man who has been long buried in it and is reaching upward towards the light. It is painted with the same colours as the "boy" in the present Painting 3, part purple and part red.

It should be emphasized here that years elapsed between the fantasies recorded in these various paintings, and that Mary rapidly forgot her dreams and fantasies, so that there can be no question of her having copied the colours of the one while painting the other. The colours "came to her" afresh with each painting.

The healing factor in this dream is that, bad as it may look, Mary does for a moment see the boy strung up. Her animus, the woman's potential function for the understanding of herself, had always been suspended in this way. It is a feature to be found in all Mary's fantasies throughout this book: it is the knowledge of the "bad" which is the saving factor. What is not known cannot be changed. What is known can.

PAINTING 4 (DREAM) 30TH JUNE 1952

Grafting onto the Tree

One of the dreams which illustrated the healing process on the psychic level of "the Tree" was as follows:

"There was a standard rose tree. Half of it had beautiful pink flowers, the other half had been pruned right down to take new grafts. As I looked at them, I saw that each graft had human features and that you [the analyst] were one of them. Then a great hand came down and picked me up and bound me firmly to the tree."

The dream was dreamt when she was depressed after having failed at yet another job. It showed that however badly things might be going externally, internally new healing forces were at work. Mary is here being grafted onto the Tree of Life, but only onto half of it, the meaning of which will soon be seen.

Thus, for the first time in her paintings the tree specifically differentiates between the two sides of her character. These were derived from her two parents, the right side being concerned with her identification with the father—the frankly sexual desire for whom had always been so present to her mind. It is on this side that the pruning has taken place and where the new buds are being grafted on. One of these bears the features of the male analyst, symbolising the growth of the transference process, as a result of which Mary's incestuous desire towards her father is becoming less incestuous. This is the transference, however, of only one side of her nature, the loving and believing side. We must say something further about this before referring to the other side, which is as yet untransformed.

57

For it was the right side of Mary's tree from which the hanging boy had been suspended, his seeming death indicating the death of, among other possibilities, potential love-life. This was because it was hindered by incestuous desire. But the voice had said that if she pulled down the wall she would find him alive again. The lopping of the branches in the present dream has a similar significance, for the new buds now grafted on symbolise the new life growing in her.

The "gardener" or "husbandman"

The "closed garden" of her psyche, which had been revealed to her as being "neglected" in the dream illustrated in Painting 3, is here shown as being carefully tended by a skilled gardener. She is now growing within the *temenos* of the consulting room in which her scattered projections could be gathered together into a single projection onto the analyst, whom she knew to be "on her side".

Yet this "gardener" is not simply the psychotherapist; it is the patient's own psychic consciousness which has been stimulated by the psychotherapist to act as "husbandman" in place of the father who had formerly usurped this role. This is here beautifully exemplified by the action of the hand, an unknown hand and not the analyst's (although it has been activated by the analyst), lifting her up to graft her onto the twig next to him. He was she said, the most advanced of all the buds. But he was not the only bud. There were yet other buds indicating the work of psychic consciousness in a more general sense. They included not only him and her, but others too, as well as further potentialities in her.

And here a word has to be said about the "human features" on these grafted buds (no buds had been there before). Incest or incestuous desire, being undifferentiated and in-turned towards the members of one family, is featureless, since it inhibits individuality. "Features" indicate specific personality or character, something brought out by contact with society and persons outside the restrictive circle of the family. It is important therefore to note that with regard to the transference, Mary is not identified here with the analyst as might as first appear, but with the power of psychic consciousness symbolised by the Tree of Life and by the hand grafting her onto it. It is this which is the main lesson of this book.

So much for the right side of the Tree indicating Mary's progress to date, which had developed out of the primitive feeling she had for her father. The analyst till now had been careful to cherish this and to appreciate it without too much criticism of it since it was to begin with her only line of life. It was for this reason that she could now transfer part of her feeling for her father onto the analyst, as the beginning of acceptance of the world outside.

What then of the left side, which had such "beautiful pink flowers", seeming so innocent till she associated them with her mother's rose garden—which Mary hated. For one of her mother's passionate interests had been gardening, which the father loathed and would have nothing to do with, nor would Mary herself if she could possibly avoid it. The mother loved roses, and there were rose trees in front of both study and drawing-room windows in the rectory garden; in her feckless way, however, the mother would not prune or otherwise look after them, but left this to the gardener. Mary was roped in from time to time to cut off their suckers, an occupation which she thoroughly disliked and only did because they were so close under her mother's eye.

This throws a very different light on the apparent innocence of the "beautiful pink flowers" on that side of the tree. It thus became evident that it was connected with the mother and with Mary's identification with her. The identification had two aspects. One was that she had taken her mother's place with her father, including her sexual desire for him, which makes these flowers seem somewhat less innocent. The other was the hatred Mary harboured against the world, and the paranoid attitude towards it which she shared with and had adopted from her mother. She felt this hatred primarily against the mother, and so against the mother's roses too. We may connect this also with the mother's "good breasts" that had so agonisingly been withheld from her.

There is no indication of Mary's conscious realization of either of these factors in the roses she painted here. For the father-problem was so overwhelmingly uppermost in her that the mother-problem was correspondingly repressed. It was not till six years later that, in Painting 30, the double-sided tree appeared again, with its right-hand side showing the buds of Painting 4 grown into leafy branches. She then connected these with her growingly successful life in society. From its left side there sprang no longer innocent roses but an angrily inflated huge red snake, indicating what really underlay the assumed innocence.

It was this snake that in this later painting (30) was seeking union with the more tender emotions lying at the roots of her being. For though the father-problem, being uppermost, was the first to be tackled in the analysis, the mother-problem was more important still and was throughout more difficult to solve. Nevertheless, as will be seen during the course of this analysis, it was the mother-side of Mary's nature that was the questing one—more questing than the father-side of her which was the more narcissistic and self-satisfied one.

The colours red and black

This state of things may be seen in the two major colours used in Painting 4, red and black. These are the colours which, with the exception of the purple in Painting 2, Mary used throughout these paintings for depicting herself, the black being associated with her father and all that went with her relationship with him (which will be described later in much greater detail), the red being associated primarily with femininity and so ultimately with the mother. Thus in this painting she colours herself and the analyst in his role of father-substitute both black, but the hand which lifts her up is red. This is connected with the fact that the analyst had to fulfil the role not only of father but of mother too.

For the analyst, whether she or he wishes it or not, inevitably receives from the patient the projection of the Self which, in its personal aspect, is based on the two parental images with regard to their conscious and unconscious influence. The analyst had therefore to give the love and understanding which in Mary's case the mother had denied or been unable to give, while at the same time exercising masculine objectivity.

A tree having two sides to it is a frequent symbol in mythology. One such is the Tree of Life and Death, or of the Knowledge of Good and Evil[18]. If we remember the Philosophers' Tree (Figure 6) growing out of Adam's phallus—symbolising his creative thought—we may note that in this figure the Tree and Serpent occupy the same position with regard to Adam's phallic understanding, but in the latter the Tree is now separate from Adam as a thing in and for itself. As is the analyst, so Adam here is, too, the husbandman who digs and delves. If Adam represents the analyst looking inwardly into himself, and thus into the patient's psyche too, the Tree and Serpent have a much wider significance.

---

18. Often entitled a Tree of Death and Life.

Growing as the Tree does out of the earth of universal human experience, the Tree is the psyche's static aspect and the Serpent its dynamic one. The Serpent gives to Eve the fruit of the knowledge of her own incestuous desire which has to "die". This is indicated by the skull on that side of the Tree (corresponding with the hanging boy on the same side of the Tree in Mary's Painting 3), and by the black man indicating merely unconscious instinctiveness. The adumbrated death or transformation of this corresponds to the lopping of the branches on the right-hand side of Mary's Tree, the side connected with her father, which is now "pruned right down to take new grafts".

The left side of this figure is more ambiguous since it contains the crucifix. It is from this side that the Virgin Mother hands down the fruit of transformed desire indicating the renunciation of her claim over her child, to which the angel bears witness. This side, as in Mary's rose tree, is concerned with the problem of the relationship between mother and child, which in Mary's case is still quite untransformed.

Figure 12. A tree of death and life, miniature by Berthold Furtmeyer, from the Archibishop of Salzburg's missal, 1481. Bayerische Staatsbibliothek, Munich.

61

The Numbers Six and Seven

It may be chance or not that led Mary without conscious purpose, to give her tree six roses and seven twigs pruned to receive new grafts. Of these six are already grafted and waiting for her is the seventh one. She certainly had no theory about numbers, and this might have been thought a matter of mere chance but for the seven snake-headed roots of Painting 15. They are trying to anchor yet another aspect of her Tree of Life into the earth. She had in neither case noticed how many she had painted. But it may here be pointed out that even numbers are traditionally "female" and odd numbers are "male". It was therefore significant that on the left side (the mother-side) of Mary's tree there is the even number of six roses. And on the right side (the father-side) there were at first only six grafts symbolising her and her father's mutual matriarchal possessiveness. Under the influence of analysis and of the analyst's more masculinely non-possessive attitude, the six became seven. Mary was the seventh one now becoming more conscious and thus less incestuous.

An archetypal parallel is the Jewish seven-branched candelabrum or menorah (see Figure 13), a patriarchal symbol of which the central seventh branch is in line with the main stem from which all even branches grow. This is a symbol for psychic consciousness.

Figure 13. Seven-branched candlestick. "Abstract tree represented as seven-branched candelabrum or Christmas tree. The lights symbolize the illumination and expansion of consciousness." Jung, *Alchemical Studies*, Fig. 3

PAINTING 5 (Fantasy) 15 January 1953

The Tree and the Black Rotting Corpse

1. General remarks

The fantasy

We have just seen in Painting 4 how the sap rising in the tree of life can flow into someone grafted onto it. There was, however, no indication in this case of where the sap came from. But at about this time Mary had a new urge to paint. She wanted first to paint a simple riverside scene, and started by putting in the earth and grass along its bank. But then the fantasy seized her, and she became its tool, not knowing what would "come". The result was Painting 5 of a strong tree with fruit on it drawing its sap from a rotting corpse lying beneath it in the sand, at the bottom of the river bed.

It might be thought that she would show interest in such a fantasy-painting or at least wonder what it meant. But it was one of her characteristics that she did not. She might bring a painting with her to the analytical session, or she might not. If she did bring it, she might just show it as something that she had done. Once it had been painted, however, she lost interest in it and brought it partly to please me, since I seemed for some reason to think it worthwhile looking at.

Knowing that these paintings always had some story behind them, I would at first withhold any comment I might make to myself on archetypal

63

grounds and simply ask her what it was about. She was never in doubt about the story that came to her while painting and this time answered, "This picture is of a section through the earth". She knew the word "section" because she had painted in this way before. We had used this word to describe paintings, for instance, of an apple split open to show the core and burrowings of grubs in it, or of a stone split open to show that it had fire inside, or of a cave deep underneath the earth with a man praying inside it and only a narrow crack just letting in a tiny beam of light, outside which terrors in the form of birds of prey awaited him if he dared show himself. These were all deeply psychological but her comment had always been that it was just "fun" to paint them so.

When she brought Painting 5, she said directly but simply:

"The grass is growing in the earth, but has to have no fruit, so that its roots are shallow. But the fruit tree has roots, which can get through the layer of stone underneath the earth, into the water underneath the stones, and down to a dead man in the sand under the water. The tree draws its strength from his rotting body."

So ran the "story" as she first told it, to which she added, however, the comment that it was funny that the grass might have no fruit but that the tree could have such lovely fruit. Also, how surprised she was to "find" the dead man lying there, though, once she had seen him, it was quite obvious to her that he was the source of the tree's sap. She had no explanation to offer of why she should have this fantasy. Nor did she even wonder at it. It was just "so".

It was clear that, like many near-psychotics, she was in touch with very deep wisdom expressing itself in these images. This was however cut off from ego consciousness to the extent that she as yet could not apply it to herself or any practical problem of life. She was as one having a box full of treasure to which she had no key, so that she did not even know what treasures it contained.

She had however given me one key in saying that she was *"most surprised to find the dead man there"*. This showed that when she started to paint this picture the whole fantasy was not yet formed, but grew during the actual painting, which prompted me to ask, then, in what order she had painted its various parts. Her explanation was a revelation to me, if not to her. For it immediately transpired that the finished painting quite failed to tell the story of the fantasy, that had developed like a living thing during the act of painting it.

64

**Development of the fantasy while painting it. "Active imagination".
The need for "tools" and someone else's interest.**

Thus one of the revealing things about this painting was that its most prominent feature, the fruit-bearing tree, had come not first but last. Into Mary's visionary field it came not as a cause but as a result of all that had preceded it, in visionary development during the few minutes which it took to paint.

This was but one of many instances of Mary's habit of surrendering herself to something like what Jung calls "active imagination" or "active fantasy"[19], as discussed for instance by Baynes in *Mythology of the Soul*[20] and Fordham in *The Objective Psyche*[21], where he describes the relative functions of "imaginative activity". This is what takes place of its own volition in childhood as contrasted with "active imagination". The latter is a more developed form of imagining involving the co-operation of a central ego which serves to repress the repression that superego has imposed. Thus are removed the barriers erected against the flow of psychic consciousness; the images are always there, waiting to be received when ego consciousness permits. The difference between these two forms of imagining is that childish imaginative activity often just goes to waste. It is divorced from ego consciousness, living in a world of its own as in the case of Mary's "fairy tales" taking up so much of her libido but having no therapeutic effect—making her still more "scatty" owing to this divorce. In contrast, active imagination has effect because of ego's participation. Realising that the images conveyed had a real bearing on actual life, during the course of her analysis Mary gradually developed this psychological tool for herself.

At this stage Mary had at least five levels of fantasy life but little understood:

1. Her dreams;

2. Her waking fantasies, the "fairy tales" she told herself, or rather which arose spontaneously in her mind from a source she knew not of;

3. Her conscious fantasies of father-bliss;

---

19. Jung, *The Structure and Dynamics of the Psyche*, p. 202 ff.
20. H.G. Baynes, *Mythology of the Soul*. London, Bailliere Tindall & Cox, 1940, particularly Ch. 4.
21. Michael Fordham, *The Objective Psyche*, London, Routledge & Kegan Paul, 1958, Ch. 5.

4. Compensating for her frustration, yet other fantasies of omnipotent destruction directed towards any in authority or whom she otherwise disliked. She would wish them every kind of ill (which she imagined she could bring on them by simply willing it) or she would stage scenes of imaginative torture (which she thought they thereby really suffered from);

5. The only form into which ego consciousness entered at all was the fifth form, stimulated by the analysis: taking her brushes and her poster paints and deliberately recording either a vision she had seen in its entirety, or else a fleeting glimpse that took on life and changed while she painted it. Her ego consciousness was active in the act of deciding to paint, but what was then important was that she had the power to abandon any preconceived idea as to what it was that she wanted to paint; psychic consciousness then took control, insisting on something quite unpremeditated. She used her ego consciousness only to mix the paints aright so as to get down on paper as nearly as possible the shapes and colours which presented themselves to her inward eye.

She thus yielded herself to be a passive and obedient instrument, painting what psychic consciousness desired, submitting to this hidden but compelling force, through which her psyche could at that time alone express itself. Without ego's consent to honour these visionary appearances by painting them they would just have disappeared again into the darkness whence they arose.

Indeed they still would have done so but for the analyst who had not only stimulated her to paint but showed much greater interest in her paintings than she had herself. For one so infantile and thus dependent on outside influence and on material objects in general to make things "real" to her, two things were needed: a) paints, paper and brushes (something to handle) and b) the psychic factor of another human being's interest. If this interest is combined with some knowledge of psychic consciousness it may be particularly valuable, because psychic consciousness is common to all mankind and is therefore capable of becoming a new channel of communication between individuals. For the same reason, most religious systems make use of material objects such as the bread and wine or images to mediate religious truth, which otherwise might be too difficult to grasp. These, it is true, may help, but they cannot ultimately solve a person's individual problems because they are too collective, leaving the personal factor out of account. Mary had tried all these means for solving her problems, but they had failed because these problems had been too severe to be dealt with only on impersonal lines.

Thus with the aid of having the materials to hand, coupled with the feeling that someone would take an interest, when she felt too "pent-up" she would take out her paints, brushes and paper, often with no idea what she would paint. As she described it when questioned, the painting then "painted itself for her", using her hand and the materials as its own medium. Sometimes this succeeded straight off, and the picture painted itself quite quickly. Sometimes a second image appeared which would blot out or seem more vital than the first, and she would either paint over the one she had begun, or else scrap it and start again.

The spirit moves. Painting "in depth"

Often she would begin with some quite ordinary scene, to get her hand in, so to speak, and then the spirit would move her and force her to go on in a certain way. When she began to paint the fantasy which turned into Painting 5, it would seem that nothing could have been simpler than the mere painting of a river bank. But here, beneath the water, she saw something of what had literally "died" in her but was now being rediscovered, figuratively "uncovered" among the silt of repressed memories lying at the bottom of the river of her life.

This new discovery was due directly to the change of emphasis or psychic direction after she had begun to paint. It had seemed to be a quite straightforward surface view, as though she had been sitting on the bank of a river painting the other bank with the river flowing in between. While doing such paintings, however, Mary's attention was not drawn to the surface of her life, which was bleak enough. It was the warmth and depth of the analysis, contrasted with the bleakness that made her less afraid than formerly to let her consciousness during painting descend, so as to paint a section rather than a view—a picture of herself "in depth" rather than a superficial one.

2. Unfolding of the fantasy

First Stage: "Grass had to have no fruit." *The shallowness of ego consciousness.*

What set the fantasy growing was that, while she was painting initially

67

the layer of brown earth representing the river bank with the grass growing on it, she oddly realized that, as she put it, *"the grass had to have no fruit, so that its roots are shallow"*. It was quite useless to ask Mary what she meant by such a phrase. She simply did not know. So far as she knew consciously, she was just talking about "grass". She could not perceive what the grass meant with regard to herself. What appeared to her as her own harmless "innocence" was so far from being really innocent that much of the fruit or seeds that it in fact produced were such attitudes as hidden envy, malice and hatred. These attitudes had roots that were so shallow they had no contact with the real waters of life lying far down below. Therefore, from the point of view of psychic consciousness which now began to operate, this complex of false innocence breeding quite lethal fantasies just *"had to have no fruit"*. Had these not been admitted and discussed during the analyses, they might have led her into becoming actively insane on the pattern of her mother or Aunt Grace, a fact of which she had been consciously afraid before analysis began.

But now she knew, somewhere, that there was something to live for although she had no notion what. Psychic consciousness prompted her to leave a space free of this "grass" in the middle of the river bank *"for something to grow there"*. This was the first stage in her painting, shown in Figure 14 A, of a life empty but expectant.

Second Stage: The fantasy grips her and takes her "down", leading to the corpse.

What should grow there was still obscure. It was at this point that the fantasy gripped her, dragging her downward into itself. Her gift under such circumstances was that she could abandon thought for the sake of perception, and let what would come, come.

Next she painted what she described as "a layer of stones", the layer underneath the earth, which she then painted grey. She is quite capable of painting separate stones, but these were not important to her. We may think of this layer as symbolising her resistances, but she was now bypassing them so that there was no point in emphasizing them. Next came the water underneath the stones. Beneath the water there was sand, the silt which the river had made, in which, to her extreme surprise, she saw lying the rotting body of the man. This was the second stage shown in Figure 14 B.

Grass
Earth

First Stage

With grass that had but shallow roots because it "must have no fruit", and a central blank space left for something to come, she knew not what.

Fig. 14A

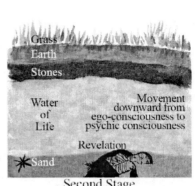

Grass
Earth
Stones

Water of Life

Movement downward from ego-consciousness to psychic consciousness

Revelation

Sand

Second Stage

Attention drawn down to the rotting corpse

Fig. 14B

Movement upward from psychic consciousness to a new ego-consciousness accepting it.

Third Stage

The tree grows from the rotting corpse and bears fruit nourished from its sap.

Fig. 14C

New life resulting from the union of ego consciousness with psychic consciousness (the tree with fruit)

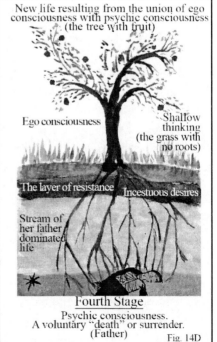

Ego consciousness

Shallow thinking (the grass with no roots)

The layer of resistance

Incestuous desires

Stream of her father dominated life

Fourth Stage

Psychic consciousness.
A voluntary "death" or surrender.
(Father)

Fig. 14D

Third Stage: Growth of the tree out of the corpse.

Till then the movement had been all downward, but now she knew that she had found what she was looking for. The body lay immediately below the space which she had left in her painting of the grass. She now knew that there grew in this place a tree with good fruit on it, drawing its sustenance from the rotting corpse by means of roots that penetrated through the layer of hard stones, down through the water to the sand in which the body lay. The last thing therefore which she painted was the tree bearing the fruit which the "grass" might not bear. This was the third and final stage shown in Figure 14 C.

The star she painted in the sand by the side of the rotting corpse was, as she said, a kind of afterthought. She said that it meant nothing, but was simply "decoration". We might think of it as a symbol for the self, or symbolising a paean of joy that at last something real had happened. It also meant "full stop". The energy that had gone into painting this moving fantasy had spent itself; it was for her, once painted, a dead thing.

It is a feature of a case like Mary's that patience is needed beyond the average—patience sustained by faith. Anyone inexperienced in the toughness of deep complexes might think when such a painting is produced that the patient is now nearing a solution and might then become bitterly disappointed that nothing seems to come of it; little change if any is perceptible in the patient's outlook upon life or overt behaviour. What has happened has happened so deep down that it may indeed get lost again if not constantly tended over the years. Or it may show itself in unexpected ways such as, years later, Mary finding herself capable of passing the examinations needed to become a state-registered mental nurse.

The redemption process

However long it may take for the tree of life to grow out of the corpse, this whole painting, provided we do not see it as a static picture but follow its growth, is a most beautiful demonstration of the course which any analysis must take. It is the same as that of any fundamental healing process or act of redemption, meaning the recovery of that which has been lost.

This universal psychic movement is illustrated in Figure 14 D. It shows how, if the fears and prides of a shallow and rootless ego consciousness can be relaxed and the force of psychic gravity can be submitted to, consciousness will "sink" through layers of resistances into the healing waters. It will do this without judgment or preconception but with a willingness to accept whatever may reveal itself. However surprising the result may be, it of itself will heal. The libido thus released will of its own momentum rise again, "scatter its enemies" and take control. The individual will cease from being restricted by the strait-jacket of unconscious prides and fears and new life will arise—the child of union between ego consciousness and psychic consciousness, which formerly had been at loggerheads.

This is a symbolic statement such as the mystics make, but it is backed by fact such as this movement of Mary's psyche.

3. Archetypes and the personality

Archetypal understanding useless unless illuminated by personal experience

Such generalized statements are, however, of little avail in psychological analysis or any form of healing unless two factors can be joined. Just as in Mary's fantasy or "active imagination" the virtue comes from union between ego consciousness and psychic consciousness, so, in order to rescue this very fantasy from once more sinking back into oblivion, or on the contrary from leading to an inflation, we have to interweave the archetypal with the personal. Thus proper proportion develops and makes the fantasy "a living thing" on the plane not only of universality, but also of intimate personal detail.

The first plane is easy to one familiar with archetypal representations— they leap to the mind on seeing such a picture as this. But it is not so easy to plumb their depths. Interpretations are quite useless to the patient unless both analyst and patient can together link them on to personal experience; this may be painful but unavoidable if they are to be dynamic in the patient's life. The process of healing is thus always as a "marriage" not only between ego consciousness and psychic consciousness but also between the analyst's archetypal knowledge—which the patient has not got—and the patient's personal background and previous experience—which the analyst has not got . It is essential to rescue previous personal experience so that the energy which has gone into repressing it may now illuminate it.

71

Since Mary had nothing whatever to say about her painting other than the bare story which she told, we may start off with what the analyst experienced when seeing it with his archetypal perception. We shall then follow the actual course of analysis in which her personal associations gradually revealed themselves and formed the link.

a) Archetypal associations
  The cross (tree) and descent into hell.
  Tree growing out of Adam's corpse. The opposites unite.

The first thing that comes to mind is the Christian image of the tree of life, the Cross, planted according to tradition in Adam's skull on Golgotha, or growing out of it. This surfaces together with the knowledge that it is a heresy to believe that Christ rose straight to heaven from the Cross, the tradition being that he first went into hell where Adam was and Abraham and all the patriarchs, waiting for him to take them up with him. This is the same movement that Mary's psychic awareness followed: first downward to the dead ("the past"), then upward into fuller present-day consciousness. The pious belief is that Christ rescued the wicked from their pains, but the truth is that all roads to heaven lead through hell and that there is no other way. Thus do the dreams and fantasies of sufferers illuminate dogma and clothe it with flesh.

Such thoughts went through my mind when seeing this painting, but I was not then aware, as I have since become, of the yet fuller concept, illustrated in Figure 15, of the Cross growing out of Adam's whole skeleton, out of his "grave", as reproduced by Jung in *Symbols of Transformation* (Plate XXXVII).

Figure 15. "The Cross on Adam's Grave, detail over West door, Strasbourg Cathedral, 1280". Jung, *Symbols of Transformation*, Plate XXXVII

Meaning of "rotting corpse". The rotting python at Delphi.

Her vision differs from that depicted in Figure 15 in that the body in her painting is not only a skeleton but consists also of rotting flesh that provides the sap from which the tree *"draws its strength"*.

We may be here reminded of yet another parallel: the rotting body of the python which Apollo slew and cast into the Delphic cleft. Its rising fumes entered, from below, the naked body of his priestess, the Pythoness, sitting on the tripod placed over the cleft, and thus inspired her oracles. These were *his* oracles delivered through her mouth.

This myth is mentioned here for two reasons. Firstly because the rotting corpse in Painting 5 corresponds to the snake at the foot of the tree in Painting 1. And secondly because the rotting corpse carries with it the same connotation as that of the decomposing body of the hanging boy in Painting 3, which symbolised incestuous desire.

The river a father-symbol

It is worthwhile pointing out, in connection with the river in this fantasy, that it is a *river* and not a pool, nor the sea. This gives an indication of what this fantasy is mainly concerned with, namely what in mythology is called the "river god". The sea symbolises the primordial mother-image from which we all arose (depicted for example by the Babylonian primaeval goddess Tiamat, who, as the sole parent and mother of all gods, seeks to devour them back into herself till overcome by her own youngest son, the hero-god Marduk). The pool or fountain represents this same femininity transformed because contained within the land. The human psyche has absorbed it so that it has now become a well of psychic life (the Virgin as the fountain, Christ as the well). But in the West all rivers tend to symbolise the father-principle and are called "father", such as Father Thames, Father Tiber, or Father Rhine. This is because the river flows between two banks, fertilizing the land through which it goes. Thus also in Egypt Osiris is the Nile. In Painting 5 the corpse is, too, the "river god". (See also the description of Orpheus, commenting on Painting 6.)

    b) Personal associations
      Black colour for (i) the rotting flesh,
      (ii) her father's clerical clothes. White ribs indicate her tuberculosis.

This brings us to the personal side of this archetypal fantasy-painting. When asked whose corpse it was, Mary first said that she had no idea. It simply was "a man". Such a reply means "animus" and in this case "unconscious animus", still as unconscious as the hanging boy. But this man no longer hangs. Like Odin, he has fallen from the tree, and she has psychically "dived down" to him.

Such unconscious perception is, however, of no use unless connected with actual memories of facts or feeling tones. In a case of repression as deep as this one was, the memories can be obtained often only indirectly through associations. These on the surface look harmless enough for ego consciousness not to be frightened and therefore to repress them into yet further concealment.

What had impressed me, however, was the blackness of the corpse, so that I asked her why she had painted it black. She answered without hesitation that the black parts were the putrefying flesh still clinging to the bones. Having apparently forgotten the purple rotting flesh of the hanging boy in painting 3 (see also that of the "unknown man" in Painting 11), she now said she thought all rotting flesh would look black like this, but didn't remember ever seeing it. This therefore drew a blank so far as personal associations went. As "black" can mean so many things (see later in this book), I in my mind had to fall back on archetypal concepts such as those of the *nigredo* and *mortificatio* of alchemy (as the first stage in self-realization through the achievement of "not knowing", that is to say abandonment of preconceived assumptions), or such as the *massa confusa* or primitive "chaos" (*prima materia*). Such blackness also symbolises the latter—that out of which any new thing may arise as well as memories formerly repressed. Another traditional meaning is that of melancholia (from the Greek *melan*, black, and *chole*, bile) and of the "darkness" of all physical and psychic illnesses,[22] symbolising ignorance of how they are self-caused.

This still took us no further on the personal level until, when I had ventured to mention the meaning of "mortification" as meaning the "death" of some kind of illusion, she suddenly came out with the statements that she

---

22. Jung, *Psychology and Alchemy*, p. 218 ff. and *Von den Wurzeln des Bewusstseins*, pp. 467-8.

had really painted the rotting flesh black because her father's clerical clothes were black and that it was " his parsonic side" that she had always objected to and thought to be "rotten".

That was significant enough, particularly because in alchemy "black-ness" means also "projection", which comes not from the object that is thought of as black but from the subject that can see only the other person or thing as "black", the blackness coming really from the inside and belonging to the person who "sees black" rather than to that which "is seen as black". Therefore, however true it may have been that Mary's father's "parsonic side" was rotten, there was something rotten also in the fact that she had never dared to tell him so, thus creating an incest-bond of mutual deception which was part of, from Mary's own angle, the real "rot" in this relationship. The alchemist thus says to the sick one that in the healing process "darkness will flee" not from the object but "from you".[23]

That all this rottenness should be connected with the beloved father was an eye-opener for her. My next question was why the flesh on the chest was not also painted black. She answered at first quite simply that *the flesh had already rotted off the chest and this is why there is no flesh on it and the ribs are white*.

But what astonished me more even than her saying that the rotting flesh was black because it was the colour of her father's clothes or parsonic atti-tudes was that she next said of the "white" chest *this is my chest, where the tuberculosis was*. When she was 16 she had nearly died of it and her father had moved his bed into her room. He had undressed naked before her where-by she had been saved from death probaby only by her conscious realization at that moment of her overwhelming sexual desire for him. This he had seemed quite oblivious of.

4. Her pulmonary tuberculosis.
Psychosomatic considerations. Psychic father-incest.

Psychotherapy is an exciting profession. One never knows when some unexpected information of this kind will come to light up the darkness of a

---

23. Jung, *Wurzeln*, p. 467, note.

deep complex, in this case by showing the extent to which she and her father were identified and were, from her angle, "as one". We may remember how she used to think he was "the only man". This means that he totally swamped her animus, which practically did not exist independently but was at one and the same time subservient to him and possessive of him. He had told her that she would of course never marry but would always stay with him. She in turn thought of him as her own.

Here, in Painting 5, they are not "as one" but they *are* one. She has tuberculosis in the place where his lungs are. It is a picture of extreme psychological incest. It is also a portrait of her psychosomatic self.

The "self" is in any case hermaphrodite. The infant at the breast is but one half of the mother-child unity. In the infant's totality one half is its own body. The other half is split between the images of the mother when she is there, and of the absent mother when she is not there. The latter is the empty space in which the psyche grows, for good or ill. Since there are two sexes and two parents, there are likewise two worlds, the mother-world and father-world. In the beginning of the infant's life before the development of that third thing, the infant's own ego, these are the only two. As father is the outsider in the primitive mother-world, so all that is outside the mother-world is psychologically "father" too, for better or for worse. This is, for the infant, the "father" world of frustration. Father comes in between mother and child. But it is also the world of opportunity. In a good marriage both worlds may cooperate well. What is not found in the mother the father may supply. But when there is a bad mother he is expected to supply too much. Frustrated longing for the breast may get transformed into longing for the father's genital, as happened in Mary's case.

Mary's desire was "black" in that it was compulsive and also unsatisfied. But "black" also means the darkness of the womb, out of which anything may come, devils or saints, instinct or animus-possession. It symbolises the unknown contents of Pandora's box containing all the ills mankind may suffer from; or on the contrary Persephone's casket with all the beauties of the world in it, which Psyche was to bring back from the underworld.

Thus Mary's problem was extreme. She had transferred her frustrated mother-longing onto her father. The tree here draws its strength from him, but only after he is dead and his corpse is rotted, symbolising not only him but her projections onto him. These were in process of "dying" now that she had a counter-attraction, which was the person of the analyst who had handled her father-problem. It had been done well enough not to arouse too many psychotic defences while new light was being shed on it.

The tree "sucks from" the corpse just as in actual life the babe sucks from the mother, or, nearer to the imagery of this painting with its sucking roots, as the foetus does from the placenta with its many veins. This had been uncreative while her father was still for her the "only man". But in this instance it is highly creative, being in a fantasy in which the dead body symbolises the psychic father-principle from which, in contrast to physical birth out of the mother, all psychic birth comes. It is in this case a symbol for the transformation of incestuous desire and also of that personal possessiveness which constitutes death for psychic freedom and real personality.

In wanting to possess one is unconsciously "possessed", a fact here symbolised on one level by the "blackness" of the corpse, which in the fantasy of Painting 5, though rotting, has by no means yet rotted away. Possessiveness is more evil if it is unrecognised than if it is available to consciousness and therefore to the possibility of change.

Dreams and such fantasies as this one work by opposites. What has been the most devastating factor in external life becomes the most healing factor when the psyche can "reverse nature" in order to draw sustenance from the knowledge of evil, thus transforming it into good. Mary's psyche was symbolised by "the earth", and when painting she had realized that the "grass" of supposed innocence which had grown out of it must not flourish. This unreal innocence must be replaced by the knowledge of what had been so maimed—that central element of psychic consciousness represented by the father-principle, functioning in its own right and not merely as a mother-substitute.

Therefore, whereas in Figure 7 the tree of knowledge grows out of Eve's head, Mary's tree was as yet not fully joined to ego consciousness. But, though it flourished inwardly, it did not yet give her conscious awareness. There was only a deep psychic movement of hope, which she was no more able to express than she had been able to express to her father what she wanted from him.

It was not till years later that fantasy joined with reality and she began experiencing physical love. But this awakening and her deep longing for trust and affection still had the greatest difficulty in coming together. The "blackness" of her still unresolved incest desires was too intense.

In my experience all chest or pulmonary diseases are apt to be idealists' diseases having to do symbolically with "air". The first thing that the infant does after issuing from the warm security of the womb into the outside world is to breathe air. The traumatic effect of this may well be gauged from the word "atmosphere", derived from the Greek *atmos*, breath, and *sphaira*. Conventionally the latter is thought of as meaning a ball or globe but its derivation means, according to Skeat[24], probably "that which is tossed about". This may well indicate the feelings of the newborn infant in being tossed out into the cold world—the father-world in opposition to the mother-world from which it comes. In the act of breathing it takes this outside world into itself. The indication that it breathes is the first cry that it emits.

We know how the father is also an "outsider" to the primitive mother-world. So "air" and "father" become psychically synonymous and are connected with conflict, without which there is no life. The infant's first act is to breathe in, absorbing something from outside which is not part of the mother-world but is creatively opposed to it.

But the importance of one opposite may be exaggerated at the expense of the other one. This is what happened in Mary's case when, feeling herself rejected by mother, she fixed a double load of hope and expectation onto the father. For her the father-world then swamped the mother-world and there was an excess of psychic "air" or father-influence which thereby became "poisoned air". This led, I suggest, on the one hand to her over-valuation of the father and on the other to the tuberculosis in her chest as a somatic protest against this.

Diseases are "attempted cures".

All diseases may be regarded as "attempted cures" on the part of psychic consciousness. It is doing its best to call attention to what is in fact a psychological disease which, if not recognised, turns into a physical one in an

---

24. Walter William Skeat, 1835-1912. English philologist and lexicographer.

effort to shock the ego into consciousness. The outcome depends on whether ego can learn its lesson or cannot. If it resorts to drugs or merely physical treatment, that is "mother" (matter) again. All modern materialistic medicine encourages this attitude. Even if the disease is what is called "cured" by such means it does not bring with it that self-knowledge which the disease came in order to promote.

In Mary's case the tuberculosis accomplished a "half cure" in that at the point of death from it she became most vividly aware of the sexual desire for her father. But it was only a half cure in that there was nobody at hand to help her to recognise that part of her desire was frustrated mother-longing for the unconscious image of the mother's breast which she had never had. This would have linked it with the bronchiectasis that developed during her frustrated infancy.

It was as an expression of Mary's extreme form of psychological incest that the tuberculosis invaded her, with the purpose of either killing her or opening her eyes (see Painting 33).

TWO DREAMS

1. Separation from the Father, November 1953

Painting 5, which was a "painting fantasy", dealt mainly with the father-problem. Ten months later Mary had the following dream:

"I was with father (she never called him "father", but by a pet name so intimate that we will not use it here) *in a bus. We were happy to be together. The bus stopped at a large building with round windows without any glass in them. We went into a long waiting hall as though in a hospital. Men in white coats were sending the women through a door on the left and the men through one on the right. Father was angry and said we could not be separated, but we were pushed off in different directions."*

Like any vehicle a person travels in, a bus is a mother-symbol. It carries one. One does not carry it. It is thus also symbolic of fate, or of a power outside one's control. Such vehicles can be of many kinds. A motor car one drives oneself shows some degree of individual control. A bus in which one is driven shows a far greater degree of unconsciousness and lack of realization of that which one is "driven" by. The bus in question was like that in which Mary would sometimes go with her father into the local shopping town. Being *"happy to be together"* in this containing vehicle was symbolic of their mutual unconsciousness of the psychically incestuous relationship that held them in its grip and was so matriarchally possessive on both sides.

But fate operates in two ways. Remaining unconscious it may destroy. But consciousness may bring about a cure. While at the beginning of the analysis it had been necessary to support Mary's love of the one man in her life she had been so close to, lest love itself should perish if too much criticized, it had been gradually dawning on her that even her relationship with him had not been quite so blissful as she would like to think it had. Such consciousness was now beginning to be a release. Blind ego-consciousness which would defend him to the hilt was giving way to psychic consciousness; the same "bus" symbolising her feeling of inseparable oneness with him now stops outside a building which turns out to be a hospital. In dream language this means a place of psychic healing. The real life bus and the inner, dream bus reveal the two sides of

80

her nature. Thus, looked at from outside, it had *"round windows without any glass in them"*, to which she had no personal associations, so that they could be thought of as sightless eyes. The lack of glass would indicate lack of reflexion, which symbolised Mary's condition before the analysis.

But, once inside, the scene was very different. It is true that they do not get beyond the *"long waiting hall"* redolent of the long waiting period which her life up till now had been. This scene was preliminary to that which was to happen next—the separation from the mothering father and a recognition of the difference between men and women. Mary was very circumstantial in some of her dream images such as that of the white-coated hospital orderlies who were sending the women through a door on the left and the men through one on the right. The dream, however, need not have called her attention to their white coats if it had not had some purpose in doing so. We may therefore remember that it was the "whiteness" of the ribs and chest of the father's rotting corpse in Painting 5 (otherwise black) which called attention not only to the fact that this was her own chest "where the tuberculosis was" but also to the realization of the connexion of this disease with her incestuous identification. The whiteness in this case would be an instance of the *albedo* of alchemy, indicating a dawning consciousness.

The basic meaning of the division thus brought about is the separation of the male and female parent-images which had in Mary's case been so confused. The Separation of the World Parents is a well-known mythological motif dealing with the birth of individuality out of the chaos of undifferentiated womb-like life.

Although it would appear that Mary drew a sharp distinction between the mother whom she hated and the father whom she loved, as we know father had assumed the role of the good mother too so that in Mary's psyche the separation had not occurred. Furthermore she had been "mother" to him and he had been her "child", so that the truly masculine father-principle had hardly operated in the rectory. The separation adumbrated in this dream thus had to be on two levels: that of the primaeval parent-images, and that of father from daughter. Since her parents were both dead, the dream indicated that the separation was about internal events—and not external ones—and had to take place within her own psyche.

The father being "angry" in the dream hardly reflects external life since hers was outwardly so mild, but it does reflect Mary's own anger at this challenge to her possessiveness of him. If Mary had known a little more about her own hostile attitudes in general the dream would have said that it was she herself who was so angry and so hurt. But it is still only her hidden animus (the father in the dream) that so reacts, with the result that though she *is* angry about so many things she is still unaware of the reason why—the incest bond with him.

2.   **The mother, the old woman with the sores, and the dark man piping in the snakes.**

Mary's dream life, having separated her from the father, now opened up the way to an experience of the archetypal mother and to the positive animus as reached through her. The following dream, from among the many dreams that she was now having, is given as she first described it to me.

"*I was at home with Mother. A wrinkled old woman with sores on her face came in and offered us a bit of the hunk of bread and butter she was eating. I was afraid of infection and would have refused, but Mother said 'Our sister has been with the gypsies. If we eat with her we shall gain their wisdom'.*

"*So we shared the food, and at once we were in a forest clearing. It was bright moonlight, and little green snakes were everywhere. Mother told me to put my hand on one of them and let it lead me. I did so, and we came to a dark man dressed in skins. He was playing a reed pipe beside a spring of water. I felt very happy and satisfied.*"

The dream is in two scenes, the first of which is in the personal setting of being "*at home with Mother*". This was a striking phrase since Mary in her external life had had such a bad relationship with her—feared her and was afraid she might become like her or like her mother's sister Grace.

The "enemy" in overt life the "helper" in the dream.
Problem of the Dual Mother. The "three sisters". Psychosomatic "sores".

It is a fact of great significance and theoretical importance in the analysis of dreams that what we think of as the greatest enemy in overt life may be the greatest helper in dream life. This paradox is due to the fact that what would appear to be our greatest enemies in overt life have power over us only insofar as what they think or say about us has at least a modicum of truth—enough

82

to get "under our skin". However spiteful, malicious, jealous or out to do us harm they are, they would be powerless if there were not a chink in our armour which they can pierce. They may be ninety percent ill disposed, but the ten percent of truth they have got hold of is what matters. In the rough and tumble of external life, we can't acknowledge it because we hate them so. But in the dream the actors are all part of the dreamer. If we have gained this amount of awareness through some relaxing of our fears, we may then recognize in the dream the voice of what we thought to be our enemy as the voice of psychic consciousness revealing some truth that we ought to know.

The fundamental figure in the first scene was the archetypal mother appearing as the *"wrinkled old woman with the sores on her face"* whom the mother, speaking to Mary, called *"our sister"*. This is a striking epithet with regard to the psychic structure indicated in the dream: Mary was psychologically one of three "sisters". This is what Jung calls the chthonic female Trinity (compare Painting 29 in which three snakes issue from her body) here composed of (i) the mother, (ii) the old woman with the sores, who was an obvious "earth mother", and (iii) Mary herself. On another level, it meant that ego in the dream was able to perceive that she had "two mothers": her own real mother and an archetypal one who carried with her all the atmosphere of mystery that archetypal mothers do.

These three may be compared with the three Fates, Muses, Goddesses, Fairies or Witches who are such frequent figures in mythology. These all refer to psychological structure, which in the present instance consists of a) a central ego-function (the observing one) called in the dream "Mary", and b) the two mother-figures, the personal and archetypal. The latter here reveal what Jung describes in *Symbols of Transformation* as the Dual Mother role: the conscious and unconscious aspects of the actual mother—in other words the personal and the collective or supra-personal.

These two "mothers" are "shadow figures" of one another in the sense that they are opposites. The old woman with the sores reveals a very different side of Mary's mother's character than that which her mother strove to present both to the world and to herself. Her compulsive cleanliness sought to cover up facts like the chronic diarrhoea she suffered from. She tried to conceal it but actually advertised it by the commodes in every room and pas-

83

sage of the house. What the mother so desperately and schizoidly tried to conceal was uninhibitedly expressed, however, by her sister Grace, that aunt whom Mary loved as much as she hated her own mother. Aunt Grace was not schizoid but hysterical and unabashedly incontinent. She was equally unrestrained in voicing her own infantile complexes by means of a stream of fantasies. It was Mary's greatest joy to listen to them and join in with her own. At the same time she tended her, washing her dirty linen with delight.

Mary was not, however, mothered by either of these. She was brought up by her father's sister Martha, a model of respectability and of conventional behaviour. But it was not of her that Mary dreamt. It was of a "second mother" or "earth mother": the old woman with the sores. On enquiry these turned out to be "running sores"—not concealed as her own mother had tried to conceal her diarrhoea and her complexes but exposed to view upon her face and round her mouth. Mary in overt life mainly associated running sores when someone has for instance "had a cold" and sores break out around the lips.

All such "outbreaks", from diarrhoea to pimples, ulcers and so on, are psychosomatic attempts literally to "ex-press" what is psychologically repressed. If it does not succeed in breaking through in other more creative ways in acts of self-realization leading to greater consciousness, the vital life force leaks away in pathological symptoms.

Mary's devotion to her Aunt Grace was primitive in the extreme and had two sides to it. On the one hand it might be thought pathological. But on the other it was "down to earth" in a way that few have the privilege to experience. What was needed for Mary's psychic health was to bring this deeply hidden part of her personality into the light and honour it. The analyst had helped in this by showing real appreciation of her familiarity with excretion and what all this had meant to her as *prima materia* for soul-building. This had released her now to the extent of producing this dream figure of the *"old woman with the sores"*.

One of the benefits of the analysis had been, for Mary, that she was beginning to be able to "listen in" to such intimations from psychic consciousness, and to use ego consciousness as a channel rather than as a blockage to such perception. Whereas, up till now, the problem to be tackled had been the most immediate one of identification with the father, there was a far deeper identification than she had as yet suspected or could bear to think about with the mother. The dream experience was connected with the fact that, as a modicum of self-knowledge began to dawn on her, she was at this time faintly beginning to realize that her mother was not just the she-devil that she had formerly thought her to be. She was a human being with problems and even sensibilities, not unlike those which Mary was now beginning to acknowledge in herself. Further—that her mother might even have had to suffer from the father's ignorance. The present dream was one of the most momentous ones bringing these facts to light. Here the image is not of the father, but of the mother who had been the apparently "mad" one. This points the way towards a new level of consciousness through the acceptance of unpalatable fact.

"Gypsies" as the conveyors of natural "wisdom".
"Cursing" a female attribute.

What lay behind all this began to make itself somewhat plainer when I enquired into the meaning of the dream-mother's phrase: *"Our sister has been with the gypsies; if we eat with her we shall gain her wisdom"*. Mary at first had no comment to make. This was quite typical of the difficulty of getting direct associations out of her.

Knowing, however, the extent of her projection onto others, I had developed the technique of asking not about what she felt but about what others felt. This often succeeded in revealing what her own feelings were. I did it on this occasion and asked what were her parents' feelings about gypsies. This had the immediate result of opening her up. She said, rather dully at first, that there were often gypsies in the neighbourhood, some living fairly settled lives but others coming and going, camping with their caravans near the village and moving off again. They would of course from time to time steal chickens and such things, which Mary and no moral judgments about but would admire them for. She had not had the fantasies that most children have of being kidnapped or "living with gypsies"—with the combined fright and fascination that such fantasies entail. Nor did she ever visit them, since she was too homebound. They would come to the rectory, begging, or with knickknacks to sell. Her father was not particularly concerned, treating them in the same way that he would treat any beggar, giving them always some small thing.

All this Mary related without much interest, until I asked about her mother's attitude, when her face lit up with vivid recollection of how the gypsies were for her the objects of superstition and fear, since if they were not placated they could curse, and the curses would come true in bringing illness or some other misfortune. Mary herself shared her mother's superstitious dread. This was not simply fear but an admiring awe in face of unknown powers, in her view wild, untamed, but sure in their effects.

This dread was psychologically associated with her mother's fear of revengeful ghosts, which amounted in fact to fear of her own revengefulness, both secret and expressed. Mary had herself copied this in her attempts to "magic" any whom she disliked or thought might injure her. We may detect a bond of identification with this unknown power, knowing that she imagined herself torturing them. She would implicitly believe in the efficacy of this despite evidence to the contrary. In reality it served only to isolate her from the world and make her feel at enmity with many who might have helped her. Her deep suspicion of them prevented this.

The word "gypsy" is a corruption of the Middle English "Egypcien" derived from an early name for Memphis and applied to the general population of Egypt.[25] Gypsies were originally strangers coming from India into Egypt, where they sojourned long. They were subsequently always wanderers, so that for thousands of years the Gypsy life has symbolised something alien to the settled property-owning population. The latter in its bourgeois aspect has always suspected gypsies, fearing that primitive mentality which recognises no property boundaries but takes what it can as if by right. Thus, where an ordinary thief is just a "thief", gypsies have that aura about them that makes their thieving somehow romantic and much more forgivable. At the same time the gypsy has the power to "curse" which no ordinary thief has.

It is moreover not chiefly the gypsy men but the gypsy *women* who have this power of cursing. To country-bred people like Mary's mother, entrenched behind conventions of all kinds and fearful of losing what they have, the gypsies are a menace. They also exert a strong attraction which betrays the secret compensatory longing to be free. The fear of their curse has its origin in fear of the "mother's curse", which is throughout the world the worst curse there is: it is the curse of revengeful nature, red in tooth and claw.

---

25. See Eric Partridge: *Origins*. London, Routledge and Kegan Paul, 1958.

Amidst all this ambivalence it will be realized that the mother's unspoken curses were a good deal more dangerous to Mary than her spoken ones. In the same vein Mary's own consciously thought out magical cursings were the more damaging to her in that she never expressed them but kept them secret. This was tantamount to fear of real contact with any human being, for this might have shown how futile they were.

The gypsies were thought of by Mary as alien people whom she both feared and secretly admired just as she both feared and actually secretly admired her mother. Complexes are always formed of two opposite and opposing elements of which the one may be conscious and the other deeply unconscious. Two such opposing elements are symbolised in this dream scene by the mother and the gypsies: the mother stands for the domineering super-ego; her dream "sister", who had "been with the gypsies", stands for the fascination of the id. This opposition inevitably includes the motive of incest. Their appearance together in the dream, however, in which the mother as one of the opposites takes the initiative of introducing Mary to the second one, indicates the beginning of a reconciliation between the two in Mary's psyche. The fact that the mother herself says, "If we eat with her, we shall gain their wisdom", anticipates the acquisition of the wisdom of the "snake". This in the end releases her, as seen in Paintings 26 to 30 and Painting 33, and in particular in Painting 29 (three snakes issuing out of Mary's own psychic body-image.)

Among many primitive peoples incest is thought to be the cause of sores and many kinds of otherwise unaccountable diseases. This was the case with the plague which overtook the Thebans on account of Oedipus' unwitting incest. Among ourselves incestuous longings are no less dangerous for not being physically expressed. Indeed, as in this case, they may be much worse because hidden and never acknowledged, so that they cannot be dealt with. Mary was exceptional mainly in that she experienced consciously the impact of incestuous desire more vividly than most, so that she was overtly more pathological than most. This meant, however, that through her very consciousness of what she felt, the psychic tools for healing as expressed in her dreams and fantasies were all the more available if they could be but shared and understood.

The incest wish is age-old and archetypal. Derived originally from the breast, transferred later to the father, it had been in this case experienced both by Mary's mother with regard to her own father, and by Mary herself with regard to *her* father.

The signs that the earth-mother knew all about it were not only the sores upon her face. Her wrinkles showing her long experience indicated "character", a word used also for runes engraved on stone and so for ancient wisdom of an archetypal kind. She could thus potentially unite both opposites. She was a "good mother" in that she offered to both Mary and her mother the bread and butter that she was eating. Her mother surprisingly suggested that she and Mary should share in it in spite of Mary's fear of the "infection" coming from the sores.

The psychological meaning of "infection"

"Infection" is the key word here, emphasizing the element of fear, concealing the desire to love. It is the fear of love which stops us from finding in ourselves the good which we unconsciously long for but still are frightened of. The evil lies not in the basic incest-love itself but in our fear of letting it die so that it may become transformed. In this way we may live with the new insight that such "dying" gives.

This is a truth as important as the apparent enemy really being the friend. The fear of physical infection is one of the characteristic obsessions of modern life, most to the fore in certain types of paranoids. Thus Mary's mother was "infection mad". She would not go near anyone who had a cold, and took every precaution against infection of all kinds—thereby naturally catching most infectious illnesses. Mary herself, reacting against this, professed herself indifferent so far as physical illness was concerned. But she was terrified of infection on the psychic plane from her mother, the gypsies, and even her beloved Aunt Grace, whose hysteria she feared to be "infectious".

It is worthwhile therefore enquiring what the word "infection" means. It is derived from the Latin *infectus*, from *inficere*, literally to "put in", to "stain" or "colour" and hence to "dye", and secondly in a negative direction, to "taint" or to "corrupt". The first meaning is psychologically allied to "dedicate", that is to take on some loyalty such as "wearing the colours" of so-and-so or even "dying for the 'colours' of the regiment".

It is thus closely allied to the idea of being "initiated" by accepting that which is "put in", namely some kind of new attitude of agreement rather than disagreement. This is in turn connected with Homer Lane's[26] "deep knowledge" that, contrary to modern medical belief, it is a mistake in personal psychology to resist germs, which will wreak vengeance on us if we do so and thereby give us the very illnesses which we try to ward off. On the contrary, we should "love" them, so that in turn they may love us.

We all know legends of the saint kissing the leper and this thereby healing both the leper and the saint. Such facts suggest once more the theme of "necessary corruption" as a stage in transformation. At this crucial time this was the subject of many of Mary's dreams and fantasies, like those of the rotting corpse of the hanging boy in Painting 3 and of her father in Painting 5. These are equivalent to "mortification" [mortificatio]: letting the old things go in preparation for the new.

Gypsies, being at the same time outlawed and secretly desired, attract much the same feelings that we have toward psychic consciousness, and towards the germs that do much of their work at the borderline between psyche and soma.

Thus fear of "infection" has as an aspect of fear of life.

"Bread and butter." Two elements in the communion feast. Milk versus blood. "Sharing the food."

This brings us back to the *bread and butter* which the old woman was eating, which Mary was at first afraid to eat because of the infection. But her dream mother (so unlike her mother in external life) referred to the gypsies' wisdom. "*Wisdom*" is akin to the Latin *videre* meaning "to see", and is in turn connected with the Old English *witan* "to know" (German *wissen*) and with "wizard", meaning originally a very shrewd, wise man. There are many cognates to this word such as "advise", all having to do with "seeing" not with the outer eye but with the inner eye, i.e. "seeing the opposite" of what at first appears.

There are two elements in the meal which the old woman offers to share with them, the bread and the butter. These can he seen as taking the place of

---

26. Lane was an American psychologist summoned to Britain after WWI; he was instrumental in helping Layard to recover from a psychotic period.

the bread and wine of the communion rite which Mary had been in the habit of receiving at her father's hands, the body and the blood symbolising the outer and the inner truth. We have already noted the reference to bread in Mary's conversation with the snake (cf. Painting 1), which the snake then refused because, though body-conscious, Mary thought that she ought not to be. A year's analysis had made her less falsely guilty about this, so that the "bread" symbolising the body ("This is my Body" in the communion rite) has now become acceptable. But she was still too infantile to take the "wine", which would indicate full psycho-sex-emotional responsibility. The emphasis of what she needed was still on the breast, the female element, the milk, here in the form of the "butter".

If this might seem irrelevant, we may remember the huge place that bread and butter takes in English childhood life, being one of the earliest replacements of the breast. They are the stuff of life, as is the breast (spongy like bread) and what comes out of it, the milk, here condensed into the butter of the bread-and-butter meal.

It need hardly be stressed that it was the analyst who in the first place trusted where Mary mistrusted, and thus "infected" her with the notion that she might one day love and cherish her own self and fundamental right to live, in spite of all the contradictions that she felt within herself.

The dream continues *"so we shared the food"*, meaning that, in the context of this dream and of the reconciliation that was beginning to take place, fear and suspicion were dissolving and psychic consciousness getting a chance to operate.

"Drop-through" into the forest clearing.

The act of "giving in" and of accepting the food offered by the old woman with the sores had the immediate effect of causing what is called a "drop-through" into a still deeper level of psychic consciousness. Here nature heals without effort of ego consciousness, and ego in the dream has but to observe and to see what happens quite of its own accord, once fear is abandoned and resistances relaxed.

"And we were at once in a forest clearing" (see Painting 6) means that the psyche responds immediately to such agreement with its purposes. A forest is a well-known symbol for that aspect of the collective mother-world in

which we cannot "see the wood for the trees", i. e. we are blinded and do not even know the wood that we are in. "*A forest clearing*" means on the contrary that in the midst of the "wood" there is some area of consciousness, symbolising the "clearing of the mind" from some at least of the clutter that had infested it, which may remind us of the adumbrated cutting down by the scythe of the thistle (Painting 2).

At the same time we are told that "*It was bright moonlight*", symbolising that inner light which shines in the darkness and reveals the inner truth, counteracting the influence of the "sun" of external appearances and interference from elders or authoritarian misconceptions. We may remember how, in the dream illustrated by Painting 3, the vision of the neglected garden with the tree and hanging boy was ushered in by the remark that "It got rather dark". This did not mean, as it so rarely does in dreams, that the dreamer could not see. Darkness means "inwardness", a change of direction in the attention which one gives to things. There was in that dream no moonlight; what she "saw" was as yet to her incomprehensible.

"Little green snakes" as animi[27]. Lost childhood returning. Wholeness.

Now, more than a year later, the moon begins to shine within her soul, so that, under its light, she now perceives that "*little green snakes were everywhere*". These little phallic snakes symbolise her scattered *animi*, the coming to life of emotions and realizations long buried, now being admitted into consciousness.

Just as in the first scene the mother in the dream was in favour of the gypsies and the old woman with the sores, saying, "*If we eat with her we shall gain their wisdom*", so in this scene her dream mother also functions as an opener of the way: "*Mother told me to put my hand on one of them*" [the snakes] "*and let it lead me.*" This is what Mary's mother in external life would never have said. It is the reverse of all she consciously stood for. Yet here the dream mother functions as the Mediatrix, as Mary the Virgin Mother does in Catholic belief, for through following her advice Mary is drawn towards the

---

27. The animus portrayed as a group of miniature representatives of itself (the whole). As a masculine Latin word, animus in the plural form would be "animi", just as cactus becomes "cacti". The more anglicized version would be "animuses". Ed.

dark man. He is dressed in skins, a saviour-figure piping in the snakes. Of him Mary said, *"He was playing a reed pipe beside a spring of water. I felt very happy and satisfied"*. As she described this scene with unaccustomed inwardness, she wept. It was the first time she had wept since the analysis began, and they were healing tears (there is a litany including a prayer for "the grace of tears"), corresponding to the "spring of water" which her dream described. It was the first time also that she said she felt happy.

What was the reason for her relief? She had not felt this relief in the first scene, dominated by the two women (the actual mother and the archetypal one, symbolising the mother problem which she could not yet face). The relief came with the vision of the snakes and the dark man since it was easier for her to accept relationship first with the father. Finally she could accept the analyst as a figure uniting both the father and the mother principles.

The problem was acute. The two opposite dangers were on the one hand that of remaining immobilised in incestuous desire, and on the other hand that of its opposite: if released too suddenly with nothing to take its place, there was the danger of sexual promiscuity, lesbian or otherwise, the symbolism of the snakes including this.

Mary, though she was still physically virginal, had these two opposite tendencies developed to a high degree. This was the more so in that she had never tested out the workability of either tendency openly but kept them both locked up under the mentally defective mask which was her refuge and prison. One thing which the analysis had so far achieved had been an increasing recognition of the sexual content of her fantasies, but not of the bitter rejection of it. This was much more entrenched because it constituted her defence against utter collapse and thus could not yet be realized.

The analyst as "male mother"

The handling of such opposites needs more than technical knowledge. It needs humanity. In the consulting room these opposites in the form of highly ambivalent feelings are projected wholesale onto the analyst. If he or she is to fulfil the analytical function, he/she must mediate them all including male and female feelings, chaste thoughts and unchaste thoughts, inner and outer emotions, expressed and unexpressed, so far as he or she is able. Thus it is clear that, in this dream, the reference to "mother" is in fact a reference to the analyst who mediated to Mary not only the realization that she was a very sick person (which she was unaware of at first) but also the fact that knowledge of this sickness was part of its cure. One aspect of this sickness consisted of her fiercely secretive and defensive attitudes. She covered up her deep and running wounds with defective attitudes which she had used as a child against the ills that threatened her in the parental atmosphere. The "mother" in the male analyst tended to release the guilt attaching to both sides of this sickness—the uncontrollable hatreds as well as the equally uncontrollable desires. Both were inevitable in the circumstances in which she was brought up. They became inappropriate only when carried forward into adult life when both parents were dead; the defensive attitudes became in fact offensive ones directed in fantasy against others but in reality mainly against herself. A sense of balance had somehow thus to be restored. This was achieved by leading her back into childhood again in an atmosphere not of withholding as her mother had withheld, but one of giving, of trust in place of fear, boldness in place of inward cowardice, fluidity to counteract rigidity.

Such handling of the situation needs "double thinking" especially on the part of the male therapist, who must be not too afraid to use his feminine perception. This is born of acceptance of the suffering which every child experiences, though in a culture antipathetic to the expression of emotion not all therapists remember vividly enough to keep their sensitivity. Problems of adulthood originate in infancy. Thus the analyst's finger, which Mary had happily sucked from time to time in the early stages of her analysis, had been, for him, quite consciously a breast symbol as well as a phallic one. Mary, in putting her hand upon the snake and letting it lead her, was thus reciprocating this conscious act of father-mothering, which in this way gave sanction to some of her most repressed infantile desires.

All this was mediated in the dream by the image of her mother which, under the releasing influence of the analysis, had turned from being a "bad" mother into a "good" mother-image ready to give "the breast". We may think of the small snakes in this dream as "tongues" for happy breast-sucking as well as little phalluses, carriers of libido in its most primitive and polymorphous form.

93

The Ghost Man piping in the Snakes

1. The dream

When asked if she could paint any part of the dream just described Mary declared that the first scene was too difficult but that she could paint the second one—the dark man playing his pipe (flute), charming in the snakes. This was because the mother-problem was still too difficult for her to face, but the father-problem fascinated her, and this was naturally connected with the snakes.

When questioned Mary had no clue, nor any associations, even to fairy tales, as to what this man might symbolise. Nor did her memory recall the obvious similarity between this man with his long dark hair and her own painting of the "ghost man" in Paintings A and B, for her habitual amnesia had blotted out all that. So it was necessary to revive the memory of the "ghost man" in order to find out what this Piper symbolised, who had the power of uniting her scattered wits or animus projections in the form of the little green snakes that had been hiding in the grass. There is a striking contrast between her attitude towards the ghost man of her adolescent experience, a puzzled and frightened one, and the trusting attitude she now evinced towards the Piper in this dream.

Her feeling of happiness and satisfaction at this scene was in sharp contrast to the father's anger and her own distress at their being separated in the previous dream. What has happened to produce this change? It is of the same order as the change occurring in the dream-mother too. In each of these two scenes there has been a drop-through from ego-consciousness to psychic consciousness, revealing to Mary the opposite of what she had concluded from her previous experience with regard to both parents. For the "ghost man" in this dream was like the "ghost man" whom she had seen at the age of sixteen: he symbolised the hidden elements in the parents, being a combination of the mother's animus and father's anima. Whereas then he had been rejected—frightening and negative, he now appears as an accepted soul-leader. The analyst had functioned as a father-mother figure tending to release her from her fears and stimulate a more positive attitude in her.

The Central Tree. Increasing consciousness.

It will be noted that in the description which she first gave of the dream the second scene, which this painting illustrates, was said to be in a "forest clearing", and there was no mention of a central tree. As usual, however, when she started to paint, she "saw" more than she had at first described, in fact a central tree corresponding to the central trees in Paintings 2 (the Tree of the Philosophers), 3 (the tree in the centre of the garden), 4 (the standard rose), 5 (the tree nourished by the corpse). It harks back also to Painting 1 with respect to the small green snakes. The forest clearing thus evidently corresponds to the enclosed garden of Painting 3, but the male figure is no longer hanging from the tree as was the hanging boy, but is here firmly kneeling on the ground. The central tree is no longer a gallows but a "good-mother" tree which overshadows him, protecting him. The spring water cascading down symbolises not only Mary's relief of tears, but also the male principle here coupled with the female tree.

Painting 6 is also on the same model as Painting 5, though showing a great advance on it. The tree is in the same place in both paintings, but the rotting corpse has been resurrected in dual form, a), of the Piper as the central figure now above the ground (relatively conscious), and lower down, b), of the snakes, more chthonic emanations from the corpse, its rotting flesh transformed. The water also has changed its place. From being underground (life-force repressed into the unconscious), it is now visible above ground in

95

the form of a "waterfall", a symbol for psychic energy. It comes out of the rock of her former resistances which, far from being "a layer of stone underneath the earth", is now also above the ground and symbolising her growing awareness of them, as well as her responsibility for having them. We may recall the scene in the desert when Moses "lifted up his hand, and with his rod he smote the rock … and the water came out abundantly" (Numbers 20: 11). The "rod", however, is no longer a rod of anger as it was in Moses' case, but in this dream is seen in the form of the "reed pipe", which the painting shows to be a transverse flute: "ghost man" plays sweet music to charm out the snakes.

The mouth, the reed pipe and the breast

This brings us to the nature of the "ghost man" as he appears in this painting and in the dream. He plays the pipe, in other words makes music with his mouth. This is one of the most primitive ways of expressing mouth-longing in a non-dependent way. It goes back to the breast. Thus, though a phallic instrument, the pipe harks back to a time of bliss or of potential bliss before conflicts arise.

Playing the pipe is like speech in that it uses the mouth movements of sucking in the reverse direction, blowing out instead of sucking in, manipulating lips and tongue as in being breast-fed but non-dependently, creating instead of being created.

There is an infinite variety of such wind instruments[28], all depending to greater or less extent on lip to produce music to stir the heart. In all of these the instrument itself can be viewed as replacing what was the breast in infancy, which the lips manipulate. Of these, the simple pipe made of a hollow stem was among the earliest and most primitive. In many early societies, the shrill noises produced by blowing into such a pipe may be made only by men or boys during initiation rites, when it is said they are the voices of the "ghosts" or ancestors transmitting wisdom to the novices. Though the women may hear from a distance, they often may not see and certainly may not play on the pipes themselves. For they are phallic substitutes for breasts.

---

28. Information kindly supplied by Robert Donnington, author of *The Instruments of Music*, Methuen, 1949, third edition, 1962.

The earliest were hollow cylinders without vibrating reeds or finger-holes and played during the initiation rites—sometimes closed at the bottom, sometimes not. Later came flutes with finger-holes, either blown transversely across the open edge or finished with channels to guide the breath. Here the mouthpiece itself was taken into the mouth like a nipple but blown into instead of sucked.

The various modern wind instruments require differing complex manipulations by the lips. The average character of the players is said to vary with the kind of instrument they play. Reed-players tend to be thin, pale, "interesting", screwed-up and sometimes tubercular, nervous and mother-bound and occasionally homosexual, sucking their lips even when they are not playing. Flute-players are apt to be untroubled, grown-up babies who puff contentedly, are not bothered with "nerves", too childlike even to have developed neuroses.

A notable connection with breast-feeding is the fact that moisture (spittle) collects in all wind instruments, and must from time to time be emptied out. It is interesting also that in modern times if a wind-player offers to let one try his instrument it is the worst possible breach of etiquette, definitely an insult, to wipe its mouthpiece before putting it into one's mouth. The stock rebuke then is, "Do you think I've got foot and mouth disease?" This shows a community of interest on a very primitive level, such as the passing of a loving cup, or of the unwiped chalice in the communion rite. This is somewhat similar to Scene 1 of this dream, in which the old woman offers some of her bread and butter.

A picture like Painting 6 with this breast-motive of the "reed pipe" (flute) so in evidence is to my mind the greatest justification for trusting to natural feelings of sympathy when handling one so infantile as Mary was. Good breast feeding certainly does not bind the infant to the mother in a negative way but is essential for the child's future ability to stand on its own feet and give instead of always wanting to be given to. In this case, to give some comfort meant to pierce through the terrors of paranoid suspicion which Mary suffered from so that, in receiving, some flickerings of trust might be awakened in her dry, hostile and almost wholly defensive psyche. Such is the feeling which this painting conveys: not one of grasping, but on the contrary one of creative satisfaction inwardly.

Six snakes

It will be noted that in her painting there are six snakes, corresponding to the six buds on the standard rose tree in Painting 4. (This was a "tree of life" onto which the analyst had already been grafted as one of the buds and she herself was being grafted as the seventh and final one.) In that painting, about a year and a half before, she was being grafted from the outside and from above by a great hand that lifted her. Now the same process of being admitted back into life is seen at work much more inwardly. All the positions are reversed. She is no longer passively being lifted onto a branch up in the air. She is walking on her own feet and coming from below. Whereas before she was on the right side, now she is on the left. Whereas a year ago the healing was all coming from outside, meaning that the burden was then all on the analyst and that the operating factor was his, not her, dynamic force, now her own psyche is more alive, responding from inside and moving of itself. Moreover, whereas then the "hand" was lifting her passive weight, it is now in the dream her own hand that is stretched out to take hold of the snake, that is, to take her own life in her hands and make the best of it.

We shall see later, in fantasy-painting 13, how these same "snakes", now seven of them, grown to greater maturity and active on their own account, are busy bringing her tree of life out of the skies in the attempt to anchor it to earth. In Painting 30 the tree is rooted in the water under the earth, and a purple snake functions as one of the roots.

Meanwhile, however, we must look backwards and recognise their origin also in the "children" who in the preamble to the dream of the hanging boy depicted in Painting 3 had disappeared into the sky (described as going away in an aeroplane). They symbolised her lost childhood and all the unrelated fantasies resulting from the gross repressions she was then subjected to as well as her lack of childhood companions. Now they return in the form of snakes, symbolising the libido, then lost, being reaccepted into consciousness.

2. Mythological Parallels

The goal of this dream is the figure of the Piper dressed in skins and piping in the snakes. We know that Mary had no associations to him other than

98

that of the "ghost man", and even him she had to be reminded of. We have so far considered him only in the light of Mary's personal psychology. Mythology however abounds with numinous figures of this kind, reference to the better-known of which may help us to understand more deeply what he stands for as a worldwide archetype. There are two main clues to this: the fact that he is dressed in skins, and that he plays the primitive reed pipe.

Meaning of "dressed in skins". John the Baptist and Christ.

The first line of association leads to the biblical figure of John the Baptist "clothed with camel's hair and with a girdle of skin about his loins", eating "locusts and wild honey" (Mark 1: 6), the bitter and the sweet. It was this John who spoke with "the voice of one crying in the wilderness, Prepare ye the way of the Lord" (Matthew 3: 3), for "he that cometh after me is mightier than I" (Matthew 3: 11). Recalling the "ghost man" on one level as the analyst, we are reminded that the ultimate healer is not the analyst, himself or herself, but is the healing spirit which is potentially available to everyone. It is the analyst's function to call this forth from its place of hiding in the patient's own psyche. This is the spirit of psychic consciousness, which Mary's Piper here represents. The analyst can only point the way, just as John the Baptist in so many medieval pictures is shown pointing his finger towards him who "cometh after". He or she helps to remove some of the psychic clutter standing in the way.

Thus John the Baptist, who has been called the last of the prophets, acts as the main link between the Old and the New Testaments. The Old Testament represents the law, while the New Testament transcends the law. Mary was indeed one psychologically "in the wilderness". But it is said that only out of the wilderness can salvation come, meaning that the worst feelings of desolation may be the best ground in which the spirit can take root, such desolation driving either to despair, or to the search for some quite different attitude. Thus it is not irrelevant to note that John the Baptist's camel hair garment has been interpreted by some as a hair shirt. But we may refreshingly remember that being dressed in skins is also a well-known attribute of nature gods, symbolising the psychic factors tending to re-establish the link back to nature in the overcivilised. Thus the one "mightier" than John

99

inveighed not against nature but against the Pharisees. And it was said of him that "He should gather together in one the children of God that were scattered abroad" (John 11: 1-52) like Mary's snakes. As Christ when he "gave up the ghost" upon the cross cried to his Father, "My God, my God, why hast thou forsaken me", so Mary had to experience the separation from her father before his rotting corpse could be resuscitated and transformed.

Christ is himself sometimes described as a piper piping to the faithful so that they should follow him. He is thus called "that gentle shepherd who guides his flock ... mostly with the sweet sound of the syrinx" (a hollow reed used for the original pan-pipes in Greece[29]). And in the apocryphal Acts of John the beloved disciple, it is told how, shortly before the crucifixion, He gathered the apostles together, bidding them "make a ring, holding one another's hands, and himself standing in the midst", and sang to the Father the famous Hymn of Jesus which includes the words:

"Grace dances. I will pipe . . .?
Who dances not, knoweth not what cometh to pass.
I would be saved, and I would save.
I would be loosed, and I would loose.
I would be wounded, and I would wound.
I would be born, and I would bear.
I would eat, and I would be eaten.
A house I have not, and I have houses.
A place I have not, and I have places . . .
A way am I to thee a wayfarer."[30]

These words are said to be uttered by one who said he was the type of all humanity, and that what he suffered and thus gained was what mankind must suffer and must gain. But the present fantasy introduces Mary as yet only to the "forerunner", typified by John the Baptist who said "I indeed baptise you with water ... but he shall baptise you with the Holy Ghost, and with fire". This links up with all the dreams and fantasies of water in Mary's Paintings 5 and 6 and other paintings later on. The fire, which arises from within in response to the

29. Robert Eisler, *Orpheus the Fisher,* London, J.M. Watkins, 1921, p. 52.
30. *The Apocryphal New Testament*, tr. and ed. M. R. James, Oxford, 1924, p. 253.

outer stimulus and which is a transforming thing, did not appear till later, culminating in Paintings 27, of the fire inside her head, and 28, of the Flaming Dragon Man about to burn the fence surrounding her retreat.

The Pied Piper of Hamelin

There are many pipers in mythology. In Europe there is the Pied Piper of Hamelin whose story Mary knew but had not thought of when she did Painting 6. Her story has all the circumstantial trappings that myths so often have. It is said that in the year 1284, to be precise, the little town of Hamelin suffered from a plague of rats and mice.

The myth has it that the Pied Piper was a man of mystery, as symbolised by the tunic and jerkin that he wore, made of cloth of every colour to dazzle the imagination with, which may remind us on the one hand of John the Baptist dressed in skins, and on the other of the gypsies in Mary's dream. The many colours symbolise infinite possibilities such as all children have under the old name of "polymorphous-perverse" coined by Freud[31]. These in the infant, however, are not perverse at all but natural and essentially creative, but which parents often quite unreasonably fear. Freud rightly regards this polymorphous tendency as a characteristic of infantile sexuality, having to do therefore with breast feeding, so that it is not irrelevant that the crime committed by the rats and mice was eating all the food.

The Pied Piper turns up one day, saying that he will charm these "nuisances" away. His price will be the burgomaster's daughter, who is equivalent to the king's daughter of other fairy tales. The German word for the suitor for a young woman's hand is *Freier*, "he who frees", in other words the liberator or "saviour". The burgomaster and townsfolk were so desperate about the rats and mice that they would agree to anything. Thereon the Piper piped, and rats and mice all scampered after him. He led them to the nearby river, into which they followed him so that they were all drowned.

He came back for his price—the bride—but was of course refused. The rats and mice were gone. Why need the townsfolk worry any more? They

---

31. Sigmund Freud, *Three Essays on the Theory of Sexuality*. London, Imago Publishing Co. 1949, p. 69.

thus possessively withheld. He said that he would bide his time, and come back when it suited him. This is the way that psychic consciousness behaves when it its treated in this way. It did not take him long. Next Sunday, wearing a strange red hat, he came and piped again, this time to the children who ran out. Out of the town they followed him, this time, however, not to the river, but towards a hill which opened and they all went in. The hill closed up and they were never seen again, but for the two children who were left behind to repeople the town. Thus were the parents punished for their failure to keep good faith.

The mountain that opens up is a world-wide symbol for the womb, and therefore of rebirth. Externally it is a breast. The Piper's strange red hat is a symbol for the nipple and for the glans penis, so that he also is hermaphrodite like the "ghost man" in Mary's dream, a symbol for the despised and rejected one who is a saviour in disguise.

Pan

On a deeper level is the god Pan, who was the first in Greek mythology to make a pipe out of an alder shoot. Pan's home was in Arcadia, land of idyllic fantasy. His name comes from the Greek *paein*, "to pasture", that is to say, to see to the feeding of animals, and only later came to be associated with the word *pan* meaning "all"—which nevertheless expressed the feeling of his universality as a nature-god. He was by some thought of as the "devil" or the "upright man", this being a phallic image associated with one of the late myths of his being begotten by Hermes, whose power was commonly symbolised by a phallic stone or *herm* carved only with an image of a head and of the erect virile member. He was a popular god of what is called fertility, having the reputation of making love to all the maenads and in particular of having seduced the moon goddess Selene against her will by wearing, to please her, the white fleeces of sheep over his own dark goat-like limbs. Compare with this the moon shining in Mary's dream.

Pan was not always successful in his love affairs. He once pursued a chaste nymph called Syrinx, who fled from him and as a last resort turned herself into a reed called by this name (compare the pipe made of a syrinx reed which Christ piped on). Since he could not distinguish her from other

102

reeds, he cut down several at random and made a set of pan-pipes out of them. This indicates one of the positive results of frustration: turning it into creative fantasy and making music out of it. It helps to show why Mary's "ghost man", who was originally the result of extreme frustration of a double kind concerning mother and father, is here fantasied by her as playing a pipe.

But Pan was doomed to die. Unrestrained sex as a foundation had to be, partly at least, transformed. Though Pan continued to have shrines, altars, sacred caves and sacred mountains dedicated to him in country places, in the Olympian theogony he was succeeded by Apollo, who in a musical contest beat Pan by playing his lyre. This outmoded the pipe, by which victory stringed instruments took precedence over wind ones, except among the peasantry who still clung to them.

Understood psychologically in terms of the body image, this meant transferring attention from the regions of the mouth and genitals (breast-sucking, incest and general possessiveness) to that of the "heart-strings", Apollo being predominantly a "chaste" (introvert) god in opposition to the unchaste (extravert) Pan. But we cannot transform what we have not got. What had to happen to Mary was first the transformation of false spirit back into nature, so as to give her some real *prima materia* on which to build a spirit growing out of and not opposed to it.

Orpheus

The Greek mystery god Orpheus, famed for his playing of the lyre— with which he charmed and pacified wild beasts and even made the trees and rocks move from their places to follow the sound of his music—formerly played the alder-pipe[32]. So we may rank him with the pipe players like Pan as well as with the more highly developed players on the lyre like Apollo, whose son some say he was. As central figure of the earliest known form of Greek religion, he may thus be regarded as forming a link between Pan standing for nature and Apollo standing for the perceptive intellect, the lowest and the highest elements in Greek culture.

At what is called the lowest, he is said to have told more than other reli-

---

32. Robert Graves, *The Greek Myths*. London, Penguin Books, 1955, Vol. I, p.114.

gious figures crude and immoral stories about the gods, but he was at the same time ascetic, teaching self-control and inwardness. He was thus an archetypal figure symbolising psychic transformation having the power to charm wild beasts—in other words, man's wildest emotions—by fully recognising them (certainly not by disregarding them). That he can charm the trees and stones symbolises, in the imagery of trees, the power to release men from their most "rooted" assumptions and boundness to the parental complexes, and in the imagery of stones from the most apparently immovable or "stony" repressions. It is thus not by chance that the Piper in Mary's Painting 6, though she knew nothing about Orpheus, should include these Orphic attributes: those of charming the "snakes", of having already transformed the tree from barrenness to leafiness, and finally of charming the water from the rock, symbolising Mary's own tears of relief at the removal of some of her petrified resistances.

Orpheus did not, however, charm only the beasts, trees and stones, all symbolising hidden emotions. He charmed men too, that is to say, altered conscious attitudes of human beings, as he did when accompanying the Argonauts on their adventure to find the Golden Fleece. He also was a sacrificial god, being like Dionysus torn by women limb from limb, although his severed head sang on. There are grounds also for thinking him to have been a river god, his name being derived from *orphruoeis* meaning "on the river bank", which is where reeds grow for making pipes [33]. This links him with the father figure under the silt below the stream in Mary's Painting 5. And this in turn recalls Orpheus' descent into the Underworld to rescue thence his wife Eurydice, who had been bitten by a snake and died—all such descents symbolising a turning inward to discover that which had been lost or never realized. It is thus worth noting, in connection with the transformation occurring at this time in Mary's psyche, that after Orpheus had been dismembered and devoured by the maenads he was then re-created by his father who swallowed his son's heart (which had been rescued by Athene), and from his own body brought him forth whole again. This is a typical myth of rebirth due to the liberating influence of the father-principle.

Orpheus is said to have been almost a celibate, as well as homosexual-

---

33. Ibid., p.113, note 1.

ly inclined, and it is said that his severed head was taken to the island of Lesbos, which may remind us of Mary's own lesbian tendencies. Even the fingers given her to suck have their counterpart in the symbolism of the secret Orphic calendar, in which the fingers represent the gods. There is an Orphic hymn in which the goddess Night, in the form of a black bird, lays the World Egg, from which is born Eros, whose esoteric name is *Phanes* meaning "the Revealer". Orpheus himself is identified with him as "the firstborn shining one"[34], the silver egg symbolising the moon. In the Orphic mysteries "falling into the milk" was a symbol for regeneration and new life.

Krishna[35]

But the most beloved of all mythological pipers is the youthful Hindu god Krishna, who was an incarnation of Vishnu, one of the three gods forming the Hindu Trinity. The earliest records about his worship date from the fifth or sixth century BC, which was about the same time as the Orphic liturgy seems to have been written down. From then till now his worship has not ceased. The instrument he plays is a transverse flute, which is the same as that played by the Piper in Mary's Painting 6, the feeling of which could hardly be described better than by Sacheverell Sitwell when he writes:

"Rain falls and ceases, all the forest trembles:
Mystery walks the woods once more,
We hear a flute.
It moves on earth, it is the god who plays
With the flute to his lips and music in his breath;
The god is Krishna in his lovely youth."[36]

For Krishna is no ordinary god. He is the most human in all the Hindu pantheon, and is the only one that "dies", shot with an arrow through the foot, death meaning transformation from one state into another one—he having two personalities, human and divine. As human, he was the supreme earthly lover in the form of a young cowherd who, with his beauty and the

---

34. Eisler, p. 6

35. Much of the information given here is taken from W. G. Archer, *The Loves of Krishna*. London, Allen & Unwin, 1957.

36. Ibid., p. 15, quoting Sacheverell Sitwell, *Canons of Giant Art*.

playing of his flute, charmed all the cowgirls and made love to them, in ways no ordinary human lover could (though they were all married to other cowherds, but no husband seemed to mind). That is to say that, as a god, he could give them something their mere husbands could not give—an internal union of the male spirit with the female soul.

In the earlier myths it is his physical love-making that is stressed, with a wealth of humour and with passionate detail. In later ones it is his more spiritual or "ghostly" aspect. Like Orpheus, he thus linked the lowest with the highest (which it was so necessary to do also in Mary's case).

As the most noble incarnation of Vishnu, Krishna thus came to be the most beloved and adored—not only as an abstract spirit but as a lover, "rewarding love with love". "Going 'from darkness to darkness deeper yet', he solved the mystery beyond all mysteries"[37] and so, like the Piper in Mary's dream, Krishna appears in the dark forest and at night when the moon shines out. He is himself likened to the moon[38], thus bringing light into the darkness. The deep forest and the moonlight are constantly mentioned when he is about, and with them too the image of the waterfall. Thus we are told "The moon falls down, saturating the forest"[39], and "the water of life poured down from the great moon"[40]. And this reflects the fact that in all warm countries the full moon is a time for love making, when it is dark enough to hide, but light enough to see.

Figure 16. Krishna playing on the flute surrounded by adoring cowgirls. Detail from "Illustration to the *Gita Govinda*, Kangra, Punjab Hills, c. 1790. N.C. Mehta Collection, Bombay". W.G. Archer, *The Loves of Krishna*, Plate 21

37. Ibid., p. 19
38. Ibid., p. 41
39. Ibid, p. 41
40. Ibid., p. 43

Krishna himself is at one and the same time the darkness and the light that shines in it. For the word Krishna means "black", but he is always painted blue or slightly mauve. Blue (or mauve) is the colour of Vishnu too, these colours along with green (blue lightened by yellow) being "commonly regarded in village India as variants of 'black' "[41] (blue being a light form of black). Thus in one metaphor Krishna is described as being "dark as a cloud, with eyes like lotuses"[42]. At the beginning of his career as a lover of cowgirls at the age of twelve, "His flute sounds in the forest" and he "stands superbly before them. He wears a crown of peacock's feathers and a yellow dhoti and his blue-black skin shines in the moonlight". Thus he "appears as beautiful as the moon amidst the stars".[43]

This is not only beautiful. It is symbolic too. Peacock's feathers have all the colours of the rainbow and symbolise new life. The yellow of his dhoti is the complementary opposite colour of the blue of his skin, the dark colour of his skin thus being clothed with light. And just as Krishna appears first not during daytime but at night, and is the light in it, so it is not during the summer months but only when the autumn[44] comes that he begins his lovemaking: that is to say, when the instinctive life is ebbing and winter is at hand—the winter of man's discontent, symbolising the introverted state in which he operates. It is in this "season" symbolising mankind's inwardness, "the dark night of the soul", that Krishna comes.

We cannot here follow the innumerable details of Krishna's career, but can notice only those features which link up with Mary's dreams and fantasies: his flute, the snakes which he deals with, and, most of all, how he is sometimes but not always recognised as the god he is a psychic force which, though it may be stimulated from outside, nevertheless operates from within.

The flute and the cowgirls

It is at the puberty age of twelve that we first hear of Krishna playing on

---

41. Ibid., p. 115.
42. Ibid., p. 28.
43. Ibid., p. 41.
44. Ibid., p. 41.

his flute and thus attracting the cowgirls, so it is obvious that Krishna's flute itself is a phallic symbol. It is recognised to be such by the Hindus. In the *Kama Sutra* for instance, directions are given for heightening sexual enjoyment by rubbing the juices of certain plants upon the male virile member, and it is later said that "a woman who hears a man playing upon a reed pipe which has been dressed with the juices of" similar plants, "becomes his slave"[45]. Krishna's flute is first mentioned as mimicking the cry of the peacock[46] which as we have already seen is a symbol of dawn, of new life springing up. Flute playing is the cowherds' special art which therefore Krishna has learnt in his childhood.

But Krishna's playing has a beauty all its own and when they hear it the cowgirls are thrown into passionate agitation. The cowgirls are both fascinated by and jealous of his flute. The combined pleasures of mouth and breast and adult sexuality are expressed by one of them, saying, "That happy flute to be played on by Krishna! Little wonder that having drunk the nectar of his lips the flute should trill like the clouds. Alas! Krishna's flute is dearer to him than we are for he keeps it with him night and day" (as a man keeps his virile member which he cannot part from). "The flute is our rival. Never is Krishna parted from it." With reference to the relationship between mother and child, and man and god, a second cowgirl says, "It is because the flute continually thought of Krishna that it gained this bliss". A third says, "Oh! Why has Krishna not made us into flutes …?"[47]

The cowgirls know it is a "call to love". They say, "It was your flute that made us come. We have left our husbands for you. We live for your love". Like Christ in the apocryphal account, Krishna replies, "If you really love me, dance and sing with me", and causes them to dance in a circle around him (see Figure 16), consummating their love[48]—a mandala formation similar to that of the apostles making a ring round Christ with Himself standing in their midst. By means of this circular dance in which Krishna symbolically made

---

45. *The Kama Sutra*, ed. John Muirhead-Gould, Panther Books, 1963, pp. 193-4.
46. Archer, p. 34.
47. Ibid., pp. 36, 37.
48. Ibid., pp. 41, 46.

love to them all, each was induced to think that she alone was his partner: Krishna thus proved how god is available to all, the cowgirls symbolising souls, the playing on his flute being likened to the "call of god"[49].

Figure 17. The Death of Balarama, with the great serpent Sesha (part of Vishnu), issuing from his mouth. "Illustration to the Persian abridgement of the *Mahabarata*, c. 1595. Collection of H.H. the Maharajah of Jaipur, Jaipur." W.G. Archer, *The Loves of Krishna*, Plate 1

Snakes

Like Mary's "ghost man". Krishna exercises power over snakes, usually by defeating evil ones such as the many-headed snake Kaliya who lived in a whirlpool[50]. Sometimes snakes are enchanted men.

But all snakes are not evil. There is a myth regarding Krishna's ancestry describing how Vishnu plucks out two of his hairs, one black and one white, declaring that these will be the means by which he will ease earth's burden. The black hair is Vishnu's own self, to be incarnated as Krishna. The white hair is Sesha the great serpent, a part of Vishnu to be incarnated in Krishna's half-brother Balarama[51], his constant companion and alter ego, who also plays the flute. He, when Krishna leaves the cowgirls, takes his place with them as their lover[52]. Black thus means introvert, white extravert. When Krishna goes back into Vishnu (symbolically dies), Balarama goes to the seashore and leaves his body there, while Sesha the plumed white serpent of eternity issues

49. Ibid., pp. 75,76.
50. Ibid. p.35.
51. Ibid., pp. 27, 69.
52. Ibid., p. 61.

109

from his mouth. Figure 17 shows Balarama with his head against a tree down by the waterside giving up the ghost with the other snakes gathered to welcome it, in much the same relative positions as the little green snakes in Mary's Painting 6.

Demon and God: "Changeling"

In Indian mythology snakes are thus both demonic and divine. They are symbols of great phallic or possessively maternal power that can be used in either way. Demons are very real, as real as gods, if understood as symbolising passionate desires, the demons being retrograde and the gods forward looking. As an example of demonic power we have but to consider the circumstances of Mary's birth by a mother who had been so bound up with her own father, Frederick, that he had acquired a kind of demonic influence over her. This lasted on after his death so that, regardless of her husband, she was determined that she would give birth to a boy who would replace the father she had lost. But since the child turned out to be a girl the mother was outraged and had neglected her, so that Mary's father's sister had to bring her up and to protect her from the mother who had herself become demonic too.

Mary had thus become a kind of psychological changeling within the family circle in the rectory. We do not nowadays believe in such demonic influence—though it exists. Mythology, however, speaks quite openly of demons as destructive forces to be reckoned with, and called by name. Krishna's own life was overshadowed in this way by a mythical demon said to have ravished the queen of his clan by assuming the guise of her husband without her knowing it. The son resulting from this union was the great enemy who wished to destroy Krishna. To avert this fate, the infant Krishna was substituted for the newborn daughter of a simple cowherd, and was thus brought up as a cowherd's son.

Thus Mary and Krishna were both psychological changelings, and Krishna's substitution for a girl recalls Mary's substitution for a boy. This is a condition that either confuses or illuminates. In Krishna's case it operated in such a way as to unite the opposites (of human and divine). In Mary's case it tended to divide and isolate. Her "ghost man" came to her in her adolescence as though he were a god to join

110

her to herself, give her self-knowledge and offer help from the realm of psychic consciousness. She could not understand him then, since he seemed to her at that time more demonic than divine. But now again his godlike figure comes to her in the changed form of the dark man dressed in skins playing his pipe as Krishna does, a central figure tending to unite her scattered fantasies into a more integrated whole, only to disappear again until it is time for him to reappear once more in another of the many guises the "saviour" assumes in Mary's fantasies.

Forgetfulness. The fleeting visions of the god. Role of the god.

Such re-appearances are acts of psychic consciousness coming and going although always deepening. They are equivalent to those which in the Orphic mysteries are said to "flow forth" from "the lake of Memory". In life they are always fitful, as when an insight comes but then may be obscured again by everyday happenings or habits of mind. At Krishna's birth his parents recognise and worship him as god (Vishnu). But the vision then fades, and he appears as an ordinary newborn child[53]. From time to time the cowherds do the same but then amnesia intervenes. "They retain no recollection of the vision and see him simply as a youthful cowherd."[54] As in the apocryphal accounts of the childhood of Christ, Jesus is represented as a kind of hooligan with supernatural powers, so Krishna acts like a high-spirited and naughty boy, raiding the houses of cowgirls, pilfering their cream and curds, upsetting their milk pails[55]. One day he eats some dirt, which he denies. His cowgirl foster-mother is angry and tells him to open his mouth. Looking inside, she sees three worlds and knows that he is god. But then the vision fades. She picks him up and kisses him[56].

. On another occasion, when the cowherds have realized who Krishna is, they beg him to show them Vishnu's paradise. He does, "yet it is part of the

---

53. Ibid., p. 28.
54. Ibid., p. 29.
55. Ibid., p. 31.
56. Ibid., p. 32.
57. Ibid., p.40
58. Ibid., p. 46.

story that these flashes of insight should be evanescent—that having realised one instant that Krishna is god, the cowherds should regard him the next instant as one of themselves" and being "only that".[57]

He is also called "the knower of all, he who is all and is present in all.... He the unborn . . .who assumes shapes at will"[58], as does the figure of the saviour in Mary's fantasies.

When the time comes for Krishna to undeceive his cowherd foster parents by telling them that they are not his real parents, his foster mother is overwhelmed by grief at this loss of her "son", but recovers when she realises that he is actually god[59]. At the same time Krishna sends a friend to urge the cowgirls to give up regarding him as their lover but worship him as god—as someone who is constantly near those who love him even if he cannot be seen.

For Krishna's love has now become a psychic one: "I live in everyone"[60].

59. Ibid., p. 52.
60. Ibid., p. 62.

PAINTING 7 (Fantasy) 27 January 1955

Dragon Waiting to be Born

We now enter a new phase in the development of Mary's awareness of herself. There had been paintings in the past of men or creatures buried underground with only the most tenuous connections with life above the surface of the earth. These symbolised deeply repressed psychic contents. Mary was only now beginning to become aware that the extent of her own hostile feelings towards the world was something pathological. These feelings, as illustrated in many of her paintings later on, were symbolised by the dragon in contradistinction to the snake, who in her fantasies was usually a "wise snake".

Thus Painting 7 was at first incomprehensible to me since I had at that time not learnt of the distinction between the dragon and the snake in her symbolic world. Coming so soon after Painting 5, it looked at first as if here again a plant was growing out of a buried corpse. But what looked like a corpse turned out to be a living though weak and unborn animal as yet within the womb; this she explained was meant to represent a dragon on account of its claws and arrow-pointed tail. Far from the thistle growing out of it in the way that the tree had drawn its sustenance from the corpse in Painting 5, the feeding movement was the other way round—the dragon drawing its sustenance from the thistle growing above the ground. Her "story" about the painting was as follows:

"Two flying snakes are trying to fly up to a luminous globe that may or may not be the sun or moon. I don't know which it is.

113

"The plant is feeding the dragon below ground. The plant is trying to draw down the snakes so that they can be food for the dragon, who is too young or too feeble yet to get food for himself.

"The spikes on the plant-fruits are also meant to attract down the snakes."

The painting was done during one of her many times of hesitation about taking some new job. The job at the school had come to an end (there had been a change of management), and after a lot of indecision, she had decided to busy herself by carrying out menial work in a rest home for old ladies. There life was as dead as it could be, but she had at least no external sex problems and little responsibility. Her fantasy life could thus partly regress into its old parent-bound channels of idealistic unrelatedness symbolised by the two winged snakes. These were flying, like moths towards a candle, towards the luminous globe up above, of which she did not know whether it was the sun or moon. That meant that the problem of "which parent is which" was still not sorted out, although it still held part of her spellbound. This is the only painting in her whole series (apart from Painting 28) in which the snakes are winged. The fact that there are two of them shows how still split she is, the purple snake standing for incest desire connected with the father, the sky blue one symbolising the unattainable mother as well as Mary's own rationalized defence about the incest wish.

But there is another influence at work: the thistle trying to drag them down to feed the dragon underground. This calls attention to the hostile feelings in herself represented by the embryonic dragon. Her knowledge of this is still "too feeble" and psychically "too young". The dragon is not winged, as none of Mary's dragons are (except in Painting 24), so this means "coming down to earth" for her.

What is remarkable is that the operating factor in this coming down to earth is the thistle, which we know from Painting 2 to symbolise the mother —at that time such a destructive influence. But the thistle flowers are here painted green, not purple as before, indicating new growth and not incestuous destructiveness. They symbolise "good breasts" (though still spikey) instead of bad, of the same colour as the dragon in the womb of the earth. They are feeding it through its umbilical cord, which might at first sight look like the phallus growing out of Adam's body into the Tree of the philosophers

114

shown in Figure 6: but it is here a channel for rebirth through the self-knowledge which this feeding process indicates.

For as we have already seen from the preceding dream illustrated in Painting 6, Mary's mother image has now changed from bad to good, now mediating wisdom through the frank recognition on her part of Mary's own identification with the less desirable aspects of her mother's character. This opens the way to increased consciousness, and to a new understanding of her own nature.

This symbolic vision of the two sides of Mary's character is carried yet further in the fantasy shown in Painting 25, in which the dragon is itself seen to be pregnant of two snakes, corresponding to the two winged snakes in the present Painting 7, which have by that time lost their wings and are united in the dragon's womb.

PAINTINGS 8 AND 9 (DREAM) LATE OCTOBER 1955

The Luminous Snake

The next paintings to be included here, Paintings 8 and 9, were of a dream nine months later, when Mary had on her own initiative taken the bold step of taking on work in a mental hospital. She stuck to this for the next four years—by far the longest time that she had ever spent consecutively in the same employment. This work for the first time satisfied her great inner need for companionship, which she found with the other male and female nurses, and at the same time opened up a quite new interest in other people's—the patients'—psychic problems. After she had been in this employment for a few months she had the following dream:

"I was having a cup of tea with Nurse Cleenie in an untidy bedroom. I saw a dark passage leading from the room, and thought I should have time to go down it without her knowing I had gone. I went a long way in the dark, and then came into a poor narrow street with tall houses on each side. I saw a red and black snake in a window and wanted it very much, so I put my hand in at the window and took it, and in my hand it glowed."

In the fantasy of Painting 7 we had the picture of the two snakes flying up towards the sun or moon but with the intimation that they should descend so as to nourish the embryonic dragon. Mary was then in an uninteresting job which in no way inspired her. Now for the first time in her life she has taken the bold step of undertaking work that really fascinates her and has to do with patients having problems not dissimilar to hers. So now the phallic snake has entered into her to fertilise her life and give her power she never had before. The darkness of her soul is thus enlightened with new energy.

The dream is in the setting of the mental hospital. Nurse Cleenie was in a superior position to her. Mary had in external life an outwardly diffident but inwardly hostile reaction towards all authority, and would try by all means available to avoid or to withdraw from contact with it. But the Nurse Cleenie in the dream symbolised Mary's own false superego "cleanness", which the name Cleenie punningly referred to. Her dream-ego thus reacted against it, corresponding well enough with the external situation of this nurse being particularly repugnant to her on account of her "bossiness". Mary was not yet in a position to fight such superego tendencies in her own nature, so could but try to circumvent them in the dream. This led her to this very moving scene with the snake at the end of the long, dark passage which led her out of the hospital into what symbolised her own individuality. For it was there in the "*poor narrow street*" that she encountered in new form that very snake that had, at the beginning, complained that her "*hands were too clean*". It was now luminous, glowing with the promise of a more consciously accepted psychic life.

She painted one picture (Painting 8) of the "*poor narrow street*", so narrow that it was dark, with the window gleaming with light in which the snake (here painted only red) lay curled with raised head on a kind of black cushion. The light shining in the window corresponds to the light of the moon (the light in the darkness) in the dream illustrated in Painting 6, which revealed the "ghost man" and his snakes. This snake is luminous, that is to say "ghostly", possessed of mysterious power. That she should "*want it very much*" and take hold of it without more ado (Painting 9) is evidence of the inner development that was now constellating itself in her. It was based on what had become full and unashamed knowledge of her father-orientated sex desire now released from her former shame and concealment of it (which had led to so much of her defensive hostility).

That she should now grasp the phallic symbol of the snake so boldly is an indication of the new psychic power created out of the old incest desire. Also indicated was that deep inner integrity which was, in the midst of her hidden feelings of guilt, her almost miraculous saving grace. The combination of the colours red and black in both paintings symbolises the vivid feelings (the red) that she had until now hidden away in the black bleakness of her life, while the black symbolises here (among other things to be discussed later) a certain "trust" and an "unknowing" faith. Thus "ignorance", which black sometimes stands for in these fantasies, may be of two opposite kinds. It may, as in many cases, be a "superego ignorance" due to an isolated pride. But it may, as in this case, symbolise a primitive and trusting form of faith, which the mystics refer to as the "cloud of unknowing". Both aspects alternate in Mary's paintings, as we shall see.

Figure 18. The snake (usually twined round the staff) as emblem of Asklepios and of his daughter Hygieia, his feminine counterpart. "Late Roman ivory carving representing Hygieia . . . ." Karl Kerenyi, *Asklepios: Archetypal Image of the Physician's Existence*, Fig. 34

The opposite to black in this painting is red, the redness of the snake which became luminous only when she grasped it in her hand. It is now well on the way to becoming a real power in her life, a psycho-pomp or "soul leader". Twined as it is around her arm it calls to mind the snake curled round the staff which is the emblem of Asklepios, the Greek god of healing, and of Hygieia his daughter and divine companion or feminine counterpart, whose emblem also is the snake (see Figure. 18). Speaking of this, Kerenyi says, "the wisdom of the ancient physician and of those who conceived the temples ascribed the mysterious process of healing rather to the night and sleep than to the day and waking. One indication of this is the institution of the 'temple sleep'" (Kerenyi, p. 56) in which dreams were interpreted by the priests and illnesses were cured—it being said, "the healer is a snake" (Kerenyi, *Asklepios*, p. 32). Connected with such dream visions was also that of the divine child here seen in Figure 18: Hygieia is seen feeding the snake as Mary tried to do in the dream (Painting 1).

The Romans were so impressed by the healing virtue of Asklepios that they are said to have imported from his shrine at Epidauros the snake with which he was identified. The snake itself was given the power to choose where it would have its shrine in Rome. As the boat containing it approached up the Tiber and passed by the island there, the snake crawled out of the boat onto the island and disappeared into a hole, close to a spring or well. The new temple of Asklepios was created above this, while the whole island was shaped by masonry into the form of a ship (see Kerenyi Figures 1, 2 and 3).

It may be noted that the snake's two colours, red and black, are also the two colours with one or other of which Mary paints herself in illustrating her various dreams and fantasies. They are joined together in Painting 29 as the two sides of herself.

PAINTING 10 (Fantasy) 22 April 1957

The Lonely Island and the Great Fish

Eighteen months after the last dream she had two fantasies (Paintings 10 and 11), the one immediately following the other, showing two aspects of the psychic process now at work in her. The one was of herself standing on a lonely rocky island in the sea with a great fish wanting to swallow her. The other was its opposite, that of a man long buried in a coffin underground, which was being broken open by the dragon of her fantasy. The fish and dragon were both painted purple, having to do with the problem of her frustrated incest desire. She described as follows the first fantasy shown in Painting 10:

"I am alone on a rock in a stormy sea. A great fish wants to get at me to swallow me. I wonder how I can possibly escape to join the people on the land."

An island, separated off from the mainland, is a symbol for individuality and for the process of individuation. Such was the island in the Tiber, just referred to, on which the snake symbolising the healing god Asklepios chose to make his home.

But this fantasy was a frightening one for her. She was so overwhelmed by her feeling of loneliness which was coupled with her fear of plunging into life. With her childhood background of confinement at the rectory, she feared and was suspicious of life. It seemed to her like a rough sea, too dangerous to face, or to commit herself to too much because of her own internal reactions to it. For the real storm was in herself, hidden by layers of superimposed conventional thinking, of the kind generated by her isolated upbringing in a home ruled by conventional hypocrisies and here represented by *"the people on the land"*. She had indeed partly freed herself from this, as indicated by the rock that had detached itself from the parental matrix of the land. But she had done it only superficially, and when faced with problems she could not understand would constantly "escape" into the most incongruous conventional statements. These utterly belied her real feelings and were a constant source of superego repression.

Thus there is no vegetation on this island of Mary's. But there has been a great change in her now owing to her increased realisation of the perils of her life. For the first time she now paints herself red, which symbolises passion or intense feeling of any kind, including that of the terror which she is now in. This is in great contrast to the blackness of the couple on the land, who may well symbolise her two parents. They indicate in any case conventional and lifeless attitudes; these, however, still represented to her apparent safety and protection against her own real self and direct intuitions. As is shown in this painting of her fantasy, the parents' death had not brought about the separation from such attitudes. It is the analysis that has brought this change about, and that has turned her previous escapist lethargy into the disturbance needed to bring the change about.

It will be noted also that the birds are black. This alludes to the dilemma in which Mary habitually had been, shown in many earlier paintings which have not been here reproduced. The black birds flying above her head there connote her own self-destructive thoughts ("up in the air") and fears based on introjected misconceptions about life. She had all unwittingly adopted these from the parental atmosphere. (Compare Vincent van Gogh's painting "Cornfield with Crows", in which the crows are flying low over the golden corn, painted only a short time before his suicide. Van Gogh, like Mary, was a country parson's child. Like her he in his youth also aspired to be a saint.)

These thoughts fascinate her, being a part of the incestuous bond which she still has with both parents, with the father consciously and with the mother unconsciously. To live a vital life (inferred by the red) is still too frightening for her, so she wonders how she can *"possibly escape to join the people on the land*"—escape, that is to say, from the *"great fish"* on the other side of her who wants to *"get at"* her and *"swallow"* her. This may remind us of Jonah and the whale. By means of the whale Jonah was rescued from the escapist fantasies that had led him to take ship for a most distant land (in order to avoid his destiny). But, as in Mary's fantasy, a storm blew up, which threatened to capsize the ship. Then it was found that Jonah's own flight was the cause of it. Unlike Mary in this fantasy, however, Jonah acknowledged this and told the sailors, "Take me up, and cast me forth into the sea; so shall the sea be calm unto you: for I know that for my sake this great tempest is upon you". So they "cast him forth into the sea: and the sea ceased from her raging ". And "the Lord had prepared a great fish to swallow up Jonah". But far from being lost in the belly of the fish he prayed and eventually found himself, saying, "The waters compassed me about, even to the soul … yet hast thou brought up my life from corruption". This may remind us of the hanging boy and of the rotting corpse in Paintings 3 and 5. "They that observe lying vanities forsake their own mercy" was indeed applicable to Mary's case. The great fish vomited Jonah out upon dry land, whereupon he started to carry out the mission which the Lord had given him (Jonah Chs. 1 and 2. See Figure 19)".[61] It

Figure 19. Jonah: " 'Night Sea Journey' and 'Resurrection', *Biblia pauperum* (1471)". Jung, *Psychology and Alchemy*
    a. Fig. 170, Jonah being swallowed by the whale.
    b. Fig. 177, Jonah being spewed forth by the whale.

---

61. Cf. also Jung *Psychology and Alchemy*, Fig. 187, illustrating the painting of a dragon spewing forth Jason, after drinking the potion prepared by Athene.

was typical of Mary, however, that though she knew the Bible well it did not occur to her to connect this story with her fantasy, nor had she any idea of what either of the fantasies meant.

The swallowing monster is an initiation symbol in all primitive societies, and is often a sea or river creature such as a shark or crocodile. Sociologically primitive society initiation symbolises transition from the state of adolescence into that of adulthood. Mary's own adolescence had been psychologically incestuous without her knowing it. She was now in the transition stage of just beginning to recognise this fact, while at the same time having a strong emotional reaction against accepting it. It is for this reason that Mary's "great fish" is painted purple, which we have seen to be the colour of incestuous desire as in the case of the hanging boy (Painting 3). Her confrontation with this fish limns the dawning knowledge which she is so afraid of admitting to herself. Therefore she wants to flee in the opposite direction. But its tongue is painted red, as is Mary herself, symbolising the acceptance of real life, even through sacrifice of much-cherished unrealistic ideals, here represented by the black people and the birds. It thus shows her the way. For to be swallowed by the fish means "going inside" oneself (and this is what "in-itiation" literally means). Though terrifying as a symbol of transition from ego-consciousness to psychic consciousness, it attests to (could Mary but have known), at the same time (like the porpoise of Greek mythology), a kind of womb affording safety from the dangers of the storm surrounding it. As we shall see from the next painting, her "terror" was a kind of "sleep" from which she was due now to awake.

PAINTING 11 (Fantasy) 22 April 1957

The Sleeper Awakes

Immediately after painting the last fantasy, a new and quite opposite one came
to her, which she was impelled straightway to capture in Fantasy Painting 11.
She described it as follows as if it had nothing whatever to do with her own
psychological condition, but was simply a "picture" that she "saw".

*"The dragon at the bottom of the picture has pushed open and broken in half
the lid of the black coffin, releasing the man, who would much rather have been left
'asleep' in it. His body is half rotting (the red parts of it are good flesh, the purple
parts are rotting flesh), and he is groping upwards. But he can't quite get to the light."*

This is another of Mary's paintings of a section through the earth, as in
the case of Painting 5. It is as if she could stand aside and could "see through"
the earth so as to see what was happening inside it. This is a form of detach-
ment that had its good and bad results: if "under the earth" indicates the
unconscious part of her psyche the fantasy could act as a kind of revelation
of what was going on within; on the other hand she could not realise that this
was what was happening to *her*. Thus, while she had no difficulty in recognising the fact that the red girl on the isolated rock in Painting 10, terrified of
her loneliness, was her, she violently denied that the present fantasy painting
11 had anything to do with her. It was simply about some "unknown man".

But it was not difficult to see that the man inside the coffin so deep
down in the earth complemented the girl on the elevated rock in Painting 10

124

(cf. also hanging boy in Painting 3). The one was too far "up", the other too far "down". The one was female, the other male. The fury of the dragon in this painting corresponded to the fury of the sea in the last one (Painting 10). The blackness of the coffin in the present fantasy corresponded to the blackness of the people on the land in Painting 10. Both rock and earth are painted the same colour brown. The dragon and the rotting flesh are painted purple as is the great fish in Painting 10.

The dragon-mother. "Black" symbol for father.
The "unknown man". Rebirth out of the father principle.

Little as Mary would at first admit that this fantasy intimately concerned her own development, her associations to the various parts of it were among the most illuminating in the whole series. To begin with, she came out with the remark, quite unprompted by me, that the dragon was very like her mother.

What she was even more certain about was that the black coffin was like her father, which harks back to her father's black corpse (Painting 5). She had then said that the blackness was due to the black parsonic clothes he always wore. What was the more remarkable was that the lid of the coffin broken open in the present fantasy was just like the father's cassock, which she had in previous paintings (not included in this volume) depicted him as wearing with a black hood covering his head and the black cassock open in front.

But the coffin, like the cassock, was only a container and not the man himself who had been hidden inside it, just as the dream (Painting 3) had urged her to pull down the wall and find the boy alive again within. But she had not believed the voice any more than she was now willing to recognise the present fantasy as being about her. The reason for this refusal, which was then obscure in other than the most general terms, is now revealed in that the real man buried inside the father's cassock is being exposed and shaken out of it. This gives us quite another insight as to what the "blackness" of the father means. Black is an archetypal symbol for the womb, or for the darkness inside it, here symbolic of the father having become in Mary's life a mother-substitute. She having herself unwittingly fallen into the role of virgin wife for him, her own love life had been totally absorbed in him. The

125

"unknown man" being pushed up towards the light was, like the hanging boy, an Eros figure marking not only the father's unlived erotic life but Mary's too. This was dawning recognition of all that she had missed in love and free expression of her individuality. Like Jonah, who had been asleep within the ship before the storm arose, she said in her description of the fantasy that he *"would much rather have been left asleep"*. The waking of him brings about the same disturbance of her escapist lethargy—her terror of the great fish—in Painting 10.

We have referred to the personal associations that Mary had linking the father with the coffin and the "unknown man". This is an instance of personal associations, which, if followed up, lead to archetypal truths. In this case it is the universal theme of rebirth out of the father principle.

Tombstone

But Mary, with her sexually repressed father, had been so ignorant of this that "black" had become for her a symbol for her own repressed nature. So now instead of the tree growing out of the father's corpse in Painting 5 there is the object on the surface of the earth outlined in black barring further progress upwards towards the light. This symbolises, like the birds in Painting 10, her own reflection of the father's repressive influence.

Asked what this was she said scornfully, *"A tombstone, of course. Can't you see that?"* A tombstone is another symbol for the womb of death. Such heavy tombstones covering the grave are sometimes said to have had as their purpose the preservation of the contents of the grave intact. When further asked "What will happen to him if he does get up there, because the heavy tombstone will still be on top of him?" Mary replied, *"Oh, if he once gets to the top, he won't have much trouble with that. He'll easily push it aside."* This showed to what extent her own repressions were now being relaxed.

When further asked for her associations to this actual tombstone she said that it reminded her of the graveyard around her father's church, where she had buried him and also her mother. She had taken it upon herself to ignore the mother's schizoid wish to be buried in the father's other parish. The tombstone in the fantasy did not cover this joint parental grave, but was more like another older tombstone in the churchyard which had the inscription:

126

"Farewell vain world, I've had enough of thee.
I care not now what men may say of me"

which she had always liked. The inscription, as was on this occasion pointed out, could well be taken in two ways, both relevant to her own life: either as a gesture of cynical despair and of desire for death as the only solution, or as a living conquest of fear.

She was now beginning to see both sides of her father problem. This may account for the fact that instead of the single large tree growing out of the corpse in Painting 5, there are now two small trees, attesting to the two points of view which she was developing with regard to her two parents.

Dragon reflects the dual mother role

But underneath all this there lay the problem of the mother represented by the dragon—the dynamic force breaking open the coffin.

Mary was also developing two points of view about the mother. In Painting 7 the embryonic dragon underground was being fed by the prickly thistle up above. For while the phallic snake is almost always a positive influence in Mary's fantasies, the role of the dragon oscillates. It varies between bad and good according to her mood and according to the nature of the actual mother. In overt life the latter was so schizoid and antagonistic to Mary; at the same time she had deep and worldly-wise perceptions which she could not implement, but she expressed them from time to time in proverbs and in penetrating remarks.

The purple dragon indicated the basic incestuous connection that Mary had with her mother (only overlaid by the emotionally incestuous relationship with her father). From the position of the dragon in the coffin beneath the "unknown man", it may be seen that the coffin here contained them both, the man and the dragon. This symbolised the repressed sexuality not only of the father but of the whole family, on both the father's and the mother's side.

We can recall that Mary had buried her mother not only in the same grave as her father but on top of him. Here in the fantasy however, the dragon is underneath as a dynamic force bringing about the resurrection of Mary's hitherto repressed creative animus. The fantasy is a dynamic one in which, on the parental level (also a deep level in Mary's own psyche) we may well see the mother in her repressed fury. She is now released, pushing at the lethargic father as she did in real life. She used to complain bitterly at his sexual incompetence—which corresponded to her own frigidity. They had had no sex intercourse after the first year or two of marriage. He on his part had complained equally bitterly (but with more external resignation) of her schizoid attacks on him. It will be noted incidentally that in this case the sex roles are reversed. The initiative and the dynamic force lie with the dragon (mother or mother's animus) in contrast to the sleeping man who is only aroused due to her buffeting. In Mary's own psychology the sleeping man thus corresponded to her own external lethargy, and the dragon to her fantasies. The latter of course had the strength to assert themselves as she painted as in the present instance. The fairy stories which came to her autonomously were also evidence of this energy. So long as she did not apply them to herself, this foiled her awakening consciousness.

Increasing awareness of her psychological incest

The more horrific Mary's fantasies became the better it was for her: they opened up the problems which she had repressed and which so fettered her because repressed, and brought them thus nearer to consciousness. They were for her the problems clustered around her incest fantasies: the purple of the dragon and of the partly rotting flesh of the man, contrasted with the red parts symbolising "good flesh" (in her ordinary talk she called this "raw" flesh). These represented those aspects of her psychic life that had been uncontaminated by the "rot" (incest).

But there is another thing here to be emphasized. How is it that the purple dragon (incestuous desire on its deepest level connected with the mother) should be here actively destroying her father-incest bonds? There are two reasons for this: firstly because the deepest incest bond was with Mary's mother herself, here functioning as archetypal mother (the dream of the old woman with the sores). Both "mothers" resented the incestuous desire for the father and so combined (as they did in that dream) to release her from it; secondly because self-knowledge is itself the cure. Until Mary could "see" or recognise the incest "rot" in her she could not cope with it. The cure is "know thyself".

128

This had been helped, of course, by Mary's contact with the world. Her continued work in the mental hospital functioned as a new "parent" for her, serving to push "father" more and more into the background as "the only man". There were male nurses as well as female ones, with whom she had contact there. It also helped her with her mother problem since she had found "good mothers" in the form of an understanding matron and in a ward sister who was sympathetic to her. Another factor helping to "bring her out" was the collective nature of staff life in the mental hospital, which she now regarded as her "home" and identified with.

The fact that in this fantasy the dragon and the unknown man are both painted with the same colours—purple and red—is yet another indication of the identity between the mother and the "child" (in this case Mary's animus). Compare also the thistle and the embryonic dragon in Painting 7 or the thistle flower and the girl in Painting 2. But there is more red than purple in the unknown man. This indicates the beginning of freedom for Mary's animus, now struggling upwards of his own accord (though he can't yet *"quite get to the light"*).

One might well think, on seeing such a fantasy painting and hearing her description of the story which it told, that she was near a solution. But such was the enormous power of habitual attitudes that Mary still had far to go. As has been said she at first stoutly denied that this powerful fantasy had anything to do with her. It took some time to bring it home to her that what she had painted was her own animus arising from the sleep of "incest-death". How this realization gradually came to her we shall see in its initial stages in the following fantasy painting 12.

PAINTING 12 (FANTASY) 30 MAY 1957

Two-headed Serpent Issuing from Boiling
Cauldron

(Preceded by Mandrake dream)

Mary was by now gradually becoming aware that her fantasies were not just unrelated fairy tales but were very urgently about herself, about her "moods" as she would now describe them, so that the painting of them now began to afford some conscious as well as unconscious relief for her pent up emotions.

Nine days later than the last fantasy, after considerable crisis brought about by the upheaval following her new psychic experiences, during which she had reacted violently against them and had been very much "on her high horse" and even threatened to break off the analysis, she had another powerful fantasy which brought her quickly back into it. The fantasy was preceded by the following dream:

"I was helping a farm man to lift potatoes. It was a sunny day and I felt contented. Suddenly I pulled up a plant that looked like a potato above ground but had long pointed roots. I was frightened when I saw it and ran away."

She did not of course know what this meant, other than to wonder vaguely whether the roots might have been like a man's naked legs. Why should these roots so frighten her? This is a case of archetypal imagery concealed under the guise of ordinary external fact. For it is clear that underlying

130

the potato-pulling in this dream is the archetypal myth of the *mandragora* (mandrake), which Mary consciously knew nothing of, but which is a plant spoken of in mythology which screams like a man when it is rooted up.

It is undoubtedly the "unknown man" in her as shown in Painting 11 with his outstretched hand only just underground that is referred to here, conveying the truth about her incest fantasies. This man was "in" Mary, an animus figure symbolising her own potential understanding of this problem which she could still not quite accept—*"he can't quite get to the light"*. This meant that Mary was herself feeling now "torn up by the roots" out of the bog of those same incest fantasies. The waking fantasy (Painting 12) now following the dream was more explicit still. She says:

"I am naked, and going down steps into a cellar, and see this serpent with two heads in a cauldron full of boiling water. I have the idea that the boiling water is somehow giving the snake or snakes (I don't know which to call them) life. Of the two I like the left-hand dark one best. I am a little scared of going nearer."

Both dream and fantasy were frightening, but the fantasy was less so than the dream, and this gives us an opportunity to understand one of the differences between her dreams and fantasies. For the dream involves no conscious effort on the dreamer's part. But the fantasy, though·also coming of itself, comes during waking life, and the painting of it involves consciousness. The meaning of the dream was thus far more obscure to Mary than that of the fantasy. In her recollection of the dream, she has no notion why the long pointed roots of the potato should so frighten her. This is due to the repression of her animus as indicated by the archetypal association to men's legs. It is Mary's unconsciousness of this that makes her so frightened since there is nothing that her consciousness can get hold of to explain the fright. Unconsciousness comes first, and then the fright.

But in the case of Mary's fantasies the fright, the anger or some other disturbance almost always comes before the painting of the fantasy, which then gives her relief. (Even the desire to escape in Painting 10 has not the strength of the panic in some of her dreams.) This is somehow connected with the act of painting, which is a conscious one done by a woman with her woman's mind. But the dream comes *only* from "the other side", from the unconscious, which for a woman has a large component which is psychically male, and in

131

this dream is concerned with the resurrection of a male figure. It has to do with the contrasexuality of ego consciousness and psychic consciousness, the latter being less accessible to Mary's ego consciousness than it is when she sets out to paint her fantasies. Thus in this dream the nakedness is underground, or only just emerging from the ground (like the naked man in Painting 11) with frightening effect. But in the present fantasy it is Mary herself who for the first time in these paintings is naked. Her bare body is also painted red indicating strong emotion, which in this case is one of fear. But it is a fear that is a conscious one, for she is now herself going underground down into the cellar—meaning into the unconscious, as if to see (though she did not think of it like this) what this terrifying mandrake thing was. As usual, it is in the "darkness" (of the cellar) that the truth reveals itself.

In the unconscious everything is upside down. This indicates another difference between Mary's fantasies and her dreams. In the dream the potato roots recalling the man's legs were underground. The fantasy helps to explain her fear, for here the "roots" or "legs" are seen in the form of two dragon-like heads spitting fire, both issuing upwards out of a central stem. This was the first time she used the word "serpent", which suggests a mixture between snake and dragon as the painting shows, the dragon element in it being shown by the creature's pointed tail. She calls this creature a *"serpent with two heads"*. It issues out of a black cauldron full of boiling water painted purple— the colour of incestuous desire—which she describes as *"somehow giving the snake or snakes (I don't know which to call them) life"*. Just as Mary's own naked figure is here painted red, so is the cauldron heated by red flames of fire, the first time fire has appeared in this series of fantasies.

The cauldron is an archetypal symbol for the psychic womb. There are many instances of it in Irish and other mythologies. We have it in our own "witch's cauldron" in which the fate of men is brewed. Cooking in the cauldron is, among other things, a symbol for psychic activity giving birth to hitherto unacknowledged or repressed psychic contents, or bringing them to consciousness. Both snakes arise out of the cauldron of Mary's conflicting emotions, which had once been so paralysed but are now waking up. The cauldron is a black one as it usually is, both in fact and as a symbol for the unconscious, out of which anything may come. But black also symbolises the father in Mary's fantasies, so we may now compare the fire which agitates the water boiling in the cauldron with the dragon bursting open the black coffin in Fantasy Painting 11. That dragon symbolised the power of the archetypal mother and of the basic incest desire between the mother and the child, the recognition of which is now giving Mary more ability to cope with it and thus deprive the father-incest bond of its former power over her. The purple of the boiling water in the cauldron symbolising the father is of the same incest-colour as the dragon of Painting 11. It is thus out of the recognition of both these incest-bonds that Mary's vision of the double-headed serpent is born.

So we may now see the connection between this somewhat terrifying sight and the potato roots of Mary's mandrake dream with their association to human legs. Mary's two "legs" or psychic standpoints symbolise the two parents (of psychologically undifferentiated sex), which Mary later came to recognise in this male-female serpent with two heads. For one of these is painted black flecked with red spots, the other is painted red flecked with black spots, showing how each has some of the characteristics of the other one. Compare the two-headed male and female dragon (represented by the sun and moon), both heads growing out of one body, in Figure 20, which Jung describes as "The *prima materia* as dragon, being fertilized by the Holy Ghost".

Figure 20. "The *prima materia* as the dragon, with male and female symbols (sun and moon). 'Hermes Bird', *Theatrum chemicum Britannicum* (1652)." Jung, *Psychology and Alchemy*, Fig. 267

Mary, fascinated by this vision as she was, said that she liked the left-hand dark one best. This is the one that does not threaten her, but points towards the left in the direction which she also is facing. This, as she later said, was like the father whom she wished to follow yet farther into the bowels of the earth—or her own psychic consciousness. But the red snake, which she came to think of as symbolising her actual mother, threatens to drive her back into her former illusions by spitting fire at her. Can she face up to this one and pass it by so as to reach the other one?

It will be noted incidentally that, to the right, seen through the opening leading down into the cellar, is our old friend Mary's small fantasy-tree, first met with in Painting 2 (in which it symbolised her world of unrelated fantasy). So long as it still shows such unrelatedness, she rightly turns her back on it so as to face the problem of her own fierce duality.

This dream of going down into the cellar is an initiation one, equivalent to plunging into the mouth of the great fish in fantasy painting 10, which she was then too afraid to do. The painting of these fantasies helped her to "take the plunge". Part of this process is the acknowledgement of what one is, symbolised by Mary's nakedness and by the redness of her body showing emotion undisguised. In all initiation rites the novice has first to undergo trials before reaching the goal. This corresponds to Mary's feeling about the double-headed dragon as it is here revealed to her.

13. Worshipping the square-headed snake

14. Dragon giving birth to small fantasy tree

IX

15. The tree trying to root itself

16. Girl chained in the air

X

17. Snake in the jar

18. Fiery escapist duck

XI

19. Cavern beneath the field

20. Falling into the sea

21. Dismemberment

22. Suffering snake

XIII

23. Hooking Leviathan

24. Purple dragon and purple incest-mist

PAINTING 13 (DREAM) 7 JULY 1957

Worshipping the Square-headed Snake

In Painting 12 the "serpent" seemed to be part snake and part dragon, but from now on these two symbols start to be sharply differentiated. Three months later the snake began effectively to constellate itself as a ruling and highly positive symbol in Mary's psychic life, and with this her self-confidence increased.

The dream to be related now was founded directly on the memory of that phase in her life already mentioned in connection with Painting 3: at the school where she had a menial job, she was attracted by an adolescent girl and went as far as she could to satisfy the craving that she felt for physical contact and the recognition of her own bodily femininity. I have mentioned how delicate this situation was, and how carefully it had to be handled while supporting fully Mary's awakening emotion. That incident had passed off without the physical satisfaction that she had desired because of the girl's ultimate lack of response. Far more important, however, than satisfaction or non-satisfaction was that Mary's basic emotion had been honoured and supported by the analyst as her most precious heritage. Mary's psyche responded to the analyst's belief that the acknowledgment of human nature and personal desire in whatever form it manifests itself, is a necessary condition for ultimate transformation.

One of the many signs of the integration now beginning to take place was the following dream, together with Painting 13 illustrating it. Though it was now several years since the break-through of emotion with regard to the girl had taken place, the memory of the experience and of its basic acceptance still remained a recurring theme at moments of crisis in Mary's life, and now came up again. We will call the girl "A" as a reminder of the "alpha into omega" nature of all such psychic transformation—from an externalised alpha into an internalised omega (the snake). Her account of this dream was:

"I was with A in a rather dark wood. I was happy to be with her again, but I noticed a big black swelling on her left hand. I had a knife, and cut the swelling off.

"Then A disappeared, and the lump which I had cut off from her turned into a black snake with red markings. At first I was rather frightened, but as the snake swayed to and fro he seemed lovely, and I wanted to worship him in some way, so I knelt before him."

Mary could not paint the first scene with the girl, which was far too obscure for her to understand, but she could paint the second scene of worshipping the snake. We may first note that the whole atmosphere is painted purple like the purple in the cauldron of Painting 12, indicating the full acceptance of the incest wish. She is immersed in it as was the two-headed serpent in the purple water in that fantasy painting. Mary herself is painted "red", indicating the acknowledgement of her desire. The snake which she is worshipping is *"black with red markings"* as was the left-hand serpent head of her desire in Painting 12. In that dream she had wished to follow it if she could but circumvent the fury of the other, the red-headed serpent head barring her way.

The atmosphere of this painting *"in a rather dark wood"* recalls that of the moonlight scene in Painting 6 when Mary had for the first time caught hold of one of the small green snakes which the "ghost man" was piping in. There is the same serenity in both. But now there are two trees—not one—which we may recognise as the two small trees in Painting 11 now grown to full maturity. They correspond also to the two serpent heads in Painting 12, which there symbolised the two parents. The head symbolising the father was painted black with red flecks, as is the snake in Mary's present fantasy. But it will be noticed also that the two colours of black and red have changed places. This seems to indicate that Mary was now in process of overcoming her fear of womanhood as symbolised by the red serpent head in Painting 12. This fear, however, had two sides to it: the incest wish towards her father, and the fear of womanhood in general. The latter had been engendered by her mother's hostile attitude as well as that of the aunt who had warned her against looking at herself in the looking glass. The desire which she had had towards the schoolgirl was in compensation for these fears. What she had desired from the schoolgirl was to be intimately touched by her just as she would have liked to have been touched by her father, so that the desire towards her father and her lesbian tendency had the same origin. They are here merged in the general need for recognition of her sexuality. As a woman, she can now worship the male principle symbolised by the black father-snake.

Figure 21. The resurrected Christ, or Christ internalised. "Noli me tangere", Duccio di Buoninsegna, Cathedral, Siena. New York, Art Resource

We may be helped to understand her problem if we compare this painting with Figure 21 of the woman worshipping the figure of the Saviour, which also has two trees in it [Mary Magdalene and the risen Christ in the Garden of Gethsemane]. The Saviour holding up the cross indicates sacrifice—withdrawing of projections—and so internalising the power that had previously been externalised.

Black symbolises among other things "the unknown". This might have been most frightening but for the redirection inwardly of her own warm emotions (indicated by the red markings) onto that psychic function in her which the snake symbolised. This was the reason why she could overcome her fears and yield to a feeling of delight, in its turn becoming adoration. That he "swayed" meant that he had life in him, and at the same time some power of reflection, not "pouncing" as her schizoid dragons, but in fact "thinking" reflectively and gently, and (still more important) subtly and flexibly. There

137

are many instances of this swaying movement—both of trees and of snakes—in mythology indicating a many-sided flexibility. We should not forget that the serpent in Genesis was also "more subtil than any beast of the field". This painting may therefore be related to such archetypal images, indicating a confrontation of the female dream-ego with the psychic male element, the snake.

The fact that there are also two trees shows how Mary's life is now getting "doubled". For the load of misery that her life has been to her till now has been due to the lack of differentiation between the two parental trees—now separated out, the one associated with the woman (herself), the other with the black snake (the father principle). This lack in the past had maintained a state of unconscious conflict in which each side was exhausted, clinched in a dark embrace, while conscious living, thinking and feeling were thus drained of their potential energy. What is depicted in the present painting is on the contrary one of the first instances in Mary's dream-life of a new and positive form of "confrontation with the unconscious", which is found to be so much less horrifying once it is embarked on than is the fear of it when it is not. We have seen its former refusal in Painting 10, which the transference has now reversed.

This dream is in strong contrast with many of Mary's earlier dreams and fantasies which have not been included here. In these she had encountered what appeared to her as "a priest" or "monk" or "nuns" in woods or in some splendid temple. She had these dreams when she herself had the feeling of "not belonging" and so of being lost or in despair. It was as though everyone else in the world had value but she had none, and they knew something which she did not know and that she never would. In waking life she did not ultimately believe this, but often thought she "should". Now the configuration is a very different one. She is now "in herself".

What is, however, most essential, and more to be noted than any other feature in the dream, is what may literally be called "the transference", closely connected indeed with the transference situation in the analysis, which has thus penetrated into the archetypal layer of Mary's psyche. It is the transference of libido in the dream from what looked like a disease, namely from the *"big black swelling"* on the left hand of the girl (whose love she had so desired but had not obtained), onto "the snake", which was hers and no one else's. Thus her own individual psychic power, which would henceforth be inalienable, would gradually free her from dependence on others, including her necessary but temporary dependence on the analyst. This would indeed fulfil the prophecy of the serpent in Genesis saying, "Ye shall not surely die", a phrase referring not to the body, but to enduring spirit now being formed in her. Mary had truly "eaten of the fruit". She had acknowledged her humanity, and had not despised or thought she should conceal her own desires.

This does not mean that she was becoming less capable in her limited way. It means the reverse: that with the real foundation of inwardly acknowledged truth she was becoming able to face the world with greater confidence, whatever troubles might be in store.

The snake symbolised a kind of "subtle" body, something akin to immortality, meaning that, once constellated, though it can suffer mightily, it cannot be destroyed or taken away. It symbolises a knowledgeable animus. For Mary and the snake are here like mutually accepting anima and animus, related to one another as "bone of my bones, and flesh of my flesh" (Genesis 2: 23). Just as the anima is for a man a bridge to deeper psychic consciousness, so is the animus for a woman. As Adam went on to say, "She shall be called Woman, because she was taken out of Man". Mary was indeed now being reborn, not out of the actual father with whom she had been unconsciously identified, but out of the father principle active in the analysis.

But she has as yet no actual boyfriend. The image of the snake is a subjective one symbolising something that is going on inside her as a result of the analysis. One of its characteristics is its square head, which has been a feature of all Mary's fantasy-snakes from Painting 8 onwards; this will continue to be so with the exception of Painting 32—in which the snake has her own head. The meaning of the squareness was obscure until much later when in a fit of rage (see Painting 31) she daubed a large piece of paper over with angry smears in the middle of which she felt impelled to paint a large black square. This symbolised her basic differentiated personality which, as the large snake's head in Painting 33, may be seen bursting into consciousness.

We may remember, however, that in this dream it was the "big black swelling" on the left hand of the desired girl that had turned into a snake with its enlarged square black head. So now the infantile incest desire, originally for the breast, which Mary had transferred from her mother onto her father (in which connection it became associated with the colour "black"), and from her father to the schoolgirl as a "young mother" substitute, was now experienced internally in the dream-image of the snake. It being the girl's left hand on which this swelling was ("left" symbolising "introverted" as opposed to extravert), this is a yet further indication of what the dream appears to illustrate: the withdrawal of projections and the formation of that solid inner personality which the square-headed snake represents. A further stage in the internalisation of the black snake will be seen in Painting 33.

One further feature of the dream that has not yet been mentioned is the *knife* with which Mary "cut off" the big black swelling. It was the first time in Mary's analysis that this symbol of the greatest importance, the knife, appeared. It has been mentioned that she had as yet no positive animus in the form of a lover, either in her waking or in her dream life. This knife is, however, a deeper symbol for the actively creative animus. It is more powerful even than the snake since it is something that she has in her own hand, which she can *use* and not merely "adore". The knife in any form, whether as the knife with which Abraham was prepared to slay his son (Gen. 22:6-10), as the "sharp stone" with which Zipporah, Moses' wife, cut off the foreskin of her son (Ex. 4:25), as the knives used for circumcision (Josh. 5:2,3), as the sword, the "two-edged sword" and so on, is, as a dividing instrument, basically a symbol for the operation of the incest taboo. Here it quite certainly functions as such, being used by the dream ego for internalising her incest desire. It severed projection on to the schoolgirl where it appeared as a "swelling on the hand" (a phallic symbol) and withdrew it inwardly where it became the "snake".

Many dualities as a result of such a severing now made their appearance in Mary's dreams and fantasies. Among them were Janus-like heads with two faces looking in opposite directions and having opposite characteristics: cats with two bodies but with a single head; snakes in couples, sometimes one red, the other black; two houses facing one another; two men; two women; and so on. At first the were very much alike, then they became more differentiated. The only one included here is Painting 29 in which Mary herself paints the 'two sides" of herself. Many such images might be taken to be so psychotic as to be a warning not to proceed. But here they were all transforming symbols, and were taken as such, so that their effects were healing.

PAINTING 14 (Fantasy) 27 February 1958

Dragon Giving Birth to Small Fantasy Tree

In Painting 13 Mary in her worship of the snake had been enveloped in a purple mist of creative incest-fantasy. Seven months later, just as the blue light pervading Mary's room when she was in danger of dying from tuberculosis had become concentrated into the figure of the Death Woman about to carry her off, so now the purple colour becomes concentrated in the figure of what she calls a "dragon". In its womb these appears the image of the small tree, symbolising her unrelated fantasies as seen in Paintings 2 and 12 but now internalised. They are incarnated within the dragon—which clearly symbolises part of herself.

We have already met with the dragon as an unborn foetus (painted green and fed by the thistle as through an umbilical cord in Painting 7), and as an already powerful figure, though still underground (painted purple and bursting open the coffin of the man in Painting 11). Now the dragon is for the first time above the ground, itself pregnant and wanting to give birth. Mary's description of this fantasy is as follows:

"This is a dragon painted as if lying partly on its side and partly on its back so as to show its underbelly. I have painted one leg on the ground to show how it could support itself in this position. It has a forked tail as all dragons have, and of course it has fire coming out of its mouth and nose. The black scales are meant to show the outside of its skin on back, head, feet and tail. The part where no scales

141

are painted in is the soft underside on which it is actually lying, though it has turned it towards me so that I can see it.

"The underbelly is painted in section so as to show what is inside it. Inside the belly is a tree. The tree has been nourished and kept alive by the warmth from the fire coming out of the dragon's mouth."

The dragon here symbolises part of Mary's own nature, in which fury (the fire) and psychic pregnancy go hand in hand. The fire, though furious—as may be seen from the painting—is at the same time a warming fire helping to incubate the tree. It is a symbol for the aggressive self-assertion that had been so stifled in Mary's home life but which it was so necessary for her to bring out. Mary having been too frightened to assert herself in ordinary life, these furies naturally vented themselves on the analyst. He could accept them not only with equanimity but even with pleasure. For they indicated her growing release from fear of "punishment": open abuse from her mother and her father's "feeling hurt". These two quite opposite reactions on the part of her two parents had produced in Mary an ever-present doubt as to what would happen if she did indeed express her real feelings of cynical scorn—especially towards her father in his parsonic aspect (which she so despised). With the small tree evidently symbolising her real thoughts, is it, she wonders, yet really safe to bring them out into the open, even in analysis? This was expressed in her next remark:

"The question is, which of two things is happening. Either the tree is not yet quite ready to come out, and the fire is still providing warmth for it to grow inside; or else the fire is going to burn a hole through the skin, so that the tree can come out".

In her past fantasies and dreams she has been quite certain it would be too dangerous. The fact that *"the fire is still providing warmth for it to grow inside"* shows her increasing acceptance of her own personality. The fire burning *"a hole through the skin, so that the tree can come out"* expresses what actually happened during the course of analysis when she let herself go and was not afraid to pour out the bile of her anger against the analyst. (For the solution of this problem see Paintings 26 and 27.)

Asked why she called this creature a dragon apart from the fire which belched from its mouth, she said quite simply, *"Because of its tail"*, by which she meant its arrow-headed tail. This is a distinctive feature of the dragon in all her fantasy-paintings as opposed to the snake with its forked tongue (with the exception of Paintings 19 and 32). Those familiar with the myth of the tail-eating *uroboros* will note that the dragon is here near to biting its own tail, which in this case would symbolise a closed circle of incest-fear. No such consideration, however, entered Mary's mind, and when I asked her about the dragon's tail, her reply was that it was simply *"the kind of position the tail would naturally get into if the dragon rolled over like that"*. The knowledge of that kind of animal movement shortly before delivery she derived from watching mother cats rolling over on the mat at home not long before kittening.

But here the circle is unclosed, leaving room for the tree to "be born" and to grow. It is the same space in which the fire issues from the dragon's mouth in order to promote its growth. If we compare this fantasy with Painting 7, we may observe that the fire now takes the place of the thistle there nourishing the foetus of the unborn dragon. It symbolised the mother's deep wisdom so overlaid by her schizoid nature that she could not implement it in her life. In the same way the fire issuing from the dragon's mouth symbolised Mary's own internal hostile reaction to the parental atmosphere. Her reaction had been a justified one; now, through its release, if was producing its results.

The direction of growth is now also quite different. Whereas, three years ago, in Painting 7 the movement was downwards towards the foetus-dragon within the womb, that same dragon, above the ground, is now itself pregnant. The tree is ready to grow upwards (in a more adult way). Whereas in Painting 2 the tree trunk was entirely pink or flesh coloured, now it is black (the father-principle), as also is the ground on which the dragon lies. The dragon's teeth are also black, as are the scales of its body.

Black is also associated with unconsciousness. It might have been thought that the image of this tree would recall to Mary's mind the small fantasy-tree which the girl held in her hand in Painting 2—but nothing of the kind. When she was reminded of it she remembered, and the memory made some impact.

Behemoth and Leviathan

There is a great contrast between the active dragon pushing open the coffin and the passive dragon giving birth to the tree. The first is long and lithe, the second heavier and more compact. These are two aspects of an elemental mythological creature referred to in the Bible respectively as Behemoth and Leviathan. The pair of them are beautifully illustrated in Fig. 22 reproducing Plate Fifteen of Blake's *Illustrations of the Book of Job*. It shows Behemoth as a land creature and Leviathan as a kind of sea-serpent like the one that Mary later painted as being hooked by the tail (Fantasy Painting 23).

Figure 22. Behemoth and Leviathan. *Illustrations for the Book of Job*. William Blake, Dover Publications, Inc., New York, 1995, Plate 15

Inhabiting the sea, the mother element, Leviathan with its long sinuous body seems male, possibly symbolising a mother's animus. The pregnant dragon on the other hand is much more like Behemoth. Though in the Bible both creatures are referred to as "he" it would appear that the land creature Behemoth with its shorter and thicker body would be symbolically the more female of the two, as would be appropriate in a creature associated with the Earth.

In the only biblical reference to Behemoth God says to Job, "Behold now behemoth which I made with thee" (Job 40:15) almost as though in contrast to Leviathan it were Job's mate or anima. As a creature of the land, not of the sea, Behemoth "eateth grass as an ox". "His force is in the navel of his belly" (Job 15:16), which indicates the mother-child relationship. "He is the chief of the ways of God; he that made him can make his sword to approach unto him" (ibid. v. 19). What better symbol could there be of God's phallic approach towards his female creation? "Surely the mountains bring him forth food, where all the beasts of the field play" (ibid. v. 20)—an image of a mother feeding her babes. "He lieth under the shady trees, in the covert of the reed, and fens. The shady trees cover him with their shadow" (ibid. vv 21, 22), as the Holy Ghost "overshadowed" the Virgin Mary when she conceived. We have already noted such an overshadowing by the tree in Mary's Painting 6. "The willows of the brook compass him about. Behold, he drinketh up a river, and hasteth not; he trusteth that he can draw up Jordan into his mouth" (ibid. vv 22, 23). With the mouth symbolising the vagina as it does

144

in so much mystical imagery, what more striking symbol could there be for the female aspect of coitus? The symbolism is of Job accepting the Lord's word, and being fertilised by it. The incarnation of the Word is symbolised in Mary's painting by the small tree of which her dragon is pregnant, the tree grown of the acorn, the seed which the old father-tree had dropped (Painting 2). In Blake's painting Behemoth and Leviathan are depicted as a pair encircled in one womb to which the Father points.

Mary was now in the course of being released from the torment of unconsciously conditioned schizoid misery by the emergence of such powerful archetypal figures, the meaning of which she was at last beginning to understand. For her habitual system of fears and counter-fears, of which there had been innumerable instances during the past eight years, was gradually giving way to hope. She was however still doubtful as to how soon it would be realised, as symbolised in this fantasy by her question: was the fire issuing from the dragon's mouth meant only to incubate the tree or to bring about its more immediate "birth"? There is no conscious knowledge about things unborn, which is apparently why Mary, although painting this tree within the womb, failed to remember the similar small trees in Fantasy Paintings 2 and 12. A womb so sluggish as that of this feminine Behemoth-like dragon is loath to yield its treasures up, so that memory here hardly operates. The relevant association tracts cannot be got at without immense patience, which an analyst can only have if he has at the same time the vision of the reward which will eventually come of it.

It is not to be supposed that when the fantasy tree gets 'born" out of the dragon it will remain a simple tree and thus so "innocent". It was quite obvious in the analysis that it would not, but that there would be such a new uprush of sex desire combined with fear of expressing it, that there would certainly be new conflicts. Thus in the next Painting (15) what are potentially the tree's roots appear as seven snakes. In Painting 25 there is another dragon pregnant of two snakes, but this has a different significance.

145

PAINTING 15 (Fantasy) 25 June 1958

The Tree Trying to Root Itself

Up to this point in the analysis Mary had been so occupied with getting a footing in the external world (for her, the mental hospital in which she worked and lived) while still heftily projecting almost all her unrecognised psychic contents onto it, that it was only on rare occasions that she had consented to enter into anything like a regular course of analytical treatment, and that for only short spells of a week or two.

Now that she was beginning to have some small idea that the world was not entirely against her, and that it might possibly rather be she who was against the world, it seemed time to press for more intensive analysis. After many hesitations and changes of mind, she finally consented. While she was still hesitating she fell into the fantasy (Painting 15) which helped her to come to the decision that it was really time to go more deeply into things.

The fantasy was of an uprooted tree-trunk floating in the air. Above it is a purple cloud. The seven roots, still unattached, end in snakes' heads reaching downwards towards a depression in the earth the shape of a dew pond.

For the first time now I had persuaded Mary to write her comments on the back of the sheet on which she had painted the fantasy. Her comment this time was a simple one. She wrote: *"The snakes want to burrow into the ground, so that the tree would be planted again. But the tree does not know if it wants to be planted, or to be drawn up into the cloud."*

The dragon in Painting 14 has now given birth to the tree of which it was pregnant. "Birth" means birth into consciousness. From the beginning the small trees of Painting 2, 12 and 14 had been to Mary mere fantasy-trees, part of her world of "fairy tales", which she in no way realised as being central to her personality. This is connected with the fact that she had up till now been very unaware of the divorce between her and reality. The tree in Painting 15 which we are now considering is furnished with eyes and mouth. This was not the first of the trees that she had recently painted (though not illustrated here) with human features such as these. They had all been trees growing by the side of a river, like the tree in Painting 5 which had mythological associations with the river god.

Apollo and Daphne. Mary's expanding life. Conflict.

What Mary did not know was that in Greek mythology such riverside trees were dedicated to Daphne, that father-bound maiden whom Apollo passionately pursued. When he was on the point of embracing her, she turned into a tree drawing its sap, or psychic libido, from the river father-god to whom she was so wedded inwardly that she could give herself to no other man. There are paintings indicating the agony on Apollo's face when he realised this. In none of the fantasies thus painted had Mary, unacquainted with such mythology, the faintest suspicion that these trees symbolised her own father-bound self. The present fantasy was the first in which she knew that the ambivalent feelings with which she had endowed the tree were indeed her own.

For Mary had by now sufficiently come out into the world, though only the restricted one of the mental hospital in which she worked, to be aware of other men. There were, as previously indicated, male nurses as well as female ones. Sex jokes were there the order of the day, and though Mary herself did not make any intimate relationships she was at least aware that others did. The image of her father as the "only man" was thus considerably weakening, his place having been taken also psychically by the analyst. But it was not he who was now uppermost in her sex fantasies, or there would have been but one snake to the tree. There was a more general awakening. She was beginning to feel that the tree had some connection with her own uprooted self

147

since it was endowed with feelings and a wish, not knowing if it "wanted to be planted" as the phallic snakes would have it be, "or to be drawn up" again "into the cloud"—whose purple colour shows it to symbolise the father-incest fantasy that had until now ruled her life.

It will be noted that the tree-trunk has no branches but two kinds of "root". What should have been the branches are here seen as all broken off. But if we turn the picture upside down we may perceive that the broken-off branches look more like "roots", so that the tree-trunk has two sets of roots: one set furnished with snakes' heads trying to root it in the reality of earth, the other still hankering to be rooted in the incest-cloud. In Mary's fantasies, and in the paintings which she made of them, she thought of snakes as always being "wise". The phallic snakes here indicate also "intelligence", which belongs to the archetypal father-principle or consciousness of self, now slowly replacing her former father-fixation. They symbolise efforts tending towards psychic consciousness.

Seven snake-heads

There are seven such snake-heads, a number she was unaware of when she painted them but which was found to correspond with the seven main roots in Painting 5, and with the seven branches of the rose tree on to which she was to be grafted in Painting 4, and the seven branches (now also noted for the first time) of the central tree in Painting 6. This number has creative meaning, but it is also made up of three added to four, which means the male element added to the female one.

The seven snake-heads wanting to root her to the ground mean the exact opposite of the purple cloud, which is the fantasy cloud of incestuous desire for her actual father—now dead and therefore completely unattainable. This had surrounded her literally as a purple mist in many previous fantasy paintings, symbolising the "safety" of incestuous self-deception. And this had carried her (like the tree) quite "off her feet" and made her into the rootless creature she had become. The seven snakes now want to bring her down to earth in order to get her rooted in her own reality-starved psyche—in touch with basic humanity perhaps for the first time since early infancy, and tending to unite her with herself and with others.

The World Tree

So much for Mary's own personal problem. But those familiar with Norse mythology will not miss another significant association with the tree, this time a powerfully archetypal one. This is the "World Tree" (Figure 23), rooted partly in the sky, called *Yggdrasill*, meaning literally "the horse of *Yggr*"

Figure 23. "Yggdrasyll, the world tree of the Edda. From Finner Magnuson's edition of the Elder Edda, XVIII century." Erich Neumann, *The Great Mother*. London, Routledge and Kegan Paul, 1955, Fig. 55

(the Terrible One). This was a nickname for Odin, who is said to have discovered the secret of runic wisdom by hanging himself upside down on the tree. And we can recall Mary's Painting 3 of the boy (the dying and rising 'young god') hanging on the tree.

The World Tree is a cosmic tree having three roots, one of which stands in heaven, and beneath it is a sacred spring where the gods have their judgment seat (note also the spring beside the tree in Mary's Painting 6). Another root is connected with a well called Mimir's Well, wherefore the tree is also called Mimir's Tree. There is a nest of serpents underneath this tree, and a dragon gnawing at its roots, and there is also a Tree Snake, which is equated further with a cock which crows to awaken the gods or giants to battle. This tree "has troubles of its own", for it is attacked from above and from below by birds and "wriggling worms", so typical of Mary's own conflicts.

Yggdrasill is regarded as the agency by which the fabric of the universe is maintained, "the universe" meaning "the mind of man".[62] It was thought of as an evergreen tree and sacrifices were made at it, not only by hanging human victims on the tree, but also by drowning others in the well—mixed motifs recalling both the crucifixion and baptism. We can remember the references of "being drowned with Christ" in our own baptismal service, meaning to accept

---

62. See Brian Branston, *Gods of the North*. London and New York, Thames & Hudson, 1955, pp. 76-83), from whose description I take this account.

death and so gain psychic life. No one knows where the roots of the tree Yggdrasill come from, but its fruits were said to be beneficial to childbirth and the labour of women, thus also symbolising the labour of man's anima.

All this speaks of regeneration, which Branston connects with the Hindu lingam as a phallic symbol standing for internal fulfilment of the individual as well as for procreation and the continuance of the human race. The wells supply its roots with the sap of life. It has a female counterpart in a well called Roaring Cauldron (compare here Mary's Painting 12), which is the source of all rivers and comparable to Okeanos. But this myth states that the tree must one day be felled (see the sickle in Painting 2) to make way for a new phase, though we are not told when or how.

There are innumerable archetypal pictures illustrating this theme, two being here particularly relevant: Figure 24 showing a tree with its reverse reflection in water, and Figure 25 of a tree with twisted roots and manifold branches in which sits a man who has taken refuge from two dragons which threaten from either side. Both these are taken from Jung's *Von den Wurzeln des Bewusstseins*, in which he writes about Figure 25, "The emphasis on the twisted roots indicates disquiet in the unconscious".[63]

Figure 24. Tree reflected in water. "The tree is painted a vivid red, and grows in the water simultaneously upwards and downwards." Jung, *Alchemical Studies*, Fig. 6

Figure 25. Two dragons are threatening a man who has sought refuge in the tree. The emphasis on the twisted roots indicates disquiet in the unconscious. Jung, *Alchemical Studies*, Fig. 9

---

63. See also sections on "The Tree as Man", pp. 337-341; "The Inverted Tree", pp. 311-315; p. 318, g 420, in *Alchemical Studies*.

The Girl Chained in the Air

This fantasy is a striking commentary on that of the uprooted tree in Painting 15 and provides a clue to the reason for its uprootedness. Mary is here seen, naked and red, suspended in mid-air by golden chains, framed against the sky in a kind of archway or vault. She is not unlike the girl in the old song who was "only a bird in a gilded cage", recalling also many tales of the daughter imprisoned in a tower by a jealous father fearful lest any young man should release her from his bonds. The fantasy may remind us of the image of herself crucified in a corner at the bottom of Early Painting F. It will recall also the hanging boy, though here there is a great advance since she now realises that it is herself (albeit the boy symbolised her animus) and not some unknown "boy" who is thus "tied up". She is now much more conscious of her situation than she was then. This is shown also by the colouring since red (the colour which she paints herself) and blue (the colour of the sky) together make purple (cf. Painting 15). This differentiation shows how she is now sorting herself out, her passion being now shown separated from the blue of unattainable desire. The blackness of the vault reminds us once more of the blackness of the womb, associated with the father in her fantasies (as a mother substitute).

This painting is included here to show how the uprooted tree with its red eyes and mouth in the last painting portrayed her own uprooted self. Her only comment on it was:

"*Feeling strung up at the Hospital. This painting didn't help much, but the next one did.*"

The next painting was done immediately afterwards on the same day, and forms a great contrast to it.

PAINTING 17 (FANTASY) 14 AUGUST 1958

The Snake in the Jar

This is the second instance of Mary painting two fantasies in rapid succession on the same day just as she had done with Paintings 10 and 11. Each time the first picture was a despairing or self-pitying one with the figure of herself "up in the air" and painted red (the anguish of her loneliness), while the second was of an "underground" and much more lively scene showing the internal response to the surface despair. Thus in Painting 10 the red Mary was isolated upon a rock, terrified of being swallowed by the great fish—which she failed to recognise as her potential rescuer. The opposite creative fantasy (Painting 11) which this despair called forth was of the awakening of her unknown animus out of its tomb. This is what Jung would call enantiodromia, a swinging from one extreme to the other in a potentially compensating and thus healing way.

Mary was now becoming aware of the danger of "false starts" leading into a kind of arid self-dramatisation or unrelated introspection. This was, however, quickly corrected when she allowed her inner fantasy life to come up by way of a contra-image to it. She had already said of the last painting that this fantasy *"didn't help much, but the next one did"*. This meant that, dissatisfied with what she herself perceived to be the unhelpfulness of her own self-pitying—the girl chained in mid-air—her psyche then threw up the contra-image of the present fantasy:

153

"The snake is imprisoned in a jar buried in the ground. The top of the jar is shut by a heavy stone. There is a fire underneath the earth, which may break the jar and free the snake. Or it may not. I don't know.

"I was thoroughly miserable when I painted this at the hospital. This helped to relieve things a bit. The last painting (16) was thought out too consciously. This one grew more naturally."

The relief came from the fact that instead of pitying herself for her external loneliness she now turned her attention inward towards the potential riches of her own psychic life. This until recently had made itself felt only in the form of the fantasies which she had thought to be quite unrelated to her life. But she was now beginning to see in them a reflection of herself and of her own predicament: she felt imprisoned like the snake. Now, instead of being strung up unrelatedly in passionate impotence, held by the chains, she—in the person of the green snake—although "shut in" now is longing to get free. And the green colour of the snake, the complementary opposite colour to the red of her own impotent fury in Painting 16, is the colour of hope and of new life. It is seen against the same background of blue as was the figure of herself in that painting.

"Under the earth" means happening to Mary inwardly. The jar might at first sight look like an alchemical vase, hermetically sealed by the heavy black stone on top of it. The fire beneath it would symbolise the force transforming unregulated instinct into psychic power. But this would be illusory for the black stone covering it is not here positive but is a negative symbol having to do with her father-incest fantasies. The cauldron of Painting 12 with the fire burning under it as somewhat similar, the matter to be transformed there being the purple liquid of incestuous desire. The cauldron then itself was black and was not closed, so out of it came the revelation of the fierce two-headed serpent—the fierceness of Mary's externalised desires and fears regarding both parents.

But now the jar is closed giving Mary a feeling rather like that which she had when working in the mental hospital; there she preferred night work ("black") to day. During the daytime she felt herself continually harried by the ward sisters and the doctors over them, driven by fear to perform daily duties she disliked. But when on night duty she felt more free to be herself. She was not supervised, and could use her intuitive faculties to ease the patients' lives much more than in the day. She was then free for instance to cope with their excretory problems in a sympathetic way (as she had done for her Aunt Grace), instead of having all the time to keep them clean. She could take them to the lavatory and there let them do what they liked instead of saying "Dirty", thus inhibiting their fantasies and the overt expression of them in excretory playfulness. If the patients wished to masturbate, she would let them instead of tying up their hands. She could at the same time, during the night, indulge in her own fantasies, and in the patients', too, to everyone's relief. For she was popular with them, and felt that she could be herself, and let them be themselves during these nocturnal hours.

The black stone covering the jar thus had a dual significance. On the one hand during the daytime it symbolised authority by which she felt herself imprisoned and her own personality denied. During the night however the darkness liberated her. During the daytime she wished that the *"fire underneath the earth"* of her own longing to be free might *"break the jar and free the snake"*. But in this fantasy she is uncertain since she says that *"it may not"*. This is, I think, because she does not yet distinguish between being imprisoned by external authority and being imprisoned by herself. This may remind us of the fire (Painting 14) issuing out of the dragon's mouth, which may be to provide warmth for the incubation of the tree, but also may be to burn a hole in the dragon's skin so that the tree can come out. Mary still feels herself to be in the same state of uncertainty.

But future fantasy paintings will show which of these two interpretations is correct. Paintings 19 and 23 show the continuation of the motif of the black stone in the layer of black earth, underneath which her psychic life was seen to be imprisoned (although she could catch glimpses of it through an ever-widening gap). In Paintings 26 and 27 it is her own head that is painted black, and in Painting 27 the fire is inside it, not outside as here. For there are two aspects to this alchemical fire in relation to the jar, as there are two aspects of alchemy: firstly, the illusory attempt to transform base metals into gold with the fire *outside* the jar, and secondly, the soul-making aspect in which the fire is *inside* the jar (see Figure 33). The transformation of base metals into gold is but a symbol for the transformation of instinct into psychic power.

The jar is thus an adumbration of the psychic womb here overshadowed by the blackness, indicating the personal father in his mother-role keeping her bottled up. The snake here is twisty, as is the life process. Its tongue is forked (as it is in most of her paintings), indicating the possibility of joined opposites and of the "two-edged sword".

The importance of the order in which Mary painted the different parts of her fantasies has already been seen (Painting 5—tree and rotting corpse). About the present fantasy she said:

"I drew the jar first because of the enclosed feeling. Then I put in the snake. Then I put in the earth, and left a space underneath knowing that something would come, but I didn't know what. Then the stone, and then the fire. I put the tree in last, but I don't know why. I felt like the snake shut up in the jar. The painting relieved this feeling."

What is most striking here is the space Mary left underneath the jar not knowing what would come, What came there was the fire symbolising the psychic force—generated in opposition to the black stone paired with it in her mind. The stone came first, representing on the personal level the father in his mother-role preventing her form realising her own individuality. This fact she was now becoming so aware of as to call forth the image of the fire in the empty space, though the fire was still outside (the analyst) and she had not yet got it inside. The small black tree came last, indicating the introjection of the "black" father influence.

The objectification of all this by painting it relieved her, although the symbolism was to her still obscure. The ruling principle at this juncture was hope—the hope of further contact with herself by means of the more intensive analysis that was now beginning.

What now follows is a selection from the fantasies that arose during this more intensive treatment, insofar as they concern the development of the "snake" and the "dragon" motifs, and her own descriptions of them written after painting, together with a minimum of comment necessary to explain their continuity.

PAINTING 18 (Fantasy) 30 September 1958

The Fiery Escapist Duck

Mary's psychology was nothing if not self-contradictory. Having achieved some degree of inwardness she would then constantly take fright and rush off into escapist thinking of all kinds so as to mask her own conflict. This painting is an illustration of such headlong flight. The fire which in the last painting was to have cracked the jar so as to release the snake of her potential psychic power, is now like a volcano. It is chaotically bursting out, thus losing its energy and taking the form of a fiery duck rising out of a stormy sea—the emotions which Mary could not yet adequately face. What she wrote of this fantasy was:

"The duck is trying to escape from the sea, to find a resting place. The bats are flying round its head to confuse it. The little snake is laughing to see the duck's agitation (like the little dog in the nursery rhyme). I feel like the duck, really powerful but too 'batty' to be able to find any rest or to make sense of the rest of my life."

While working in the mental hospital she had developed (along the lines of her previous life) a technique of masking her emotions so successfully that few of her superiors or fellow nurses there knew that she had any. They just thought her rather odd and "vague", which was an opinion she liked to encourage as it saved her the trouble of ever trying to explain herself. It masked two things: the deep intuitions that she had about the feelings of the patients that were ignored by the authorities, and the cold, bitter and cynical hostility which she inwardly experienced against all those who she thought did not understand. This could not be allowed to pass unnoticed during analysis with the result that, when challenged by the analyst, she would sometimes pour out streams of opinionated thought of the most absurdly conventional kind to hide the conflict she was in. Thus while on the one hand she hated and despised the doctors who would inflict shock treatments on the patients in their care, she was so proud of having learnt how to arrange the syringes and other medical paraphernalia upon the doctors' trays that with this other side of herself she would coldly but passionately defend the treatments which otherwise she so objected to.

When not responded to or argued with, such psychic storms would sometimes end in shrieks, which would of themselves sooner or later show her the state of mind that she was in. One kind of release for this was to go and paint a painting such as this one: she was the duck escaping from the problem of her own self-contradictions so as to *"find a resting place"* in a state of self-deceptive unreality. It will be noted that the duck (which here might look so innocent) is in exactly the same attitude as is the right-hand part of the two-headed serpent (the angry and insane mother influence directed against Mary's entry into her unconscious) in Painting 12. Both are painted the same red colour as Mary is in her escapist mood in Painting 10 (the black birds symbolising her own destructive fears and thoughts). Mary now says regarding the painting of the duck that the black bats *"are flying round its head to confuse it"*, but in this case the confusion is a necessary one tending to show how stupid the duck is in trying to escape. Mary herself feels *"like the duck, really powerful but too 'batty'.* The *"little snake"* (which in Mary's paintings almost always symbolises psychic consciousness) *"is laughing to see the duck's agitation"*.

The reader might think, from the considerable insight that the above description of her fantasy might seem to convey, that she by now knew quite a lot about herself. But an essential feature about Mary at this time was that her modicum of self-knowledge was still largely encapsuled in her fantasy life as a kind of self-picture that was only partly felt to be herself at all. Her emotions were still so much projected into this fantasy life (which she still regarded as a kind of fairy tale on a different plane from that of her living reality) that she was able to recognise only a small portion of the truth expressed

158

in it as applying to herself. Time after time she produced such fantasy knowledge, encouraging the analyst to believe that much more progress had been made than was the case.

It will be noted that the transforming fire hidden beneath the earth (Painting 17) is now exposed to view. For with her gradually increasing trust in the safety of an analytical situation (in which she could rely on the analyst not to turn his back on her because of the confusion she was in, just as she was afraid the world would do), her psychic consciousness could now allow her turbulence to come into the open. That is, she need not fear to expose her chaotic and unformed feelings since in fact she was encouraged to live with them and to express them in analysis. In this way she was gradually to be aware of and thus come to terms with them. Although the fiery duck was a symbol for escapism, it was a good thing that it should be exposed as such. The same principle applies to the fact that what in Painting 17 had been the harmless earth was now a raging sea, in which nevertheless the knowledgeable purple snake of psychic consciousness could swim, calmly observing it.

PAINTING 19 (Fantasy) Undated

The Cavern underneath the Field

Mary having recovered from the scare illustrated by the escapist duck in Painting 18, her psyche settled down again to drawing her attention to what was happening within. It was one with the same half-knowledge that, as in the previous painting, she could become aware of it:

"I am walking in a very dull meadow, and don't notice the hole that I am about to fall into. This hole is half full of water. A dragon and a snake live there. They don't agree with each other, but I think they will join together in attacking me when I fall into their pond.

"The meadow is so dull that I can't understand why I don't notice the hole and the more interesting things underground."

We may remember Painting 2 in which the thistle had hoisted the girl "up in the air". Whereas in that fantasy she did not recognise the unknown girl to be herself (and the girl was so unobservant as not to see the thistle she sat on), now the girl was fully recognised as being herself. She was still walking unobservantly, however, in a dull field and was only half-aware of the cavern opening up under her.

For in the second paragraph of her account there are two "I"s which mean different things. Her ego consciousness does not notice the hole which she is about to fall into. But with her fantasy consciousness (psychic consciousness which takes over when she paints) she does see it and what there is in it. Knowing how much more "interesting" the things in her psyche or "underground" can be, could she but contact them, she cannot understand why her ego consciousness does not see also. For the dull meadow with root-less grass (like that in Painting 5) symbolises that dreadful dullness and barrenness of life that the paranoid lives in, in which everything and all people look just the same since they all are plastered over with the paranoid's own lifeless projections. These allow no character and no differences to peep through the everlasting monotony of "one-way" thinking and perceiving— one-way because no positive and linking emotions flow out towards people, and so none can flow in from them.

"The girl" in Painting 2 was so divorced from life that she (Mary) could concentrate on nothing but her fantasies without relating them to her actual predicament: she was blaming others for the misery that she was in. But there is a great contrast here to Painting 2. For now, in place of the prickly thistle growing upward, i.e. projecting her combined incest desires and fears into an uncomprehending and therefore rejecting world, there is the small hole or gap in the black earth. It affords entrance to the cavern underground in which the real cause of her conflict can be seen and its solution thus made possible.

In this cavern we may recognise the "vase" (Painting 17) with its black restricting stopper now removed. The heights of escapist fantasy '(the Purple Thistle and the Fiery Duck) have now given way to the depths in which everything is changed and has the opposite meaning to that which it has when it is projected outward onto others and the world in general. In Painting 2 Mary appears to be "at rest" in the purple of her incest fantasy. The purple atmosphere above the ground (Painting 13—Mary worshipping the snake) is almost equally serene.

But the internal truth is very different, for inwardly her incest problem is a battleground, indicated by the whirling brush-strokes of the disturbed purple atmosphere inside this cavern of her soul. Note also that the snakes in Painting 18 as well as in this one are purple too, and that her snakes are usu-ally "wise". The purple in this case means "awareness of incestuous desire"—knowledge of which is itself part of the cure. But Mary, although so unaware in ego consciousness, is now inwardly so disturbed that, though she knows that the dragon and the snake in her psyche are natural enemies (the

161

snake symbolising calm wisdom and the dragon the fury of her own uncontrolled emotionality), she is consumed with fear lest *they will join together in attacking me when I fall into their pond*". The universal nature of such archetypes may be realised if we consider the subterranean waters of Australian aboriginal belief—the dwelling place of the great father-snake and of the spiritual and the yet unborn. These mythical subterranean waters underneath each tribe's own water-hole were supposed to join in a great reservoir of psychic consciousness common to all, uniting them on the same level of psychic experience.[64]

A feature of this fantasy peculiar to Mary is how the blackness of the stone (a stopper) has been transformed now to the blackness of the earth. Through the gap in this, owing to the removal of the stopper, she can now peep and become more aware of what is going on within; what is now revealed besides the snake is the existence of the dragon. This is painted red as she also is painted red, thus suggesting her own dragon-like nature beneath her assumed innocence. That the purple snake was later over-painted red is in accordance with her fear that the otherwise "wise snake" may join the dragon in attacking her.

In contrast to her nakedness (Painting 16) she is now clothed again. This indicates the self-defensive armour with which she would think of herself ("just an ordinary girl") with no problems, such as she seemed to think herself at the beginning of this fantasy. Her ego consciousness fails to recognise the gulf beneath her feet, but she must sooner or later fall into the gulf so as to encounter what awaits her there.

---

64. See for instance W. Lloyd Warner, *A Black Civilisation*, New York and London, 1937, p. 253.

PAINTING 20 (Fantasy) Undated

Falling into the Sea

As usually is the case, what Mary fell into, or nearly did, was a surprise. About this fantasy she wrote:

"In this painting I am hanging onto the branch of a tree, afraid to let go. The crab is hungry for me, and I dread meeting it. The snake is watching all that happens. I feel that he is interested in me and quite friendly. In the end I shall have to let go of that branch from exhaustion. Perhaps it would be better if I could do so before I am quite worn out. The crab may not be as bad as I think it is."

One of the revealing features of this picture is the black branch of the tree onto which Mary still clings. It may remind us of the branch in Painting 3 (the chained hanging boy). There she had painted herself black (the fantasy "had nothing to do with her"), while the hanging boy was red (her deeper emotions that had been sacrificed). Now and in Painting 19 she is herself red though clothed, the redness symbolising now her own aroused emotions, the clothing symbolising her armour of fear making her still *"afraid to let go"* and sink with trust into the sea of life. We shall have little difficulty in recognising the persistence of black—the black stone covering the jar, and in the black layer of earth: the illusory security of her father-boundness. Quite naturally when she lets this go what she is due to meet with is of course the Great Mother—the Crab. This replaces the dragon of the previous painting.

163

The Crab

Quite naturally Mary is afraid that the Crab is *"hungry"* for her. But this is just what she had previously avoided with the Great Fish (Painting 10). Since that refusal of relationship, the Fish, as always happens when friendly but feared unconscious factors of this kind are rejected, has now become more primitive and has sunk further down, till it is now guised as a Crab right on the bottom of the sea. Analysis has now shown Mary that her clinging to safety is an expense of effort that no longer profits her. She knows that in the end she will *"have to let go"* from sheer exhaustion. *"The crab may not be as bad as I think it is."*

For the Crab itself is "human" as she is, with red eyes and large red mouth. It too is conscious of its isolation and too great self-protectiveness (typified by its shell). Unconscious factors mirror conscious ones and yearn to be accepted just as ego does. So the Crab sends out long claws which seem to threaten but are really to embrace. Its mouth is soft and ready to receive, as is the womb. What seems so frightening is really loving too. The Crab, a well-known mother symbol (cf. the astrological Cancer) here indicates the Archetypal Mother who has lost her Child, longs to receive it back and to incorporate it so that their mutual loneliness can be assuaged. Having been ignored so long in Mary's life, however, this archetypal mother-image is herself angry (or appears to be) at this neglect. Thus the first encounter with her is, as it always is, a terrifying one. So in its dual aspect of attacking and loving the Crab functions as the Initiating Mother too. This is at first so frightening to ego consciousness, and in particular to Mary's, (cf. her association with her actual mother). Once the fear is *"let go"* the Great Mother gives of her best as any loving mother would.

This dual aspect is the essence of all initiation rites. The novice is first hurt and terrified and then accepted into the larger world of social and psychic adulthood, which becomes a new "mother" to him or her, instructing and protecting. The process may be seen at work in Mary's fantasy, not only in her encounter with the Crab but in the nature of the Crab—indicated by the colour she has painted it. This is a dirty green (the same as the water, Paintings 18, 19) now concentrated in the Crab. It appears as the personification of that Great Mother the sea, from which all things arise and into which all shall return. Mary's attention being concentrated on the Crab, the sea surrounding it has lost the angry aspect it formerly had. It is now a tranquil blue so that Mary is not afraid of it, and is already immersed in it, although still frightened.

But is this terror really of the Crab, or is the real fear that of letting go the branch? The answer to this question will be found somewhat surprisingly in the next painting, which will show what happens when the "Crab", in a new form, does swallow her.

The Snake

The snake looks on approvingly, watching and taking note as in Fantasy Painting 18, no longer feeling "shut in" as in Painting 17, and she is no longer afraid of it (Painting 19). She feels that he *"is interested in me and quite friendly"*.

As in most of the fantasies she had during analysis from Painting 1 onwards, the snake, as well as symbolising her own calm and knowledgeable psychic consciousness, represents the analyst onto whom she has projected so much of her hope of getting well and solving her problems. He for his part stimulates what hopeful forces there may be in her and stands by her in the troubles she goes through. For there are always, in any analytical treatment, "two analysts", the "external analyst" who helps, and the "internal analyst" which his presence calls forth in the patient's own psyche. There it may have been formerly unrecognised or long asleep, like the Kundalini Yoga snake which we shall meet with later in Painting 33. There is always such a correspondence between external and internal factors, each mirroring the other and co-operating when circumstances allow. The snake, whom Mary thinks so wise, symbolises her own growing internal power of self-observation and of trust in whatever her fantasy or dream life may bring forth, counteracting and tending to dispel her conscious fears.

For the only time in this series of Mary's fantasy paintings the snake is painted brown, the colour of the earth, or "common sense". The colour of the sky also reflects the earth. The snake here is quite confident that what is happening is right. It has no fear of what will happen if the Crab devours her. It stands for the male principle of psychic consciousness which complements the female nature of the Crab so that the two may be regarded as male and female. This suggests a kind of "sacred marriage" in the sea in which, in several primitive mythologies, the gods have their being, and live. Or, on another level, if the snake is indeed representing the analyst, the Crab might be a symbol for the dynamic process of analysis, the two working together like man and wife.

We may conclude this brief review of Mary's Painting 20 with a comparison with Painting 5 (the brown tree sending its roots down towards the mother-substitute). This blackness depicted for Mary what was at that time a quite unconscious fear, lying as the rotting corpse then did in the silt under the riverbed. In the present fantasy the danger is now a conscious one (the black branch at the top of the picture). The father's rotting corpse is now replaced by the living Crab whose claws reach upward for Mary. The libido is now flowing in both directions: from Mary downward towards the Crab, and from the Crab upward. The unconscious is now recognised not as a dead but as a living thing, from which her new life may be born.

PAINTING 21 (FANTASY) UNDATED

Dismemberment

Rebirth always entails a sacrifice. In this painting we see the naked figure of Mary; it is painted black, chained to a red pillar by golden chains. It is shorn of her arms and legs which are seen inside a cave within a mountain painted green. The sky is blue. Below the pillar is a purple dragon guarding the cave. Mary's description is:

"The person chained to the red pillar is probably me. Her legs and arms have been cut off and hidden in a cave. The dragon is guarding the cave, but I don't think he put the limbs there. I should probably be even more helpless on the ground without arms and legs, so perhaps it is as well that I am chained."

Compare Mary's Painting 16: she was herself red, suspended in the air by chains fastened to a black vault which limned the father's possessiveness of her. Now there are similar golden chains but the other colours are reversed. Mary herself is black, and the pillar she is chained to is red. But she is not embracing it for Mary said, on being asked, that the black figure had its back to it.

The positive meaning of dismemberment. Mythological parallels.

The fantasy of her mutilated body without its arms and legs which have been thrown aside would seem to be at first glance a tragic one. It will be noted however that the arms and legs were just those parts of her by which she had been chained in Painting 16. Those chains seem therefore to have

167

been removed, and to have been replaced by chains which bind only her torso to the red pillar which supports her now. And it is not Mary's life force, symbolised by the red colour of her body in Painting 16, that is now mutilated. It is that part of her nature which is so often painted black and which till now has been too father-bound.

This fantasy is thus no tragedy, since it depicts the process of "dismemberment" which is an essential part of every transformation myth. What has to be transformed is not the life force (painted red) but the "blackness" of unconscious infantile desire originally projected onto the mother. This is a natural phenomenon in early infancy but as the child develops has to be sacrificed or "cast aside". If by the time of puberty this has not taken place it is apt to turn into incestuous desire. This is an infantilely god-like "enclosed" thing which must be sacrificed in the interest of those wider and deeper relationships which distinguish the life of humans from that of animals. It is for this reason that the "saviour" gods have to be sacrificed by being dismembered. Osiris was dismembered by his brother Set, his limbs being torn off and his whole body divided into twelve parts which were buried in different places throughout the land. Osiris thereupon became Lord of the Underworld, meaning the world of the psyche. We know from Mary's paintings and from psychology in general that what is symbolised as being "underground" or else under the sea or in a cave is psychic life that operates unseen. In Greek mythology Dionysos and Orpheus were similarly dismembered. In the case of Christ, it was his garments that were thus divided up: "And they crucified him, and parted his garments, casting lots: that it might be fulfilled that was spoken by the prophet: They parted my garments among them, and upon my vesture did they cast lots." (Matt. 27:35). This might seem less fundamental than bodily dismemberment, but it may also be more psychological since garments are not the man but are protective clothing— like the mother or the mother's womb which they replace. Thus it is also the symbol for incestuous desire that is dismembered and removed afar.

Dismemberment as preparation for rebirth

This motive of dismemberment is one that is not infrequent in modern dreams and phobias. A certain patient, not Mary, came into analysis because

168

she was so terrified of seeing "cripples" out of doors that she was unable to go out to do the shopping or see friends. She said that she could never go out without seeing some kind of cripple in the street. I thought this statement rather exaggerated until I realised that she included among cripples not only those who had an arm or leg removed but even those who limped. I tested this myself and found out that if one was really on the lookout for such things one could not in fact go out without encountering one or two. The question was: Why did she mind so much? Asked whether she ever dreamt about cripples, she exclaimed, "It's bad enough to see them in the street; it would be ghastly to dream of them!" The obvious reply was that it was her psyche that was crippled, but that, not realising this, she projected her own emotional crippledom on to the physically crippled whom she saw, and was compelled to see, wherever she went. However, in the containedness of the analysis and with this possibility in mind, she did in fact quite soon start dreaming of cripples. She met them not in the streets of the city in which she was living at the time of the analysis but in those associated with her childhood and the repressed emotions she then had. In these dreams she met dream-figures with arms off or bandaged up as though injured, with ears and noses or other parts of their bodies cut off, or with their heads bandaged.

Since psychic contents cannot be seen but can be expressed in dreams only in terms of what is called the "body image", and since it is the purpose of all dreams to heal, it gradually became clear that there was a healing purpose in such dream-crippledom. Since arms and legs and other bodily protuberances are in fact "projected" out of the body as its executives, they portray psychological projections. The dream told her they had to be "cut off" or of themselves "drop off". This meant that the projections had to be withdrawn and in effect were already being withdrawn on the deep level of the dream work. Subsequent dreams showed that the aim was to reduce the whole body image to the condition of a foetus so that her psyche might be reborn.

Another patient dreamt that she was by the side of a canal into which bodies covered with sacks were being thrown. Horrified at the sight, she ran away, but curiosity drew her back again. She became aware that the analyst himself was with the bodies at the bottom of the canal, not drowned but very much alive, and—as she thought—was "torturing" them. Later she saw the dismembered parts of these bodies laid out on the quayside, and the figure of the analyst was there "re-sorting" them by taking arms or legs, or calves or breasts, noses or ears, from several bodies, and building up quite different bodies with them. She thought this terrible, as the new bodies would be quite different from the old ones. This meant that quite new personalities were being made. What ego consciousness had thought of as a torturing was in fact a reconstruction or transformation of her own psychic contents brought about by the autonomous psyche or psychic consciousness. This was in the dream by the figure of the analyst, so as to sort out her complexes and help her to find out who she really was. Immersion in the canal had been a kind of baptism indicating a rebirth.

Dismemberment as creative sacrifice.
Mountain and Crab. The Self

In Painting 20 Mary was herself immersed in water fearing that she might be being tortured or devoured by the Crab. Part of her had suspected, however, that it might not be a bad thing if she was. But the Mountain with the cave in it, in which her severed arms and legs are to be seen in the present fantasy, is painted the same dirty green colour as was the Crab. Although the imagery differs, it would appear that the image of the Mountain, another symbol for the Great Mother, replaces that of the Crab. If this interpretation is correct, it would in fact be the Crab's claws that have pinched off her arms and legs, and swallowed them into what is here depicted as the cave, corresponding to the Crab's mouth—both symbolising the psychic womb. It will be noted that the Mountain leans over towards her as the Crab's claws had done.

This might seem fanciful were it not for the fact that the Crab, the Mountain, and the cave or hole in it are often mythologically connected. There is a belief in Malekula[65] that the spirits of the departed ancestors live on a volcano called the Fire of the Devouring (and Initiating) Mother Goddess. They dance in the form of skeletons all night until the dawn, when

---

65. Layard, *Stone Men of Malekula*; Malekula is an island in the South Pacific country of Vanuatu. *Ed.*

their bones fall asunder until the next sunset and they are joined up again and so resume their nightly frolic. The Initiating Goddess is the transforming Fire which issues from the bowels of the earth. In yet another form she loiters as an enormous crab on the path leading up to the volcano to devour the spirits of the dead before they can get there.[66] The encounter with this crab is part of the mythological initiating ritual. In other myths, in the form of a Crab Woman she digs a pit in which to trap unwary men in order to eat them, but they survive this too[67]. In yet another version, in which she is described as "that which draws us to it so that it may devour us", she lives in a cave at the foot of a mountain by the sea. Men spend a large part of their lives sacrificing black pigs to her, symbolising the sacrifice of their incestuous impulses. When a man dies yet another black pig, which was reared for this purpose, is cast alive into his grave. As the spirit of the dead man passes through the cave on its way to the volcano and she launches herself at him to devour him, he throws the spirit of this black pig to her. She is so intent on devouring it that the spirit of the dead man himself slips by and passes on into the afterlife. The pig is thus like a projection of himself which he discards, and the discarding of which procures for him his immortality. It is the last vestige of his incestuous desire which is thus cast into the cave[68].

Christ says "I am not come to destroy, but to fulfil" (Matt.5:17). All things must be fulfilled, even incest desire, for what cannot be fulfilled externally must be fulfilled internally. Incest externally (whether physically expressed or not) means a projection of infantile desire; incest internally means oneness with oneself. Oneself is at the same time the universal self. The cave in Mary's painting is a symbol for the self. It contains four primary parts, seen here as two hands and two legs, all painted black. They have been severed and thrown into the cave—discarding of the projections of incestuous desire like the black pig in the Malekulan myth. It is in the context of rebirth that we may here understand Christ's sayings, "Except ye be convert-

---

66. Layard, *Stone Men of Malekula*. London, Chatto & Windus, 1942, pp. 221, 228 note.
67. Deacon, *Malekula*, p. 627 and Layard, "The Making of Man in Malekula", *Eranos-Jahrbuch 1948*, Rhein-Verlag. Zurich, 1949, p.253
68. Layard, *Stone Men of Malekula*

ed, and become as little children, ye shall not enter into the kingdom of heaven"; "Wherefore if thy hand or thy foot offend thee, cut them off, and cast them from thee: it is better for thee to enter into life halt or maimed rather than having two hands or two feet to be cast into everlasting fire" (Matt. 18:3,8). This would be "maiming" only from the point of view of a non-comprehending ego consciousness. From the point of view of psychic consciousness it would be like the dropping of a hampering burden.

But since no "jot or tittle" may be lost, the withdrawn projections act as "food" for the psyche into which they have been withdrawn.

Dragon guarding the Cave. Mary's ambivalence.

An unusual figure in these fantasy-paintings is the very formalized purple dragon looking rather like a boat of which the pillar is the mast, with Mary chained to it. This may remind us of how Ulysses had himself tied to the mast so that he should not be seduced by the sirens tempting from the rocky shore. From the position in which it is, this dragon is not unlike the purple dragon in Painting 11 which freed the unknown man from the black coffin. Mary herself is awakening from the sleep of at least some of her father-boundness. The problem is: What is the dragon's function here? She writes, *"The dragon is guarding the cave"*, which is the traditional function of the dragon guarding the treasure in the cave. But Mary says, *"I don't think he put the limbs there"*. This is probably correct since it was the analysis which had done this. The somewhat heraldic formalisation, which is in such strong contrast to its writhing activity in most of her other fantasies, may indicate that the dragon is now losing some of its power and has become an object for aesthetic contemplation rather than a real immediate danger. Yet it may still have a positive function in preventing Mary from reaching out for her arms and legs again. Mary herself had no opinion either way. But she does say, *"I should probably be even more helpless on the ground without arms and legs, so perhaps it is as well that I am chained"*. This shows once more how little she yet understands of the creative meaning of her fantasies.

It is a frequent feature of both dreams and fantasies that, however deep the transformation symbolism in them may be, towards the end the misconceptions of waking life creep in to introduce a doubt or even to deny the

172

meaning of the dream or fantasy. This final sentence of hers is thus a typical-
ly doubting one. For she appreciates indeed how helpless she would be if on
the ground (meaning "down to earth") without her arms and legs, but fails to
recognise such infantile helplessness as a necessary pre-condition for rebirth.
She prefers still the golden chains which bind her to the image of the father's
phallus which she cannot enjoy. Nor, having her back to it, can she face up
to it or recognise the potential life force in herself which it represents.

The next fantasy painting will show the conflict that this leaves her in.

PAINTING 22 (FANTASY) 13 OCTOBER 1958

The Suffering Snake

The conflict that Mary is now consciously in shows itself in this painting, of which she wrote:

"This started by being a fountain, but as I painted it I found that it was an unfriendly plant. It grows out of the poor snake's mouth, draining its strength, and the branches bend down and root themselves, fixing the snake to the ground. The snake's tail, which is the only free part of it, is lashing about and fighting the plant."

The fountain is a symbol of gushing joy and of new life such as the rebirth motif in the last painting would adumbrate. This fantasy painting thus started with a feeling of real release. But no sooner did it start to flow than the feeling of "not being allowed" to enjoy life as a child and "not allowing herself" to now overwhelmed her, and the fountain then turned into an *"unfriendly plant"*. Plants allude to psychic contents of a primitive kind. This one is growing out of the snake's mouth and thereby suffocating it, *"draining its strength"*. All this calls to mind once more Mary's frustration at the breast and her negative interpretation of the helpless foetus in Painting 21.

Her experience at the breast had indeed been a disastrous one, but it was her continued reaction to it which produced the impasse she was now in. By the time of life Mary had now attained it is "Not that which goeth into the mouth" which "defileth a man; but that which cometh out of the mouth", for "those things which proceed out of the mouth come forth from the heart; and

174

they defile the man" (Matt.15:11,18). The colour of the plant is the same dirty green as that of the stormy water in Paintings 18 and 19 as well as of the Crab in Painting 20 and the mountain in Painting 21. It in this regard "dirty" represents her elemental fears and consequently hostile attitudes. For instance, she still finds it almost impossible to disentangle the introjected fears of her father from the reality of the analyst, and of all others with whom she is in contact. These are of a paranoid nature, leading her to think that she is being criticised when she is being approved of, and prevented from doing what she wants to do when there is no such external prevention. On the contrary, it is her own sense of guilt and her not allowing herself to live or to express her feelings that makes her so suspicious and so cruelly stands in her way.

So here the "poor snake" depicts her own self-persecuted outer and inner life, leading her now to desire to persecute others. She often expresses this by saying that she could imagine only one good thing to come out of her getting well, and that would be to be in a position to "give hell" to anyone inferior to herself in her employment. But since this very paranoid feeling kept her at that time from ever rising to such a position of external superiority, even this desire was largely baulked.

The red snake here indicates passion, not only to dominate but also to love and to be loved. It is associated with the father, as was the red pillar in Painting 21, and it is writhing with unhappiness, being pinned down by the very plant which has issued from its (Mary's) own mouth. The only part of it that is free is its tail, lashing about trying to fight the plant. Experiences at the breast influence later sexuality. This fantasy illustrates that fact: the branches of the plant issuing from her mouth and its associations of frustrated breast feeding, instead of growing upwards towards the light, bend down towards the ground again. Her sexuality is pinned down in frustrated incest-desire, and doubles her distress. The only part of the

Figure 26. "The cosmic tree is caught by the earth and cannot grow upwards." Jung, *Alchemical Studies*, Fig. 18

175

Figure 27. "The same regressive situation . . . but coupled with increased consciousness." Jung, *Alchemical Studies*, Fig. 19

snake's body which is free (the phallic tail) is lashing out. This corresponds to Mary's frantic attempts to free herself from her self-inhibiting and paranoid attitudes which the plant represents.

Figures 26 and 27 are copied from paintings, made by two different women suffering from the same kind of complex that Mary was. They were reproduced by Jung who says of Figure 26, "The tree … cannot grow upright. It is dragged down again by the earth and again grows into it," while of Figure. 27, "The same regressive situation, but joined to increased consciousness".

PAINTING 23 (Fantasy) 16 October 1958

Hooking Leviathan

After the last masochistic fantasy about the writhing snake I had discussed with Mary several instances of how she unnecessarily persecuted herself. This had disturbed her usual assumptions of being a victim of the ill will of other people to the extent that, three days later, to relieve her feelings, she sat down to paint again.

The innocent green bank

With customary external mildness covering the conflict she was always in, she started to paint what she described as *"a grass bank which was going to have something disturbing, I don't know what, buried beneath it, and this would have been dug up by someone, but that story didn't carry itself on but turned into this instead"*.

There had been many grassy banks in earlier fantasy paintings, covered with daisies and other signs of childish innocence. In those days she was quite unaware that there was anything at all underneath. But now the "innocence" is wearing a bit thin and the grass bank turns into the curved back of a dragon symbolising the disturbing factor underneath. These were the emotions surging inside her, which might be *"dug up by someone"*, on the analogy of the archaeological excavations which she used to visit with her father in his rural deanery. These emotions were in fact now being exposed in the analysis.

177

Leviathan

The painting now assumed much the same form as Painting 19, with the dragon swimming in the waters underneath a layer of black earth. There was a gap through which could be seen operating a tall and a powerful man painted red (while she is black); he has caught the dragon on a hook. Mary's description is:

"The dragon which lives in a lake underground has been hooked by its tail and is struggling hard. The red man thinks he will be able to kill it, even though it is so much bigger than he is. I am looking on at the struggle between them, and am not certain whose side I am on. Two of the little fishes which would have fed the dragon are swimming away. The third is waiting to see what happens."

"This was painted in a very bad temper, and I feel that I am fighting to get free as much as the dragon."

This painting cannot fail to remind us of the biblical verses:

"Canst thou draw out leviathan with an hook?
Or his tongue with a cord which thou lettest down?"
"Canst thou put an hook into his nose?
Or bore his jaw through with a thorn?"   (Job 41: 1, 2)

We have already noted the contrast between Mary's two kinds of dragon; one comparable to Behemoth, such as the dragon giving birth to the small fantasy-tree (connected with her father's influence); the other to Leviathan, a sea-serpent or creature of the sea (standing for the mother's animus). Figure 22 reproducing Blake's engraving shows them both together but facing in opposite directions in one womb, with Behemoth on top and Leviathan partly hidden in the waters underneath. Their relative positions correspond to Mary's far greater consciousness of her problem about the father, contrasted with her lack of consciousness about the mother, many of whose dragon-like qualities she imitated. It was these latter which she hid under a mild exterior illustrated by the innocent-looking grassy bank. In the discussions about the writhing snake in Painting 22 these qualities were now being revealed to her. So she could no longer think of herself as being quite so innocent and had to recognise her own partly dragon-like nature, and that she was not only a victim but was internally a cynical aggressor too.

178

Mary of course was not unique in this. Such opposites exist in every human breast, though in her case the contrast was extreme due to her unconsciousness of the compulsions that so dominated her. In the book of Job, Behemoth and Leviathan are described as the twin powers of God, when, at the end of Job's struggle with his self-righteousness, God speaks *"out of the whirlwind"* (Job 40: 6), that spiritual womb or melting-pot in which all things are changed. For the word "God" means many things. What is known by his name can be an elemental force beyond control[69], which can be destructive in a person if not recognised. Such was the incest-wish that Mary had, and which had ruled her life without her knowing it, making her almost unapproachable. The biblical description of the power of Leviathan, when operating uncontrolled by consciousness, so vividly describes this aspect of Mary's character that we may quote parts of it here. To begin with he is proud and will not compromise: *"Will he make many supplications unto thee? will he speak soft words unto thee?"* It is a risky job approaching him: *"shall not one be cast down even at the sight of him? None is so fierce that dare stir him up"*. He is seductive as the devil is: *"I will not conceal his parts, nor his power, nor his comely proportion"*. But on the other hand *"his teeth are terrible round about. His scales are his pride, shut up together as with a close seal"*. Nothing can describe better Mary's fierce secretiveness. *"Out of his mouth go burning lamps, and sparks of fire leap out. Out of his nostrils goeth smoke, as out of a seething pot or caldron"*—compare the cauldron with the double-headed dragon in Mary's Painting 12—*"His breath kindleth coals, and a flame goeth out of his mouth."* (Job 41:3-21)

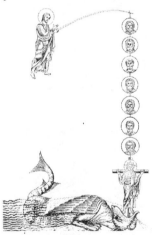

Figure 28. "Capture of the Leviathan with the sevenfold tackle of the line of David, with the crucifix as bait. Harrad of Landsberg's *Hortus Deliciarum.*" Jung, *Psychology and Alchemy*, Fig. 28

But he is not only evil, for through him *"sorrow is turned into joy"* (Job 41: 22). It is not said in the book of Job how this is done, but

---

69. See also Jung, *Psychology and Alchemy*, p. 443.

there is a twelfth century picture reproduced by Jung in his *Psychology and Alchemy* showing Christ as a fisherman rescuing Leviathan, who lies in a contorted position in the sea not unlike that of Mary's writhing snake in Painting 22, by hooking it with a line, with the crucifix as bait (Figure 28). Leviathan is thus proud, and pitiable in his pride. Sorrow is turned to joy only by means of sacrifice, which is in this case the sacrifice of his concealment in the depths. Only by being sacrificed himself could Christ, after the crucifixion, descend into the depths called Hell. The Fisherman had been born to "save", to draw mortals to him, and to redeem.

One sacrifice entails another sacrifice. Pride must be wounded before it yields. And so in Mary's Painting 23 the dragon has its tail pierced by the hook that will eventually draw it up onto dry land. It is not to be killed as Mary thought but to be brought up to the light of consciousness where its activities may be unmasked (as in the next painting).

The tall red man. The transference. The analyst and "inner analyst".

Who therefore is the tall red man who lets down the line and hook to catch hold of the dragon at the point immediately underneath the place where Mary stands?

He is clearly, on the one hand, the analyst who thus for the first time in Mary's fantasies is here shown as providing a visible link between her conscious and unconscious processes—between Mary above the surface of the earth and the dragon below. For it is a function of the analyst to mediate between two worlds: those of the patient's limited ego consciousness and of the vastly greater area of psychic consciousness, from which the patient is divorced in varying degrees. The diagram shown in Figure 29 may illustrate roughly how this type of mediation works.

The horizontal line represents the threshold between consciousness and unconsciousness. The patient's limited awareness of him/herself is repre-

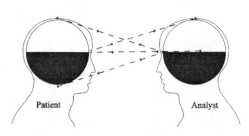

Figure 29. Diagram: mediation between conscious and unconscious.

sented by the white semi-circle above the line. In the ideal situation here described, the analyst's mediating function is that he/she can see both sides, the conscious and unconscious, while the patient is aware of conscious "sides" only. An individual's full circle is both white and black.

While fully appreciating the patient's conscious attitudes and difficulties in relating to unconscious ones, the analyst can nevertheless act as a go-between, functioning within the limits of his or her own ability as a kind of mirror by means of which the patient may become aware of what is happening inwardly and unconsciously. The hook and line in Mary's present fantasy symbolise the link with the unconscious which the analyst provides, as indicated in this diagram. The upper sloping line between the analyst and patient represents the link with consciousness. As the patient becomes more and more aware of the contents of the unconscious, a process of mutual attraction sets in whereby the conscious and unconscious become more reconciled (as indicated by the small arrowed lines) until in the imagery of this diagram they meet in the central black and white circle representing the integrated self. This is of course never wholly attained but can only be approximated to.

But the analyst is not the only healing factor in this reconciliation process. As Mary says, the dragon *"is so much bigger than he is"*, meaning that the unconscious can never be wholly apprehended by anyone. But the patient's psyche itself provides a powerful helper. For the tall red man not only stands for the analyst but, more important still, the patient's own internal animus or power of perception—stimulated into action by the analyst. It is an invariable process in a successful analytical treatment that, through the transference, the person of the analyst is complemented by or calls into being the patient's own "internal analyst", who is far wiser and more knowledgeable about the patient's problem than any analyst could be.

We may recall her Fantasy Painting 11of the "unknown man" or animus figure. He now stands on the earth as an element of consciousness, rid of the rotting flesh and using his knowledge of the dragon who at that time helped him towards consciousness.

The fantasy depicts the strong link between the analyst and the dragon. So long as the dragon remains underground, much of Mary's own dragon-like nature is projected onto the analyst. She sometimes thinks of him as if he were the dragon too, and says *"I am not certain whose side I am on"*. For the "bad temper" in which the fantasy was painted had been due to one of the discussions which had taken place regarding her fantasy of the writhing snake (Painting 22) only three days before. There the analyst had been actively instrumental to her dawning realization that she was a victim not so much of others as of her own dragon-like hostile attitudes. She had naturally been partly resentful about this, which may account for her saying, *"I feel that I am fighting to get free as much as the dragon"*.

Locked door. The colours red and black.

This raised the question: how much did Mary want her incest fantasies exposed, and how much not? What was the nature of the barrier that Mary's psyche had set up so as to keep her ignorant? To illustrate the kind of process that had been at work and the extraordinary assumptions that were now coming to light, there was the example of her going one day into the village. It was a considerable distance from where she worked. She wished to find out something from some of the villagers but came back without having done so. When asked why not, she said their door was locked. I happened to know that their door was never locked during the daytime as they kept open house: people were constantly going in and out, as she herself had often done when others went with her. When this was pointed out she said blankly, "But I thought everybody kept their front door locked". I reminded her of other houses where the front door was not locked and she knew it. It turned out that in a certain corner of her mind she thought that all front doors were locked because the front door of her father's rectory was always locked. In spite of all the evidence of her senses it took some time to convince her that this was not true. She had sufficient humour to see at last what this assumption meant in terms of the difficulty she had in opening doors within herself.

Assumptions of this kind are symbolically "black", indicating not only a passive unawareness of a certain group of facts but also an active and compulsive force to hide them up. Ever since her painting of the father's black rotting corpse we have known the colour black in her work to be associated with the father in his unconscious mother-role—and with her more general amnesia designed to cover her desire for him. But this compulsion to conceal

182

is now gradually lessening under the pressure of the analysis. She is beginning to acknowledge more what her own real feelings are. Thus the black stone closing the jar (the alchemical vase) expressed on the personal level her feeling of being bottled in. But in Painting 19 the black earth similarly imprisoned her in her inner world. And now in Painting 23 this gap has widened, and through it she can clearly see the dragon underneath being hooked up.

This brings us again to the relation between the colours black and red. Red in these fantasies invariably symbolises passion or strong feeling of some kind. In Painting 19 Mary, red with blind emotion, almost fell into the cavern. In the present painting, however, red has been transferred to the tall man, externally the analyst, actively engaged in fighting for her. She remains black as the earth is, father-bound and with the paralyzing conflicts that entails. She is unable as yet to take any active part.)

Fishes. Last of the dragons underground.

The three little fishes may well indicate her psychic state. Two are in active flight from the dragon who is trying to devour them. It may be prevented from doing so by being hooked. The third fish faces the dragon calm and unafraid, and like the snake in Paintings 18 and 20 "*is waiting to see what happens*". We shall meet this fish later, painted purple and talking to a snake, in Painting 32.

It may be noted that the dragon in this painting is facing the other way round from the writhing snake in Painting 22, symbolising the beginning of a real change of attitude on Mary's part. This is the last time her dragons were painted underground (7 and 11—in the earth) or in water, Painting 19 and the present one. Henceforth the dragons are all above the ground and their influence on her can no longer be concealed.

PAINTING 24 (FANTASY) UNDATED

The Purple Dragon and the Purple Incest-Mist

Mary was now in a spate of fantasy painting stimulated by the analyst's continued attack on her false assumptions such as that of the "locked door". There were times when she would scream out in her defence of them, and would continue screaming even after she had left the room. In the next interview she might relent, but a new instance would arise calling forth similar reactions as though she were possessed by something outside her control. One of the few means she had of relieving these feelings was sitting down to paint, not knowing what would "come". We have seen how the feelings overwhelming her were sometimes so intense, though at the same time confused, that they could be expressed only in terms of colour. These later took on shape as in the case of the blue colour that suffused her room when she was on the point of death, and which became condensed into the form of the Death Woman clothed in sparkling blue bending over her to carry her away.

The colour that now "came" to her and which she had to paint, was again: blue mixed with red—a mixture of coldness and frustration (blue) and of warmth and passion (red).

Purple, as has been previously stated, in its negative aspect is a disturbing colour which may be a warning of a hidden psychosis. If handled with due care it may promote a resolution of the conflict through acceptance of its evil side, which in its turn releases and reveals the good.

Thus Mary's present fantasy was in two parts, or "scenes" as they might be in a dream. The first was about the dragon which the purple colour had congealed into, and the second about the delicate and tender tree symbolising its opposite. This Mary seeks to reach if she can escape the power that the dragon exercises over her.

Scene 1.

"I started this painting by mixing purple paint. I knew it was for something threatening, but I didn't know what it would be. When I started what turned into a dragon I was not sure if it would turn into a snake. Then I knew that it was a dragon and that its hand was hovering above my head, squeezing it from time to time, like a headache."

Scene 2.

"Then I knew that I wanted to go forward, but didn't know where, and the mist came round me in the picture. I think it came from the dragon. The tree started by being meant for a bullrush leaf. It is carefully protecting its fruit by folding leaves over it. The pond might just as easily have been a fountain. I found it very difficult to get this part of the picture or the feelings belonging to it all clearly, and it does not seem nearly as real as the dragon. The dragon also wants to get at the fruit, but I don't think he will reach it."

SCENE 1. The purple dragon leaps. Incest desire and amnesia.

In the initial scene we see the dragon of Painting 23 now hauled onto dry land, meaning that what it symbolises is being made more conscious to Mary than it has ever been before. No creature of the sea likes to be hooked, just as Mary had felt recently that she was being "hooked" by having some of her secret complexes brought to light. She naturally resisted this, which may explain the fact that while she knew the purple colour would turn into "*something threatening*", she said she was not sure whether it would turn into a dragon or a snake. Snakes symbolise for her "wise" things: so if this creature had become a snake, she would have learnt nothing but to admire herself yet more and to repress the secrets of her dragon-like nature. Wisdom consisted in the opposite of this: acknowledging the truth. The key to the change now taking place in her are the two words "I knew": *"Then I knew that it was a dragon and that its hand was above my head, squeezing it from time to time, like a headache"*.

This is a great advance on her saying of Painting 23 that she was not sure which side she was on. But such realisations do not come easily. During the analyst's recent attacks on some of the unconscious subterfuges which she used against herself, she had had several headaches. They are often symptomatic of resistances against acceptance of a painful truth. This fantasy helped her to understand the cause of these resistances.

It was with this painting that it first became unmistakably clear to both of us what the use of the colour purple in Mary's paintings meant in terms of incest fantasy. For we had now come to a kind of breaking point in which it was becoming apparent that the basic reason for all her secrecies on the pattern of the "locked door" and her hidden hostilities, was the need to conceal her longing for her father's genitals as a breast-substitute. Many personal associations had recently accumulated around this fact. It was never referred to between us by the technical term "incest" but in terms of her growing awareness of the conflict which this desire entailed. This was expressed symbolically in what she now described as the difference between the dragon and the snake. For there was a dramatic session in which she described the difference between the two. The snake was basically wise and up till now had rarely moved, mainly observing in a detached way what was going on. But the dragon was a huge thing that leapt. In terms of the long walks she made to the neighboring village up and down steep hills, she would envisage the dragon as getting there in no time in two great leaps without having any contact with the country in between. Mary herself, being small, would take enormous strides, which we came later to describe as her dragon-strides, hardly observing the countryside. Mary enormously admired the dragon for being able to do this. In fact, however, the "leaping" indicated "amnesia" of the intermediate steps and also of the track of personal associations that would have led back to the mother-problem so overlaid by the relationship with her father.

The elements comprising this amnesia that made it so difficult for Mary to cope with were the same as we have found elsewhere. They were basic in the formation of her character—namely the mother's animus which "leaps" and the father's anima which had enveloped her. The "leaping" aspect is emphasised by the dragon's wing(s) enabling it to cover vast distances without contact with the world. The incest-mist which emanates from it expresses Mary's engulfment in the father's anima to which the mother's hostile animus had driven her.

The dragon looks as though it screams when leaping on her and clutching her, just as Mary sometimes screamed when her identification with it was pointed out.

There has been much use of purple in these fantasies, sometimes as good, sometimes as sinister (Painting 15: to be rooted, or drawn back into the cloud). Now for the first time Mary experiences *herself* as being pounced on by the dragon and enveloped in its purple mist. She feels it to be something sinister. So "purple" as an echo of the involuted state of mind that she was in, was no longer for her a theoretical concept but a very real experience.

SCENE 2. The purple incest-mist. "Mothering tree".

Figure 30, from a sixteenth century manuscript[70], is included here because of its striking similarity to Mary's painting—though she had of course

never seen it. In this figure the man is being beaten down, but is thereby being brought "down to earth", crawling on all fours just like an animal or like a child. For all devouring monsters have a dual or paradoxical significance. Like dreams, such visionary creatures have both bad and good in them, depending not on the vision itself (which just "is" as a revelation from psychic consciousness), but on the extent to which its message may be understood in ego consciousness. It is

Figure 30. "The assault by the dragon, from Vitruvius, *De architectura*, Venice, 1511." *Symbols of Transformation*, Fig. 35

---

70. Jung, *Symbols of Transformation*, Fig. 35.

well known that in primitive initiation rites the novices are often forced to enter into the simulated body of some devouring monster so as to experience the horror of being enclosed in it. This substitutes for regressive mother-longing or incestuous desire and is done in order that the initiants may be reborn out of the "womb" into the world of balanced psychic reality. It always entails the abandonment of pride—of the possessive pride that is an element of every incest fantasy. It is also a "coming down to earth" so as to find the Earth Mother or instinctive power within and to emerge from the isolation of the uninitiated child so as to face the world effectually and play an active part in it.

Mary, though being so mild externally and having usurped her mother's place with him, had nursed the secret pride of being the apple of her father's eye. This was one aspect of the "dragon" with which she had unconsciously identified herself. Now that it was out in the open and clearly seen for the monster that it was, she could for the first time disidentify with it. She "wanted to go forward", to escape from its hypnotic power over her so as to get on with her life.

It is important to note, therefore, that it is the realisation of the dragon's power that is itself the means of overcoming it. But being so used to being hypnotised by it she "didn't know where" to go. It is significant that it was at this point that "the mist came round me in the picture". The "mist" and the "not knowing where to go" are one and the same thing. This is the second time during this fantasy that the colour purple or a vague "purple" feeling without a form dominates Mary's consciousness. It is of note because while the dragon echoes something that was originally external in the parental atmosphere, the mist signifies something now exclusively her own.

Moreover if we follow Mary's own account of how this fantasy painting grew (the tree appearing now as a solution of her doubt), it will be clear that her vision of this tree was like "a dream within a dream". This means that it reveals a deeper layer of reality than that of the fantasy that the dragon mainly represents.

For the mist is egg-shaped, with Mary as a partly foetus-like creature with huge head and painted red, passionately desiring to be hatched out into the world. This would naturally entail being less dominated by the fascination and frustration of her father-incest desire. So what she sees in her mind's eye now is a *"tree … carefully protecting its fruit, by folding leaves over it"*. The fruit thus cherished is like something growing in the womb; the tree is a tender mother-tree underscoring the mother-love she had so missed in childhood.

This is the first "good mother" tree Mary has had, contrasting with her "father trees". What it ultimately records may be seen in Figure 1 of the Tree Mother with a tray full of fruit and other foods which she offers as though issuing from her breast. Mary has travelled far enough by now to catch a glimpse in her psyche of such a tree, meaning that there is an element now growing in herself of tenderness towards herself.

This is in strong contrast to the destructiveness of the dragon overwhelming her, which occupies most of the space in the painting. Her father-incest fantasy had been the only emotional "reality" that she had known. This substitute reality masked the more basic need for mother-love. There is a great contrast, too, between the splendid painting of the dragon (although she is beginning now to know how dangerous it is), and the uncertain, frail and careless painting of the much smaller "mother tree". The relations she had had with her own mother had been so bad that she could scarcely conceive of a "good mother" at all. As Mary says herself, *"I found it very difficult to get this part of the picture or the feelings belonging to it at all clearly, and it does not seem nearly as real as the dragon"*.

It is for this reason presumably that the earth is still black and that she says *"The tree started by being meant for a bulrush leaf"*. Bullrushes are phallic symbols. Also, they grow by the water (cf. Painting 6). The tree grows by a pond with a wading bird close by. Her father-love was a necessary link for her in the process of relating to the yet deeper mother-love which was now springing up within her.

The concept of new life springing up is contained also in Mary's saying that *"The pond might just as easily have been a fountain"*. This may remind us of the fountain Mary started to paint which turned into the "unfriendly plant"(Painting 22). In the short space of time of a week or two since Mary painted that, the "unfriendly plant" has now turned into the "mothering tree", which has a shape not unlike the fountain that Mary had in mind for Painting 22.

The fountain is a symbol for new life as is the tree bearing and cherishing its fruit. The tree, the pond and wading bird are comparatively disjointed symbols when contrasted with the direct and simple image of the dragon, looking as it does so much more unified and formidable and able to do just what it wants. It bears witness to the fact that it is the dragon that has for so long dominated Mary's world. The concept of the mother-tree is still so new to her that its associated elements are not yet properly joined up.

Nevertheless, now that Mary has become aware of the dragon's greedy destructiveness and that it *"wants to get at the fruit"* of her new life, she can say, *"I don't think he will reach it"*.

PAINTING 25 (Fantasy) 24 October 1958

Dragon Pregnant of Two Snakes

The pressure on Mary's pockets of defensive secrecies, and the rather gruelling experience that she was going through as a result of it, continued to produce the spate of fantasies, of which the next three were all painted on one day, beginning with the present one. This does not mean by any means that these were all the fantasies that she had that day since they were apparently continuous. But the act of painting in each case served to fix one phase of fantasying in her mind, like an act of a play or chapter of a serial story. This one then demanded a sequel and got it in the next painting she made, which marked some new advance on the last one and a new level of realisation. Through the painting of it this could be "caught" instead of sliding off into a chain of fantasies that could be without end.

The horror of the last fantasy thus "fixed" in Painting 24—the purple dragon leaping over her and giving her the kind of headache which she knew to be connected with her resistances in the analysis—produced the present painting, of which she says:

"This is a dragon which is going to be crushed so as to release the two snakes inside it. A stone has been dropped on the dragon, but it has a hard shell, and as the stone is rounded it was trying to wriggle out from under it. So a booted foot is now on the stone and will push it down on the dragon.

191

"The dragon is me, but I am not sure what the snakes are, or how they will escape unhurt when the dragon's shell is broken."

This is a great advance on Painting 24, in which Mary had thought of the dragon as being something extraneous to her and not part of herself. She now realises what it is: *"The dragon is me"*. And there is another difference. Since the dragon was no longer thought to be outside herself, projected all her life onto her environment through thinking that she was the victim of other people's hostile or stupidly interfering attitudes (*they* were the dragon, and not she), there was something now growing *inside* her. It is represented by the two snakes of which, now that she can acknowledge herself to be the dragon, that dragon is pregnant.

The dragon's pregnancy betokens her own psychic pregnancy resulting from the hard work done during the past few months of uninterrupted analysis. During this period Mary found herself in head-on collision with the analyst over the unremitting attacks already referred to. These in turn produced counterattacks from her, releasing some of the aggression that had so long been bottled up. Now she could become aware of it and was sometimes horrified at it. The conflict, however, had been tempered and sweetened by the humour which is essential to all creative work, and without which the analyst's attacks would have been unavailing since they would only have increased resistances. For humour is like grace, oiling the works so that otherwise insurmountable barriers may yield and reveal the treasures they conceal. Humour includes being able to withstand the tension of two points of view at once. For instance, when Mary produced her Painting 24, the analyst could share her admiration for the leaping dragon (while at the same time knowing how dangerous it was). In the present fantasy he could laugh with her at the somewhat inane look upon the dragon's face, while inwardly rejoicing at the transformation it portrayed.

Meaning of black and red. Function of the analyst.
Thinking and feeling, intellect and love.

This painting is a picture of the work of the analysis. So that we may appreciate the movement of Mary's mind it may help us if we realise the order in which she painted the three main elements of this fantasy. She painted the dragon first—representing herself—then the black stone that had been "dropped" on it, which underscored the shock (and there had been many such shocks recently) of the analyst's attacks. One of these was his refusal to accept such surface explanations of her withholding herself from life as her belief that others wanted to dominate or criticise her way of life for their own purposes. She associated the black stone with the headaches caused by her resistances to the analysis. So the black stone represents the analyst's critical attack as it was experienced by Mary. The meaning of the red boot which she painted in last to complete her intuitive representation of what was happening to her, is revealed by her explanation of another painting made some time before (not reproduced here) of a basket of pears gathered for "the family". One pear, a windfall, was lying on the ground and a great booted foot was about to crush it into the earth. Mary said that this pear was like her, so that at first sight the imagery seemed to indicate despair. But then she said to me, *"But you don't seem to understand. The other fruit will all be eaten up, so that no fruit trees will grow out of them. This pear is being crushed into the ground so that its seeds will sprout and grow into pear trees".* This helps us to understand the meaning of the red boot in the present fantasy. Just as the pear had to be crushed and pressed into the earth so that its seeds might grow into new trees, so in the present fantasy the dragon (herself) had to be crushed so as to release the life within.

This crushing was no simple but a most complex process. Mary herself was so much more complicated than a mere pear that a straightforward "boot" alone could not prevail over the toughness of her hide. This brings us to further reconsideration of the meaning of the contrast between "black" and "red".

Let us recapitulate some of the outstanding instances of the use of these two colours through the series. The colour "black", originally referring to the safe darkness of the womb, had come to mean for her the manifold frustrations of her life, together with the barriers that had grown up in her which caused her loneliness. We know, too, how the colour "red" symbolised the more dynamic elements in life, including the potentiality of love, and is used as the colour for the various potential "saviour" figures that occur throughout the fantasies.

There is the hanging boy (Painting 3) with his red and partly rotting body hung by a black chain to a black-grey tree, with Mary herself painted black and being so frustrated that she cannot think of anything to do. Nevertheless in Painting 4 the black Mary is lifted up by a loving red hand and grafted onto her tree of life. In the dream illustrated in Painting 8 Mary, deep down in her unconscious (in an underground city), saw in a shaft of light a red snake rearing itself upon a black cushion in the same relative positions as the red boot and the black stone in the present fantasy. She took it in her hand (Painting 9) where it became luminous; the red snake also has a streak of black in it. In that painting Mary was black (standing for her external dumbness), but the red snake called attention to the force, stimulated by the analysis, by which she had overcome her usual lethargy. On her own initiative she had got a job where for the first time she met men on a footing of equality (male nurses). In Painting 11 there was a violent eruption from underground and the dragon burst open the black coffin from which appeared, struggling upward, the red of the body of the "unknown man". In Painting 13 Mary was painted red and was worshipping the black snake. In Painting 16, however, the real state of affairs was evident: she was strung up by golden chains to the sides of a black-grey vault. In Painting 19 she caught for the first time a glimpse through the black earth into the cavern which it had hitherto obscured. In Painting 20 Mary, still painted red, was about to plunge into the sea to face her complexes but as yet could not let go of the black branch of the tree symbolising her father-fixation.

In almost all these paintings "black" stands for something negative, based on the frustration Mary had experienced at the breast and later with regard to her father-incest fantasies.

But a turning point came when in Painting 21 Mary, then painted black and chained to a red pillar, had her black arms and legs cut off and hidden in a cave signifying the womb where they belonged. In this way she might be rid of the incubus of her self-frustration tendencies and be reborn with a new view of life. This was indeed soon followed by the breakthrough of Painting 23 in which the tall red man, limning the dynamic aspect of the analyst and Mary's own response to it, through a gap in the black earth was hooking up Leviathan, so that the dragon could be seen in Painting 24 for what it was.

In Painting 24 the black earth of Mary's basic inner frustration is still there. But in the present painting (25) the earth has a more natural colouring of brownish green not unlike that of the "mother tree" in Painting 24, and the colour black has changed its place. Instead of supporting the dragon from below, it is now above the dragon as a black stone.

With this change in position, the colour black has also changed its character with regard to the kind of frustration it now represents. For it must here be emphasised once more that, like all archetypal representations, any colour may have two opposite meanings within the framework of the same main one—depending on the context in which it is used. The black stone in the present fantasy also frustrates but it is a creative frustration since what it is frustrating—trying to "crush"—is the "hard shell" (thick hide) of the dragon. This is Mary's tough wall of resistances.

In Painting 25 red and black are thus used as symbols for analysis and stand for not only what Mary projects onto the analyst, but also for what she intuitively understands to be the two main parts of analytical technique. It is in fact less a technique than a deeply felt necessity, not only for the patient but for the analyst in dealing with a situation in which the whole being must be involved. The analyst must use both feeling and thinking, "feeling" to make relationship by "feeling what the patient feels" as nearly as is possible; "thinking " to understand and to evaluate what all these feelings are about. In ordinary language the analyst must love, and at the same time have the clear sight to criticise. Love without critical faculty is blind. Critical faculty without love to temper it is blinder still. These two are delineated in this fantasy by "black" for the thinking or critical faculty, "red" for the feeling and the love.

In most people's lives it is the feeling that comes first in infancy and in favourable circumstances turns into love. It is the thinking faculty, that criticises and in normal development creatively frustrates, which is developed later on. But Mary's case was an extreme one in which severe frustration came right at the start, so that the normal loving mother-child relationship never flourished. The vacuum thus caused was filled by a flood of bitter or puzzled infantile thinking which was frustrating in an uncreative way and became basic to her character. Even the love of her father became frustrating too since it could never be physically fulfilled. This is, in the main, what "blackness" meant to her.

It symbolises also an attitude of mind which she maintained in her relation to the world, and is also what she with her paranoid projections presumed was the world's attitude to her. But the critical faculty of the analyst, which mirrors her own self-criticism, has an opposite intent: to release instead of hiddenly to bind and to destroy. For Mary had acquired a new father-figure who by his criticism of her boundness tended to take off the burdens of self-criticism and the feelings of guilt and so of the secret defensive hostility which all her life she had inflicted on herself.

But as a function of the analyst intellect is not enough. Any woman and many men can easily "wriggle out" from any merely intellectual argument, as the dragon tried to wriggle out from under the stone. What is needed is love to temper criticism, and to combine with it. Therefore, as the last thing Mary painted in the present fantasy, and as the last thing that she could believe in, came the red "booted foot". This is the only human thing in the picture, showing the love which alone could make the attack effective and "crush" the stupid dragon's hide. As previously noted, it was the "hard shell" representing Mary's resistances and her fierce external virginity adopted in defence of the father-fixation.

The dragon's pregnancy: meaning of the two snakes.

In contrast to the dragon of Painting 24, which wanted to attack the mothering tree, this dragon is itself becoming a mother; for Mary now wishes to foster and protect the thought and feeling stimulated within her by her horror at the spectacle of her own dragon-like nature. This will be achieved by her snakes which always stand for wisdom and growing consciousness. Horror at the dragon has made it pregnant of its own opposite. In contrast to previous dragons, all fierce and active (except the embryo dragon underground of Painting 7), the dragon in the present fantasy is immobilised and passive. In contrast to the dragon (Painting 14) which is pregnant of a *single* tree, this dragon is pregnant of *two* snakes. This is itself a clue to the meaning of these valuable creatures, which must not get hurt when the "dragon's shell" is broken.

The number "one" symbolises a primitive wholeness or completeness as if in the womb, or in the intimate relationship between a good mother and her infant child. Mary only had a substitute mother in her father and this had been her problem ever since. Owing to the incest fantasies that grew up around her and her father, it came about that in her view there was only one parent. There was no outside influence to break the enclosing vicious circle of this primitive and quite unnatural identity. But the dragon in Painting 24 did not entirely encircle her (the dragon in Painting 14 had still enclosed the small tree of her father-fantasies). There had been a gap in Painting 23 through which the dragon had been hooked, and in Painting 24 there was a gap in the dragon's encircling influence through which Mary could catch a glimpse of the new "mothering tree".

And so the one-ness of her single-sided attitude was now becoming two. She had acquired another father. Now she was acquiring yet another "mother" too. All this was tantamount to a second world for her. Creation myths constantly symbolise such a splitting of one into two—which is in fact a doubling of the personality, usually thought of as the dawn of consciousness.

It is usually the masculine principle that has to be added to the feminine one. With Mary it was the reverse. It was the repressed mother principle that had to be brought into consciousness. It is not surprising therefore that, pregnancy meaning dawning consciousness, the two snakes in the dragon's belly are the same colours (red and green respectively) as were Mary and the "mothering tree" in Painting 24. The red snake flecked with green, and the green snake flecked with red, show their close affinity. Each partakes partly of the nature of the other one as in a mother-child relationship. In Mary's family there had been bitter enmity between her mother and herself.

One of the manifestations of Mary's changing attitude was the new view that she was acquiring of her mother. She realised she was not just a hated tyrant and rival for the father's love but was a fellow-sufferer who also had sensitivities that her father had not got. Thus she was now remembering not only her mother's fierce hostility but also some of her mother's better qualities. Mary herself had a surprising passion and deep feeling for poetry, which she now recognised as being derived from her mother's reading of poetry to her. For her mother would not only read poems to her, but would read them aloud to herself, a habit which Mary also had.

Mary's duality, however, showed itself in a very odd way. When asked to read aloud to me, she would read hurriedly and in the dullest of voices like some children when they are made to recite at school. When asked why she did this she would say that was the way her father had taught her to read: "count-

Figure 31. Earth mother suckling two snakes. *Codex lat. Monacensis 14399,* 15th cent. Munich, Staatsbibliothek

ing two" for a comma, "three" for a semicolon, "four" for a colon, and "six" for a full stop. This made her reading dull as ditchwater. But after I had heard her reading aloud to herself with passionate delight, I asked her to read like this to me. At first she could not, stuttering over each word. But after she had got over the fright of projecting the image of her pedantic father onto me, she began to be able to read naturally and with the deep feeling she experienced, as her mother had done. She said then how like her mother she was becoming and continued to become. When it was suggested that if her father had been something more of a man her mother might not have become as schizophrenic as she was, Mary replied wistfully, "Yes, or if she had never married at all".

Mary was herself boy-like in the toys she played with when a child: she preferred soldiers to dolls. She invariably broke the latter, tearing their hair out and breaking off their hands and feet, preferring battle scenes to nursing ones. This may have been the reason why she fell so easily a prey to the devouring aspect of her father's anima, and later for her lesbian tendencies. But the "boy" in her had actually got repressed, and was only now coming to light. It showed in her appreciation of her mother's better qualities and in taking action on her own initiative—instead of always being at her dead father's beck and call. This active side in her had been called forth by the analyst's "attacks". So there were two snakes that she was now pregnant of and soon to nourish: one of them red for the masculine analyst, the other green, showing a more feminine receptive attitude.

A mediaeval image with broad symbolic application in this respect is Figure 31: the earth mother suckling two snakes. In archetypal imagery, any two such snakes facing each other in mixed enmity and amity together form a symbol for the reconciliation of the opposites. The best-known example is the *caduceus* or "rod of Mercury" formed of two snakes entwined around a central rod, their heads facing one another in mutual recognition. It is a symbol of great healing power.

25. Dragon pregnant of two snakes

26. Hammering the head

27. Burning and divided head

28. Flaming dragon man

29. Split self

30. Fourfold tree-self

XVII

31. The black square

32. Autonomous dragon complex and
"Wise Snake"

XVIII

PAINTING 26 (Fantasy) 24 October 1958

Hammering the Head

This is the second of the three paintings all done on the same day in a passion of conflict with the analyst, which she knew nevertheless to be a creative one. Following in such quick succession, they are particularly informative as to the way in which the symbols merge, re-form themselves into new patterns, and reveal ever more clearly the present rapid progress of her development.

In Painting 25 Mary could identify herself with the dragon pregnant of two snakes without suspecting what such a pregnancy could mean, or what the snakes would do if "she" gave birth to them. Now for the first time the realisation comes to her in a symbolic way that psychic pregnancy means consciousness of self: it is in the self in contact with the outside world that the dragons, snakes and trees and other elements of her rich fantasy life exist and act as representations of her own emotional and mental processes. There had of course been previous indications to her that this might be so (cf. Painting 15—the uprooted tree had emotions similar to her own). But Mary's psychic consciousness presents her now with a vision of her own head, with a hammer from outside trying to "knock sense" into it, while the dragon inside her brain is trying to destroy her small "fantasy tree". Yet other symbols operate within her throat and neck:

"*This is my head. The dragon inside it has two heads of his own, which would*

199

pull in opposite directions if they were not both concentrating on trying to destroy the small tree. The red snake, who would perhaps fight the dragon, can't move to do so because he is caught on the points of three swords. The handles of the swords are held by a monster lower down, who is perhaps an octopus with lots of arms. The hammer blows from outside are trying to knock sense into my head, but they and the dragon together produce a bad headache.

"I thought of the swords as being part of the tight choking feeling that catches my throat when I am nervous."

The colour black

The focal point of the transition from Painting 25 to the present one is the colour black. In the previous painting it symbolised the analyst's critical faculty and Mary's resistances; in this painting it stands for a degree of awareness Mary had never had before. It is an awareness that is "black" because of the element of light receptivity in it, a power of "not knowing", of being conscious that she does not know, and thus becoming able to receive impressions both from without and from within in a way she had not hitherto been able to. This was because her thinking faculty had been so dormant that it had hardly existed for any other purpose than to create negative rationalisations (designed to protect her incest fantasies) and that inclined her to see the worst in everyone and so contributed to her loneliness. Her thinking faculty, such as it was, had thus become for her a barrier to relationship, rather than a forger of new links. It was now functioning, however, in relation to the analyst. So the black colour with which in this fantasy her head and whole outline are painted reveals acceptance of his critical remarks—which have now made her criticise herself. She now questions the validity of her dragon-like attitudes, and so the critical faculties of both analyst and client are merged to some extent in a shared conscious desire to break through the "hard shell" of her inhibiting resistances. Her thick skull here corresponds to the dragon's thick hide (Painting 25). For the accepting attitude of "unknowing" indicated by the black outline is still, out of habit, partly defensive—hence the need for the hammer to go on hammering.

Since Mary's skull has taken on the blackness of the black stone in Painting 25 (with respect both to its critical, thinking connotation, and the headache it gives her) and some degree of receptivity to the blows directed against it, it has become sufficiently yielding for these blows to have driven the dragon inside her skull. In Painting 24 it was outside (receiving all her projections); in Painting 25, it was inside and she was identified with it. It appears not as the whole of her but as a function of her brain, intent on destroying her tree of psychic life. And since it is in her head, the incest problem it represents is no longer something she cannot think about. She is becoming more and aware of it, especially with regard to her own hostile secrecies and unnatural reserves.

Whereas in Painting 25 there had appeared to her to be a heavily critical intellect backed up by a lesser or more remote amount of love, here the main force is felt to be the love symbolised by the red hammer, only guided by the intellect symbolised by the black rod or handle that directs the blows. It was this contact with the loving element in analysis, the sympathy or "feeling with", that enabled her to think of herself no longer as a dragon waiting to be crushed but as a human being—a woman with a very complex nature symbolised by all the things seen to be going on inside her.

The Hammer

Like the red boot, the hammer has a flat striking surface that can crush or crack but cannot penetrate. It is a tool that comes in close contact with what it works upon, and has a definite effect on it, but it remains detached. It may be bruised with hard work, of which it thus retains the marks, but it remains itself and may be used on other objects as well. It is thus a fitting symbol for any phase in an analysis where owing to the intractability of the material the analyst must be specially active.

Asked what kind of hammer it might be that she had painted, Mary said, *"Naturally, a hammer with two heads. There is a bulge at the other end but there was not room for it on the paper"*. Why *"naturally"*? Mary seems to have had in mind something like the double-headed hammer that is sometimes called Jove's Thunderbolt, a hammer with two heads shaped like a dumbbell stating the power of divinity (psychic consciousness) to influence men's minds or bring about a cataclysmic change. It is an archetypal symbol for the union of opposites which is recognised elsewhere, such as in the similarly

Figure 32. "Pandora rising from the earth" (her head being forged in the smithy of Prometheos and Epimetheos). Kerenyi, *The Gods of the Greeks*. London, Thames and Hudson, 1951, p. 219

shaped *dorye* of Tibetan mythology. An apt example of its use may be seen in Figure 32 illustrating the creation of the Greek goddess Pandora, the mother of all living, like the Eve of the Old Testament. She was said by some to have been fashioned by Hephaestos, the great Fire God, who in his smithy forged the armour of the gods. Others said that it was Prometheus, who stole the fire from the gods and was the "friend of man", who with his brother Epimetheus created Pandora. They first hammered upon the earth, whereby her head was forged and continued to be hammered on as it arose and until it assumed its final shape. Figure 32 shows the two brothers forging her head by striking it alternately from either side, in the same way that Mary's head is being hammered in her fantasy so as to "knock sense" into it, i.e. to give it life. In Mary's next painting the fire will be seen inside her head.

The hammer is not the only double-headed symbol in Mary's present fantasy. The dragon *"has two heads of his own, which would pull in opposite directions if they were not both concentrating on trying to destroy the small tree"*. These two heads function in a different way from the hammer's two heads. The latter have their weights combined in the force of the blow that strikes, to give life in the form of consciousness involving union of the opposites. But it is the schizoid nature of the dragon that its two heads pull in opposite directions so as to keep things apart and prevent any such union. They can combine only to destroy as they are trying to destroy the centre of Mary's being.

The devouring dragon and rescuing red snake.

The dragon represents Mary's frustrated and therefore devouring desires on two levels—maternal and paternal. Both parents thus "devoured" her, and

202

she would have devoured them both. The whole internal situation was thus a matriarchal one: Mary was attacked on the one hand by her mother's animus, and on the other by her father's anima.

The purple dragon of Painting 14, which was almost biting its own tail in a contorted effort to give birth to the small tree, is now trying to eat it up again. This is an act typical in all mythologies of the devouring mother who, in the endless cycle of birth and death followed by other births and other deaths, seeks to devour the children she has borne. This is the karma of Indian mythology, in which everything happens as it has always happened before, and there is no change. Thus one of the poems that Mary's mother used to read to herself aloud was Coleridge's *Work without Hope*, referring in her mind to the futility of living as she lived, without any prospect of development. And Mary too liked this poem. She felt herself getting more like her mother all the time. Which side of her mother would win? Would it be the mother in whose memory the wise sayings of country life were stored? Or would it be the mother worn out by endless battling with herself and getting more and more schizoid?

Regarding the onslaught of the dragon on the tree, there is striking similarity between the small tree and the primitive hind brain which in section is so much like a tree with its main branches and subsidiary ones. It is this which is connected with the functioning of the more basic organs such as those of the alimentary tract (feeding and swallowing). In contrast to this, the dragon surrounding it appears to occupy the space between it and the skull that anatomically is occupied by the much later developed cerebral hemispheres. These include the forebrain that is connected with the thinking process. Although she knew some elementary anatomy Mary averred she had not thought of any such similarity when painting this picture of her fantasy, and I believe this to be true. Nevertheless the similarity is a salient one, suggesting the attack on her basic life force.

If the dragon (her mother's negative animus combined with father's anima) had succeeded in destroying the small tree, Mary might well have lost her reason and her common sense as her mother had done. But, as with the revelation of the purple dragon leaping over her from behind and enveloping her in its own purple mist (Painting 24), it is consciousness of what is happening that counts. "The truth will heal", however bad it is. All her life Mary had been quite unaware of the circular thinking in which her incest fantasies had involved her. The present fantasy therefore had more than one healing result.

It showed her first how central to her psychic life the small tree was. It was so central that the dragon's limbs appear to radiate from it as it attacks it from all sides, gripping the tree as the purple dragon in Painting 24 had gripped her head. But she is now more knowledgeable than then. The dragon has always been there without her knowing it, but now there is a new factor causing the conflict to become a conscious one. What she says is that it is the combination of *"the hammer blows from outside"* and the dragon which "together" give her the headache. It is the result of the clash between the two. Since she now welcomes the hammer blows as *"trying to knock sense into my head"*, it becomes evident that it is the dragon that is the active core of the resistances. The headaches are felt in the "blackness" of the skull which lies between and this seems to her to be the battleground in which the conflict is raging. There is a highly creative outcome in the next painting in which the meaning of a "splitting headache" becomes clear.

Now comes the second and most revealing aspect of this fantasy, showing the healing and individuating nature of the transference. For the red colour of the hammer symbolically wielded by the analyst is reflected in the red colour of the snake symbolising that power within Mary herself which has been awakened as a result of the analysis. It is now preparing to fight the dragon so as to rescue the small tree. The snake is not yet as free to act as is the analyst in the analytical situation, for the reason that internal development invariably lags behind external fact. After all Mary has only just become pregnant of the two snakes in Painting 25.

The inhibition in her case is symbolically described by her saying how *"The red snake, who would perhaps fight the dragon, can't move to do so because he is caught on the points of three swords. The handles of the swords are held by a monster lower down, who is perhaps an octopus with lots of arms"*. The octopus is another well-known devouring monster with many tentacles, so that if one is cut off others can still operate. That it is here painted purple as the dragon is shows their affinity. It is a creature of the sea, whereas the dragon is a crea-

204

ture of the land. It therefore symbolises the deeply buried emotional force of "purple" incest fantasies connected with the mother that gave rise to the purple dragon in her brain, where the defensive rationalisations about the father had proliferated so disastrously.

Just how the golden (yellow) swords could hold back the red snake was never properly explained, except by Mary's association with the seven swords that traditionally pierced the Virgin Mary's heart when her Son was crucified. Perhaps she felt like this in defence of the dragon whom the snake, as the saviour and deliverer, is going to attack. What she actually said about them was, *"I thought of the swords as being part of the tight choking feeling that catches my throat when I am nervous"*, in other words when she is afraid of expressing what she really feels. For the throat contains the vocal cords, which may be flexible or rigid as the swords seem to be. Moreover in psychic body-imagery, in which the body symbolises the psyche, the narrow passage of the neck is the place which forms either the link or barrier between thinking located in the head and the emotions having their origin in the parts of the body below the neck. The imagery is not only symbolic but psychosomatic as well. The tautness of the muscles in the neck often corresponds with psychological resistances, so in an uncoordinated individual the term "stiff-necked" applies in both ways. Mary's stiff-necked-ness is here symbolised by the fact that head and body (thinking and feeling) are divided by a thick wedge of blackness that the red snake is as yet not able to pierce. Compare Jung's mention of a patient complaining that "a snake was stuck in her throat".[71]

The colour green

One final word may here be said about the colour green. There were two snakes of which the dragon was pregnant in Painting 25, a red one and a green. These colours are complementary opposites, and we have seen the red snake in the present fantasy to be the active or "male" one. The colour green would therefore represent passivity, or earthiness, or femininity, as in the case of the green "mothering tree" (Painting 24). As noted, there is no green snake in the present fantasy, but there is the small green tree. All trees are symboli-

---

71. Jung, *Symbols of Transformation*, p. 378.

cally passive since they cannot move from place to place. The tree here cannot fly from the dragon, but can only wait to be delivered by the active red snake. Mary's green snakes have all been passive or earthy ones, all connected with trees. There was the green talking snake at the foot of the plum tree (painting 1), the little green snakes charmed by the Piper sitting beneath a tree (Painting 6), the green snakes flecked with red trying to root the tree into the ground (painting 15), the green snake flecked with red imprisoned with a tree in the jar (Painting 17).

I can only suggest, then, that there is something in common between the green snake and the green "mothering tree" of the second last painting (24), and this is their common passivity and feminine attitude here symbolised by the colour green. If this is so, the green tree here replaces the green snake, a supposition that will be seen to be confirmed on more than one level in the next painting.

As in a serial story, this fantasy leaves several questions which are answered in the next fantasy, which followed immediately after this one:

1. What is the further effect of the hammer blows?
2. Will the dragon devour the small tree?
3. Will the red snake be able to penetrate through the stiff neck to rescue it?
4. What is the meaning of the "splitting" headache Mary suffered from?

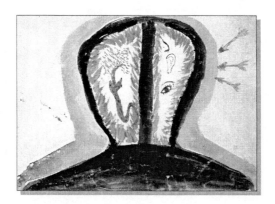

PAINTING 27 (FANTASY) 24 OCTOBER 1958

The Burning and Divided Head

This is the third of the fantasies that Mary painted on that memorable day. It was painted immediately after the last painting (26) as a direct reply to the questions that that had raised.

Mary had spent that day in alternating rages and receptiveness arising from the conflict she was in between hostility and love, sometimes hiding her secret thoughts both from herself and from the analyst, sometimes revealing them or realising them. It was a remarkable advance that she was able to break through her most unnatural reserve (which always gave her the appearance of having a blank mind), to launch attacks upon the analyst. This was to risk losing that which she had pinned her faith and hopes of getting well upon, in the spontaneous ejaculations of fury that shook her to the core. The analyst's delight in these, and the unusual energy with which he answered back, treating her now for the first time as an equal who could stand such buffeting, aroused in her yet further fury. At the same time it gave her a sense of personal relationship she had not had before, so that she felt safer in attacking than she had done before in holding back.

And so this second fantasy painting about her head showed it a mass of flames, and at the same time divided into two, symbolising her growing consciousness of the division in herself and the creativeness of the amity-enmity relationship with the analyst. The latter could no longer be disguised and was so much better than a blind belief. Mary's own description of her painting was:

"*This head is in flames of anger inside because it is divided. The right side has an eye and an ear and nose, but these are not much good to it because it is not in touch with the left side which contains a very wise snake with a tree growing from its mouth. If the two sides were together the snake would help the eye and ear to make sense of what they see and hear from outside.*

"*The head is surrounded by mist which is so dense (like me) that even friendly arrows find it difficult to reach it.*"

There are two main links between this fantasy and Painting 26. One is the continued occupation with the fate of the small tree now rescued by the snake, the other is the blackness of the head with its quite new feature—its division into two. Since Mary's own account is concerned mainly with the division into two it may be as well to discuss this first.

The "splitting headache" and "split mind".

A casual observer, seeing in this painting such undoubted evidence of a "split mind", and not knowing what had led up to it or what she said of it herself, might well conclude that Mary was getting more schizoid instead of less, if indeed she was not already lapsing into schizophrenia. But this would have been a great mistake. For human beings are all split, or have a dual nature, owing to the incest taboo. This is the primary division separating mankind from animals having no such creative taboo and which gives to man the power of observing himself as well as of controlling some of his more basic instinctive drives.

There is thus among some primitive peoples a "dual organization" into two exogamous but intermarrying halves or *moieties* for the purpose of preventing incest, so that the incest taboo tends to expand society and at the same time the psyche of each individual member composing it. Infringement of this basic rule, obliterating the taboo by the denial of the fundamental split, can only be dealt with by killing the offenders if they are discovered. Such an act, if not so drastically dealt with, would disrupt society and reduce its members to the undifferentiated state out of which the incest taboo had lifted them. The consciousness of duality which the doubling of organisations expresses externally is crystalised out in mythology (which is the collective fantasy life of all those concerned). This operates through the belief in two ancestors, two sisters or two brothers, one for each moiety or half of the social system. To one of these ego belongs but may not intermarry within it because of the incest taboo creating the frustration necessary for the development of society. This also causes *thought*, for one must know whom one may marry or have intercourse with, and whom one may not. This power of thought expands personality, making it dual too. The split thus leads to the beginning of consciousness as something different from mere instinctive urge.

But in our own much larger society there has been a subtle change, making the problem far less obvious but all the more dangerous for being hidden up. Except in some cases the taboo against physical incest has through the centuries become so ingrained in us and taken for granted that we are for the most part no longer conscious of it as are earlier peoples. This means that, though the barrier exists, and socially we are aware of it, we do not know about it inwardly. We have not had the vital experience of suffering this separation consciously. This does not matter much for ordinary folk with many other interests. But in a case like Mary's, in which there was a minimum of outside interest to draw off the libido which is naturally·incestuous, and where there is no conscious barrier, the problem can become acute. When in addition there has been no "good mother" figure to establish healthy human relationship, and the "give and take" that is bound up with it, there is nothing to prevent untrammelled flow of fantasy about a "good parent" who will give everything, without a barrier of any kind. This is a condition found only within the womb, where there is no differentiation and no conscious thought.

The schizophrenic is one who in this psychic sense has not yet been born, not having severed the psychic umbilical cord through which unconscious fantasies derived from the parents' unfulfilled desires and attitudes flow into him. This overwhelms what might have been his or her separated personality leaving the victim sooner or later a prey to them. A severely schizoid person like Mary has certainly, though not quite to the same extent, been swamped by such unconscious fantasies. In her case they were so rejected by her conscious mind as to have been thought of by her as mere "fairy tales" having nothing to do whatever with her life. Thus she was, to begin with, to all appearances unconscious of her split, of which the appearance of her "ghost man" was yet further evidence. The course of this analysis has been to make her more and more conscious of this split in her personality by linking these unconscious fantasies with consciousness so that she could recognise them as parts of herself. And most important parts at that, without a conscious link with which she could not satisfactorily regulate her life. One of the main stages of this bringing into consciousness was "hooking the Leviathan" so that she could relate to it, see it for what it was, a part of her, as she began to do in Painting 23. From that moment the stage for the battle for her consciousness was set and the intensive attacks on the closed fortress of her mind began.

As we have seen, one of the results of this was the "splitting headaches" she began to have. Whatever the physiological aspects of pains like this may be in the matter of a heightened blood pressure or similar symptoms, headaches of a psychogenic kind such as Mary's were have been described by more than one psychiatrist as being like "growing pains", derived from psychic adhesions being torn apart, becoming more "unstuck". Each realisation is thus a pain, but it is a necessary pain, not unlike that connected with childbirth.

There is a classical story of Zeus having a terrible headache until his head was split open with an axe by Hephaestos, the Fire God. Out of the split so formed was "born" his virgin daughter Athene, fully armed—a story symbolising the birth of a powerful daughter-anima. The headache thus becomes a warning and a help, if we can understand it so. This was explained to Mary, and she understood, for she could understand symbolic language where she would close up tightly against rational argument. The headache is an argument *ad hominem*. As Mary said of Painting 26, it was in the conflict between the dragon and the hammer that the headaches arose, indicating that if the dragon would only let the small tree go and stop trying to deprive it of its liberty the headaches would then cease.

This is what is actually happening now in Painting 27, in which the two sides of the head (the psyche) have got unstuck and separated out, with the division between them made by that "black" psychic substance—an element of thinking that is able to distinguish between these two sides of herself. The dragon has now disappeared and has turned into or has released the fire of anger and of passion now raging in her head. With that release her headaches for the time being also ceased, for by accepting them and realising what they were for, she had allowed them to do their work: forcing her to accept the reality of her own dual nature.

Figure 33. "The Mercurial serpent, alchemical symbol of psychic transformation. From Barchusen, *Elementa chemiae*, 1718." Jung, *Symbols of Transformation*, Fig. 6

Internal fire. "Friendly arrows". The nature of the split.

Two pictures may help us to understand what has been happening. The first is Mary's Painting 14 of the dragon giving birth to the small tree, and pouring fire out of its mouth which is in some way going to assist in the tree being "born"—in other words delivered from the very dragon that has gestated it. The other is Figure 33[72] of the mercurial serpent in the alchemical closed vase (corresponding in the present fantasy to Mary's head) pouring forth the fire that arises out of it and apparently replaces it. Jung quotes from Neitzche's *The Beacon*: "This flame with its grey-white belly hisses its desires…. This flame is my own soul flaming with "its blaze of silent heat".[73] He further speaks of an "act of union with oneself" which is "also a self-violation, a self-murder"[74], as we have seen in the case of Mary and the alchemical dragon both bursting into purging flame.

But there are in Mary's case two flames or fiery areas, one on each side of her head and separated by the black line symbolising the new growth of her thinking faculty. For thinking always does divide. These two separated fiery areas may remind us of the two divisions of early society, which are also in some places thought of as "two fires"[75]. One fire is that of the opposite moiety into which a person may marry, thus symbolising passion and activity, the

---

72. Jung, *Symbols of Transformation*, Figure 6.
73. Ibid., p. 95.
74. Ibid., p. 291-2.
75. See Codrington's *The Melanesians*.

other is that of his own moiety to which the incest taboo applies, so that from his point of view this fire is one of sexual frustration. The same applies to the two halves of Mary's head: in the left half a union is in progress between the red snake and green tree, symbolising the fire of fulfillment. But the right half contains the "eye" and "ear" and "nose" but *"these are not much good to it because it is not in touch with the left side"*, thus portraying the fire of frustration. Mary naturally experiences this division as a painful one since it threatens to disrupt her former circular thinking and emotional condition, in which each side of herself was constantly interfering with the other one. But the creative thought implied by this fantasy is her realisation that there is a split, and that there is a need to unite the two halves. They cannot be united creatively till they have been separated out and the two halves recognised for what they are: the right half containing the observing faculties or functions of ego consciousness, here painted black, and the other half containing the archetypal snake and tree belonging to psychic consciousness.

The hammer blows which have caused the splitting headache have now turned into the three "friendly arrows" trying to penetrate her head. This may be compared to Spielrein's patient saying that "she too had been shot by God three times—then came a resurrection of the spirit"[76]. Jung says of this that "the torment which afflicts mankind does not come from outside…. The deadly arrows do not strike the hero from without"[77]. But it cannot be overemphasized that this fantasy, and the transformation it symbolised, was no result of a spontaneous inner development but of the hammer blows of Painting 26. That is to say that they arose out of a direct personal relationship with the analyst and his refusal at this stage in the analysis to accept the mild but "hurt" and inwardly devouring role anticipated from him on the model of her father. Through his "hitting back", the dragon-like projections were driven back into the place they issued from (her own now seething brain): here only, in the context of this relationship, could they be dealt with and resolved.

Already these hammer blows were being recognised as the *"friendly arrows"* of the present fantasy, still coming *"from outside"*. But the thick purple

---

76. Jung, *Symbols of Transformation*, p. 290.
77. Ibid., p. 293.

"mist which is so dense (like me)" which now surrounds her head makes it difficult for them to penetrate. This is of interest since it will be remembered that in Painting 24 there was the leaping dragon *and* the purple mist, which the dragon exuded over Mary as a projection from itself. Mary had carried the "mist" with her wherever she went—the bemusement she was always in (attacks from mother's animus and father's anima). In the previous painting (26), however, there was no such purple mist surrounding her. She was then too occupied with the problem of her internal dragon to be conscious of projecting it. But in the present fantasy—the dragon having burst into the flames which for the time being had burnt it up—the purple mist symbolising the obtuseness which her incest fantasies produced in her relation with the outside world reappears. It is a defence against that love or "friendliness", that she now recognises the arrows to betoken, for fear of a repetition of the frustrations experienced by her at home. One of the interesting things about this purple mist is its apparent lack of character, for in contrast to the raging dragons of her other fantasies it is featureless and symbolises sheer stupidity—a fact she is now recognising in saying that it is *"so dense (like me)"*. This is in itself another sign of progress: her recognition of her situation. The magnitude of what this mist of apparent indifference conceals and how the defences may be stormed, will be seen in the next painting (28).

Red snake and small green tree.

What we have so far discussed has been the end product of the fantasy. We have not yet noted the subtle movements in Mary's psyche leading up to it heralded by the activities of the red snake. It is the active "hero" of this fantasy and corresponds internally to the red hammer of Painting 26. For it will be remembered that, in that fantasy, the red snake had not yet penetrated through the "neck" of her resistances to rescue the small tree from the dragon. The red snake affirms that power stimulated to activity in her by the analysis: the endeavour to rescue her individuality.

As we know "red" means active passion, whether it be of love or hate, or both combined. These two paintings, 26 and 27, are the first ones in which any of Mary's snakes, which hitherto have done little but passively observe, have taken an active role. The role of the hero in all fairy tales and fantasies is to rescue the maiden from the dragon. We have seen the "small tree" to be the potential center of Mary's life. So the snake is "red" with passionate desire for it, but, till it could get at grips with the dragon (which was the real object of its hate), the hatred must find some outlet. This it did in Mary's creative attacks upon the analyst.

This phenomenon helped the red snake to burst through the barrier of resistances formed by the muscles of Mary's neck so that she could now use her vocal cords with good effect. In terms of the last fantasy it is clear that, by this very act, the red snake had overcome the dragon and rescued the tree from it. But it shows how little Mary logically "thinks out" her fantasies so that she actually describes this union of the snake with the small tree as "*a very wise snake with a tree growing from its mouth*". Taken at its face value, this indicates a very different state of affairs from that shown in Painting 22: the red suffering snake choked and pinned down by the "unfriendly plant", being her almost total inability at that moment to express herself.

The present union of the red snake with the small tree may be understood on more than one level. In terms of Painting 24 it may be understood as the red Mary, having at last united herself with the "green mothering tree"—the fruit of which the dragon there wished to devour. In terms of Painting 25 we may think of it as a union between the active red snake and the passive green snake equated with the small green tree.

Beneath this there is a deeper level still: this concerns the meaning of the "small green tree" itself. Ever since the first appearance of this tree as growing out of the acorn shed by the old father tree in Painting 2 we have regarded this small tree as being connected with her father-incest fantasies. But we have seen (Painting 26) how Mary's intense but infantile desire for the father's rather ineffectual virile member was but a substitute for the much deeper need for the mother's breast which she had so lacked: the tree is breast-shaped with a phallic trunk so that it potentially symbolises both parents. We have seen also how Mary's defences against the whole idea of mother-love and personal relationship on a feeling level have recently been tending to be withdrawn. Indeed she has even remembered some of her mother's better qualities and sympathised with her. If we may then look once more at Mary's present painting of the red "*snake with a tree growing from its mouth*" we may see in it the image of an infant with its wide open mouth hungrily sucking at the breast. If this interpretation is correct, the "hero" or saviour in the form of the red snake in the present fantasy is on this level the infant having overcome its terrors and now eager at the breast.

Dividing to unite

At whatever level we may interpret this symbol, it is a uniting one. It results from the main division in her head, separating the personal from the impersonal in such a way that the archetypal fantasies of bliss, belonging to psychic consciousness, do not invade the sphere of ego consciousness, symbolised by the eye, ear and nose. For the purpose of dividing on one level is always to unite on another one, which as we have seen cannot be done till the parts are separated out. Before this happens there is only a mass of confused (because unconscious) opposites which get in one another's way. They distort every issue and render clear thinking and the sorting out of emotional problems impossible, or at best extremely difficult. The uniting process always starts on the deepest level of psychic consciousness, corresponding to the potentiality of bliss in earliest childhood. It is on this level also that the archetypes function. And it is only gradually, through much sacrifice of pride and due attention to these archetypes, that the wisdom which they embody percolates upward into consciousness to ease the problems of everyday life.

We may appreciate the speed with which realisations were now coming to Mary by comparing the three fantasies all painted on this day (Paintings 25, 26 and 27) with all her previous fantasies. The difference now is that while in those fantasies the unconscious contents were all seen as *outside* her, both conscious and unconscious are now experienced by her as belonging together *inside* her own psyche. She has rendered this as the two compartments in her head of which she says, "*If the two sides were together the snake would help the eye and ear to make sense of what they see and hear*" as she says, "*from outside*"—but which includes "from inside" too.

The Dragon and the Snake

The overcoming of the dragon by the red snake led me to inquire more closely still into the nature of these two opposite principles in Mary's psychic world. So I asked her if she could possibly write down what she thought about them. By this time she was becoming able to sort out her thoughts enough to say that she would try. The following is what she wrote and brought with her to the next interview.

"Snakes are very wise. They are at the same time frightening and fascinating. In many of my pictures the snake has the possibility of being helpful. He is just as dangerous as the dragon but he could be made friends with. The dragon is fierce and stupid. He won't be friendly to anyone, but simply burns or eats whatever gets in his way. He moves in great leaps, and so does not see many of the things the snake knows about.

"I think of the dragon coming out in my quite unreasonable tempers and moods. These pour out over whoever is nearest at the time and mostly have nothing to do with the person or situation they attack. I'm not sure about the snake. I think it may be some power inside me which is likely to be dangerous and destructive unless I find out more about it and give it some attention."

After some further consideration and questioning she added:

"The snake would think out who to attack and would have some reason for doing so, unlike the dragon which destroys everything in its path. The dragon leaps a long way at a time, for example he would go from here to another place about a mile away and not notice anything between.

"These snakes and dragons are rather more real than anything that happens outside me."

We have already noted the dragon's characteristic of leaping from place to place representing Mary's amnesia of intermediate links in her psychic life-history. It also symbolises her habitual escapism from any close human contact, leading to her self-imposed isolation, her life-long stand-offishness and *noli me tangere* attitude towards everyone. Among these were many who would have helped her out of her isolation had she allowed them to but whom she spurned indignantly. This is connected with the dragon's attitude of simply burning or eating whatever gets in his way. This underscores her conscious attitude regarding any who might approach her at all intimately or who she feared might in any other way dominate her.

One of her favourite fantasies was that of "crucifying" her imagined enemies by nailing them horizontally on boards, gouging their insides out so that their intestines spilt over and the horror-fascinating blood flowed out. It was quite typical of the way she projected her own fantasies that when the analyst showed an alert interest in such a gory fantasy, she said quite innocently ,*"But surely, doesn't everyone have thoughts like this?"* She did not in her conscious fantasies torture her father in this way, but she unconsciously so hated him that she used to dream of him burnt by the fires of hell. She also had wishful fantasies arranging fatal accidents for a lover whom she did not want to see, thinking that by concentrating on such accidents she could actually bring them about. We may conclude that such fantasies harked back to the early frustration of her struggle at the breast, and shifted only later onto the father-plane.

Of snakes, on the contrary, she has said with few exceptions throughout the analysis that they are "wise". They are at the same time *"frightening and fascinating"*, a phrase which she first used with regard to the "ghost man" whom she saw at puberty. He throughout the analysis has typified for Mary her deepest love-ambivalence. The snake *"as dangerous as the dragon"* differs from it in that it *"has the possibility of being helpful"* and *"could be made friends with"*. She must find out more about it. She had learnt by now to regard the "ghost man" in this way, also the analyst with regard to his recent attacks upon her typified by the hammer-blows, in that it was part of the snake's wisdom that he *"would think out who to attack and would have some reason for doing so, unlike the dragon which destroys everything in its path"*. For the snake at least can "think". It can deliberate; the dragon can only act compulsively.

Regarding the snake as an archetypal symbol Jung says, "According to Philo the snake is the most spiritual of all creatures .... Its swiftness is terrible. It has a long life and sloughs off old age with its skin .... Among the Gnostics it was regarded as an emblem of the brain-stem and spinal cord .... It is an excellent symbol for the unconscious, perfectly expressing the latter's sudden and unexpected manifestations ... while the dragon is its negative and unfavourable action—not birth, but a devouring; not a beneficial and constructive deed, but greedy retention and destruction"[78] (see Figure 30).

---

78. Jung, *Symbols of Transformation*, pp. 374-5.

Dream of skinning a snake

With regard to the snake sloughing off its skin, which symbolises rejuvenation or rebirth, Mary at about this time had a dream after a particularly abusive episode of scorning hatred for the analyst, which she had subsequently partly seen through. The dream was that she was in flat country like that of her home, the rectory, but, unlike that countryside, which has nothing but the gentlest hills, there were high mountains all around. These symbolised on the one hand her mountainous projections, which she had now "*come off*", and on the other hand an enclosing circle to keep her "in herself". A man approached and asked if she was "*glad to be at home*", meaning that she had by now withdrawn "*in herself*". But, as she said, "*I did not answer because I was busy skinning a big pink worm (it was about the size of my forearm). I thought the skin would make a good pipe to play on, but the worm hated being skinned and kept trying to get away*".

This referred partly to her love of worms and of all "creepy-crawly things" representative of the most primitive part of her psyche. But when questioned more closely about the bigness of the worm, she suddenly looked up and said, surprised, "*It was the size of a snake. It must have been a snake*". When asked about the pinkness of the snake, she said it was the colour of flesh, reminding her of the male member. But at the same time she thought it looked like her own arm, so that it symbolised something to do with her. The idea of turning the skin into "*a good pipe to play on*" recalls the Piper of Painting 6, as well as the pipe that Krishna played on (that the girls were jealous of because he loved it better than he loved them). The pink flesh symbolised her own secret phallic desires, and the skin symbolised the resistances she had to having them exposed. That was why "*the worm hated being skinned and kept trying to get away*", which she described as being "*like me trying to wriggle out of a tight corner that you have got me in*". And yet Mary is here skinning the pink worm herself, which showed the analysis had deeply bitten in to the extent that she was herself trying to remove the complexes. The difference between the small size of the worm and the larger thickness of the snake can be yet another revelation that underneath her longing for the father was a yet greater longing for the mother's breast, as she was now beginning faintly to realise.

PAINTING 28 (FANTASY) 6 NOVEMBER 1958

The Flaming Dragon Man

The fire that was in Mary's head in Painting 27 has now caught on to good effect. The discussion about the snakes and dragons led to a new fantasy of truly dynamic effect, in which the dragon now figures for the first time in human form as a flaming giant threatening to destroy her false security.

"*This is me hiding behind a fence which has stood fairly well until now. I am very frightened because the things outside (or inside me) are large and strong, and can break down my fence or climb over it. The giant is in flames all over but they do not hurt him. I think he wants to grab me in his hand, and I feel I shall be hurt when he does.*

"*The flying snake is the most powerful of the other creatures. He is also very wise and I rather like him, but he is a bit frightening at the same time.*

"*I think I shall be burnt by the flames according to how much I fear them. If I was not afraid, I might be able to live comfortably in them as the giant does.*

"*This is the first time I have had a snake with wings. When I look at it now the fence seems to be wooden, so it may get burnt down by the giant on his way.*"

It will be noted that the fence taken for the resistances behind which Mary has hidden herself so long is circular. It may therefore remind us of the circular wall around the red hanging boy to hide the sight of him from her till she could pull it down. Mary is herself now painted red, but not with rotting flesh because she is more conscious now than she was then. The hanging boy

219

was a potential animus-figure, strung up by the black chain, which is the colour that she is there painted too. But now the colours are reversed. Mary is red with fright (as she was in Painting 10 when she was trying to escape from the initiating great fish, and as was the frightened duck in Painting 18). But she is no longer high up or large in her escapist fantasies. She is low down and very small. What once had been the hanging boy and later had been the tall red man hooking Leviathan in painting 23 is now the flaming Dragon Man coming to rescue her by burning down her fence.

Her growing sense of the power of the archetypes could not be indicated more impressively than by this fantasy in which she experiences herself as being all alone within her fence, surrounded by archetypal figures much larger than she is. The fence symbolises from one point of view the mask composed of her defensive attitudes that have *"stood fairly well until now"*. Note Mary's rapidly increasing consciousness in saying this. But she is very frightened because *"the things outside (or inside me) are large and strong, and can break down my fence or climb over it"*. So there is another thing she recognises now. The things that seem to be outside her (outside her fence) are really inside her, although she still inevitably projects some of them outwards, for instance on the analyst.

No human being actually sprouts fire or has the enormous strength that this Dragon Man has. There are of course resemblances to the analyst, for the Dragon Man is trying to storm her black and spiky fence just as the hammer in Painting 26 was trying to break through her resistances. And there are further parallels. The hammer which in that fantasy was red, symbolising the element of love, has now become intensified into the fire issuing from the Dragon Man. His body is black for that thinking faculty which alone can successfully direct the love, as the black rod directed the red hammer-blows in Painting 26. The link between the hammer and the fire in the present fantasy has been the three 'friendly" arrows trying to pierce Mary's purple mist in the intervening Painting 27. The fire which was inside Mary's head is now issuing from the Dragon Man, and the blackness which surrounded and divided Mary's head in Painting 27 is now inside him.

There is here a feeling of "otherness" which indicates that Mary is now confronted with something much greater than any individual person, though

220

any individual may be in touch with it or act as mediator for it. For when Mary says, *"The giant is in flames all over but they do not hurt him"*, what is inevitably called to mind is Moses' encounter with God speaking from the burning bush: "And the angel of the Lord appeared unto him in a flame of fire out of the midst of a bush... and the bush was not consumed" (Exodus 3:2). How many times must Mary have heard this passage read out in her father's church, in a kind of stupor, simultaneously adoring her father, and, as she grew up, hating the dullness of his sermons (though he read the lessons, as she said, "so beautifully"). But the words had made no real impact, and it was not from this biblical account that Mary's vision came to her out of the archetypal depths. But the biblical account helps us to know what it meant. For when God called to Moses "out of the midst of the bush", speaking about the deliverance of his people from their afflictions, and Moses then asked God his name, God answered, "I AM THAT I AM". He emphasised this once more by telling Moses to say to the people, "I AM has sent me unto you" (Exodus 3:14). However this may be interpreted by theologians, the psychological meaning as applied to all of us (God being the centre of everyone's being) is "Know thyself". And this is what the Dragon Man is trying to help Mary to do: to destroy the defences which she had built up to hide herself from others, and also from herself.

As usual, Mary's understanding of her fantasy develops while she is painting it. At the beginning she thought the Dragon Man might break down her fence or climb over it, and was afraid that he would want to grab her in his hand. She felt that if he did she would be hurt. (Compare the much milder vision of the red hand grafting the black Mary onto the Tree of Life in Painting 4.) But as her fantasy developed so did her understanding of it. The fence as she has painted it is made of iron bars, but at the end of her account she says, *"When I look at it now the fence seems to be wooden, so it may get burnt down by the giant on his way"*. She also says *"I think I shall be burnt by the flames according to how much I fear them. If I was not afraid, I might be able to live comfortably in them as the giant does"*. This shows the insight that Mary was now gaining on this fantasy level. It corresponds with the mystical conception that the fire of hell is in fact the love of God, which torments only insofar as it is rejected but which purges and saves and gets transformed into ecstasy insofar as it is accepted gratefully.

There is thus a certain similarity between this fantasy and Painting 13 (Mary worshipping the black snake flecked with red). She may have felt this deeply as an act of adoration, but it did not arouse in her the terror of a direct impact with something like divinity. We may remember that Christ said "Who comes near Me comes near the Fire". See also Hebrews 12:29, "Our God is a consuming fire".

Of the other mythological beings outside Mary's fence one is the dragon painted green, a pathetic looking figure now deprived of its destructive power since its fire has been taken over by the saviour figure of the Dragon Man. But there are two figures that are much more threatening. One is the black head of what looks like a bird of prey behind the Dragon Man. This is quite a new feature in Mary's fantasies, apparently revealing the fear she still has of her dead father's power over her and of the analyst's critical faculty.

There remains the "flying snake" which is *the most powerful of the other creatures. He is also very wise and I rather like him but he is a bit frightening at the same time".* This may remind us of Jung's phrase about the symbolic snake's "painful and dangerous intervention in our affairs, and its frightening effects"[79]. The winged snake thus shares some of the characteristics of the Dragon Man and of Mary's feelings about the analyst. But it is a split-off part for Mary says, *"This is the first time I have had a snake with wings".* This is not strictly true, as we will remember the two flying snakes in Painting 7 with which the unborn dragon was to be fed. One of those flying snakes was painted purple, as is the snake in Mary's present fantasy, and as is the snake also which is laughing to see the red duck's agitation in Painting 18. The snake in the present fantasy seems to be

Figure 34. Christ with burning heart and flames of light. "Romanesque wood sculpture, 11th to 12th cent. Church of San Candido, South Tyrol. Heart and crown metal rays, modern." .

79. Jung, *Symbols of Transformation,* p. 374.

222

Figure 35. Shiva Nataraja, the Dancing Shiva, India, Tamil Nadu Thanjavur District, Chola Dynasty, 12th cent. Museum Rietberg, Donation Eduard von der Heydt

a kind of *deus ex machina* watching over the action of the Dragon Man rescuing Mary through her defences. The background of the whole painting is purple as it was in Painting 13, the purple colour now seeming to become more positive adumbrating "knowledge of incest desire" rather than incest desire itself.

Figure 34 is an image of Christ with a burning heart and flames of light streaming from his head. Figure 35 is of Shiva, the god of healing destruction, with a ring of fire all round him. This compares with the fire emanating from the Dragon Man and is like Mary's fence will be when it catches alight.

Figure 36 is a symbol for consciousness or emotional awareness in the centre of a flaming heart.

Figure 36. Eye (symbol for consciousness) in flaming heart. From *Theologica Mystica*, reproduced by Edna Kenton, *The Book of Earths*. New York, William Morrow, 1928

PAINTING 29 (FANTASY) 9 NOVEMBER 1958

Split Self

The process of division culminating in Mary's "split head" of Painting 27 is now carried a step further in the present fantasy. Mary's whole psychic body-image is now split into two; she painted it three days after Painting 28.

"*This is me divided into two halves. They face in opposite directions. The black side is rather wooden, but it feels powerful and thinks that other people are of very small importance. That is why the house and people are painted so small. It is threatened by a red claw, probably belonging to a passing dragon.*

"*The red side has snakes growing from its head, hand and foot. This side is only interested in its snakes. They keep in touch with each other by the vine which is friendly both to the snakes and the red half-person.*

"*The two sides pull badly against each other, and neither seems to be of much practical use.*"

This is the most self-knowledgeable of Mary's paintings up to date. Although she says that "*the two sides pull badly against each other, and neither seems to be of much practical use*", this is a considerable advance on Painting 27, of which she said that though she was aware of the two sides of her head, these two were "*not in touch*". Now they are very much in touch, and the contrast is a striking and a conscious one. Like the two faces of Janus (the janitor or door-keeper presiding over entry into a new phase of consciousness), Mary's two halves "*face in opposite directions*". We will discuss these separately since they have two such very opposite meanings.

224

The Black Side

For the first time Mary gives us her own idea of the meaning of the colour black: *"the black side is rather wooden"*. We may think of it as being like the wooden fence in the last painting (28) which was there due to be burnt down. *"But it feels powerful and thinks that other people are of very small importance,"* and *"That is why the house and people are painted so small"*. This adds to the knowledge so far gained of what black means to her. We already know it to indicate an attitude of aloofness. At the same time it has the element of compulsive thought that she had originally developed to take the place of the mother-love she lacked; this had allowed her to justify herself in some of her more abnormal attitudes. The new element Mary now adds is that of "power" and the feeling of superiority, which has been hidden under her self-effacing exterior. This is an attitude of the unconsciously "omnipotent child" claiming a kind of divine right—like that of the huge figures of the divine kings in ancient bas-reliefs towering above common soldiers or the enemies which they have slain. But it is all the same a sign of the greater consciousness which she is now achieving that she can thus express it in her fantasy. This is in marked contrast to the last painting, in which she was so small and the flaming Dragon Man so huge. It is in fact this feeling of omnipotence which she projects onto the Dragon Man (psychic consciousness) as opposed to the underdevelopment of her own ego consciousness. This has to be compensated for by just such an inner feeling of superiority.

The objects of this feeling of superiority may be seen in the two small black figures down below, which possibly symbolise the parents. If we assume this we see that the mother is the larger one and the father the smaller, in proportion to the degree in which (in spite of her father-love) she inwardly despised them both. The sky on that side of the picture is painted blue, indicating the unattainable. The house is a maternal symbol, standing for the unconscious basically matriarchal nature of this whole black side of her. The *"passing dragon"* flying through the air is an indication that, although the dragon is in process of being subdued or at least understood as a symbol for escapist fantasies, it still has power to threaten her with its red claw. This is remarkably like some paintings of her mother's hand threatening her in much earlier fantasy-paintings (not included in this book). It will be noted that the dragon's claw is snatching at her from the same direction as the hammer-blows were raining on her head (Painting 26) and as the "friendly arrows" were pointing around her head in Painting 27. A *"passing dragon"* is like a *"passing thought"*, a relic of past attitudes (not altogether overcome). It accounts for the very negative aspect of this black side of her in which she does indeed imitate her mother in a kind of general suspicious contempt.

The red side. Three in one.

The two sides of this painting resemble the two sides of Mary's head in Painting 27. For in that painting the *"ear, eye and nose"* in the right-hand side are also painted black but are *"not much good"* because not in touch with the *"very wise snake"* in the left. The present fantasy helps us to understand why this should have been so by showing that it was her own concealed sense of superiority that cut her off from the ordinary things going on in the world around.

In Painting 27 of the Divided Head, Mary had identified herself only with the stupidity of the *"eye, ear and nose"* (obtuseness of her conscious attitude). She did not identify herself consciously with the red snake having the green tree in its mouth. But the shock of having had her fence burnt down by the flaming Dragon Man in Painting 28 has helped to dissolve the barrier that had prevented her from knowing that the archetypal images of the red snake and green tree were also part of herself. In the present fantasy therefore she does not hesitate to recognise both sides of her psychic make-up. The red side of herself has three snakes emanating from it, indicating the acceptance into her personality of the saving power of the red snake in triple form, while the small green tree has turned into the vine, the whole of which side Mary is now worshipping.

Though Mary has not yet specifically mentioned the number "three" the notion of three-ness is growing strongly in her now. We have seen it functioning negatively in the three yellow swords in Painting 26, there hampering the red snake in its attempt to rescue the small tree. We have seen it negatively also in Painting 27 in the isolation of the eye, ear and nose. But in that same painting we have seen it in a very positive form in the *"three friendly arrows"*. In the present painting it is more positive still in the form of the three

226

red snakes growing from Mary's *"head, hand and foot"*. We can consider this as something like thinking, action and standpoint. As Mary says, *"This side is only interested in its snakes"*. She adds significantly, *"They keep in touch with each other by the vine which is friendly both to the snakes and to the red half-person"*. When asked what she meant by the snakes keeping in touch with each other by the vine, she said:

"The vine keeps the snakes together, so that instead of being three snakes with three separate sets of ideas (which would be tiresome as they are growing from one person) there are three snakes all of one mind".

The extraordinary thing about Mary, about the dullness of her ego consciousness and the deep perception of her psychic consciousness, is that, although this is a clear statement about the Trinity (the three in one) and Christ as the vine, she had had no conscious idea of this. She was astonished when I called her attention to it. The fifteenth chapter of St. John's Gospel begins, "I am the true vine, and my Father is the husbandman". If we may take this on a human level, which was the only level on which Mary at this time could consider things, we may observe that the Trinitarian concept applies not only to the three snakes growing out of the red (passionate) side of her, but that the whole painting of her dual self and of the vine (which is the same height as herself) is also triple. The black side stands for the frustration with its compensating feelings of superiority, the red side the passion, and the vine the object of her love.

But Mary's psychic make-up is so complex that of these three images the red side of her, with its three phallic snakes, is symbolically "male". The vine thus comes to symbolise her femininity. Since her father was the only man to have aroused any passion in her before she came into analysis (she had worshipped him almost as a god), the purple colour of the flower symbolises the incestuous element in this love-fantasy, as also does the purple atmosphere with which she paints the whole of this side of the picture. But she is herself no longer purple as she was when sitting on the purple thistle in Painting 2. For through the phallic intelligence (positive animus) which the analysis is now developing in her—and which is particularly noticeable in the enquiring attitude of the snake issuing from her head and looking at the flower—she is becoming differentiated from what the purple represents and is more able to examine it.

227

It will be noticed also that the vine itself grows from the snake issuing from her foot. The vine thus bears witness to her true nature as a woman, clinging as a vine is, and receptive as is a flower symbolising her psycho-sexuality. This is now open to be fertilised by the snake representing her intelligence. The vine is thus in direct contrast to the dragon's claw of her otherwise destructive schizoid possessiveness. It is no contradiction to equate both Christ and the essential Mary with the vine, because "Christ" means the Self, of which the phrase is true which he spoke to his disciples saying, "Without me ye can do nothing".

Mary is now recapitulating many of her past dreams and fantasies on a more mature level, so we may here recall the dream of the "three sisters" preceding the Piper of the Snakes. We may hazard the suggestion that, as Christ was not only the vine but also the bread of life, the vine with its purple flower in the present fantasy may also symbolise a more sublimated aspect of the "old woman with the sores". She had offered Mary and her mother the "hunk of bread and butter". Mary was then "afraid of infection and would have refused" had not her mother insisted that they would thereby gain the wisdom of the gypsies. And it was this acceptance that opened up the way for the Piper to pipe in the snakes.

A gypsy is an "outcast" as was Christ, and as Mary's essential femininity had also been. Anything outcast is also feared by the conventional. But Mary's fear is lessening; so that she can now look at her own femininity from a more detached point of view, now less incestuous. For things in her are getting separated out, which is one meaning of the Trinity as "three in one", not only "one". For the number "one" means symbolically "undifferentiated", indicating a primitive wholeness that is not yet conscious of itself. Such primitive wholeness has first to be split in two, so that each side of the personality may become aware that there is another side, the third factor being the awareness of this duality. Thus "one" becomes first "two" then "three". The third factor in Christian theology is called the Holy Ghost, the function of which is to unite the opposites, which have been formerly confused or else so separated out that neither can admit the existence of the other one.

The great advance Mary has made towards becoming more human since the early days of the analysis may be appreciated if we compare this painting, so full of feeling, with the arid painting of the threefold flowering plant in

Figure 37. "The crowned hermaphrodite. From a manuscript, *De alchimia*, attributed to Thomas Aquinas, c. 1520." Jung, *Symbols of Transformation*, Plate XVIII.

Painting 1. It was a lifeless Trinitarian design connected with what was then for her a meaningless dogma, and which she put in simply for "decoration".

Two alchemical representations may illustrate the archetypal nature of her present fantasy. One is Figure 37 of the winged "Crowned Hermaphrodite", standing on a double-headed dragon which it has overcome and thus can use for good its transformed strength. The other is Figure 38 of the "Hermaphrodite with three serpents and one serpent" and below it a three-headed snake. This figure of the alchemical hermaphrodite resembles Mary's fantasy with regard not only to the two sides: one side with three serpents, and the other, has one serpent—in Mary's case, one arm. The latter is her stupid and unsubtle side with little possibility of growth because of the pride that hinders it. The subtle side is the red side with the *"three snakes, all of one mind"* through their connection with the purple-flowering vine. That is the harbinger of growth as the next painting will show.

Figure 38. "Hermaphrodite with three serpents and one serpent. Below, the three-headed mercurial dragon. 'Rosarium Philosophorum', in *Artis auriferae* (1593)." Jung, *Psychology and Alchemy*, Fig. 54

PAINTING 30 (Fantasy) 11 November 1958

The Fourfold Tree-Self

Two days later the drama of Mary's search for her fundamental femininity was carried a further step forward in the painting of a new fantasy. It was started in one of her apparently inconsequential moods, she said, *"for the fun of trying out my new paint brush"*. To begin with she had merely the desire to paint the brown trunk of a tree. But as she painted it the fantasy gripped her, a red snake grew out of the tree-trunk's "head", and a purple snake emerged out of its roots, and at that moment she became aware that the tree symbolised herself.

There had been previous trees which she had furnished with eyes and a mouth to indicate her recognition that they had something to do with her emotional attitudes, but this was the first time that she had become fully aware of it. The result was the most complex picture of her emotional condition yet achieved. There was, however, the usual contrast between her description of the finished picture and her account, when later asked for it, of the order in which she had painted its various parts. It was the latter that actually led to a far greater understanding of the realisations that were taking place in her during the act of painting itself. It will be simplest to give both her descriptions here so that they may be considered together. Her description of the finished picture was:

"I am the tree. My roots are in water (not a very firm foundation). The red

230

snake growing from my head wants to make friends with the purple snake growing from my roots.

"They can't reach each other, and pull me between them so that I flap around in ineffective anger.

"I think the purple snake is the less fierce of the two, but he would grow if he came out into the daylight and could control the red snake.

"The tree branches are poor and stunted because the snakes take so much energy. I think these branches are my outside life."

The order of painting was:

"The tree was painted first, and I did not know what else would be in the picture. Then the red snake grew. Then the ground, which I made black as it is very hard and will be difficult for the snake to get through. Then I painted the water, and the purple snake grew from the tree roots.

"While I was painting the purple snake I knew that I was the tree, so then I painted the tree purple too, and put in the arms and face. The leaves came last."

There are many allusions in all this to Mary's previous fantasies; we will begin by linking this fantasy with that of her split self (Painting 29).

Purple Snake growing from its (Mary's) roots.
Transformation of incest fantasies.

As in Painting 29 (Split Self) the tree in this present fantasy is divided vertically into two halves (cf. also Painting 27, Divided Head) of which, as in all these paintings, the right half symbolises ego consciousness (*"I think these branches are my outside life"*). The left-hand side contains the elements of psychic consciousness. Another important link with Painting 29 is that the red snake here issuing from Mary's head and yearning towards the purple snake corresponds to the red snake coming from her head in the split self painting and yearning towards the purple flower. This would suggest that what the red snake is so fascinated by is not essentially either the purple flower of the vine nor yet the purple snake but what the colour purple itself symbolises. Up till now this has been her incest fantasies.

The colour purple has all along appeared in many different forms as a projection onto objects external to her own ego. This appears also to be the case with regard to the purple flower of Painting 29. But here is a subtle indi-

231

cation: these projections may be about to be withdrawn and inwardised, as the vine bearing the purple flower is rooted in Mary's (snake-headed) foot. The three red snakes emanating from the red side of her in that fantasy all being "of one mind" means that the red snake growing from her *head* must also know that the vine itself is part of her. What has thus happened is that the purple colour of the flower in Painting 29 has now descended into the purple snake issuing from the tree's roots, so that the two images of Mary and the vine in Painting 29 have now coalesced into the present image of Mary as the tree. [Her purple over-brushing is visible only on the snake. Ed.]

Part of the symbolism of the tree is that it cannot move from where it is. It cannot walk or run, as animals or adult human beings can, either to explore the world or to escape from awkward situations. A tree cannot pursue a desired object as animals can. It must accept what is. So, like the Buddhist Bo tree or the Christian cross (so often called a tree), it stands for contemplation or "inwardisation"—the withdrawal of projections and a centring of the attention upon the inner life. Thus, in this fantasy of Mary as a tree, the power that had been lost to her—squandered or thrown away in her projected incest fantasies—was now becoming available to her. It could build inner strength which is no longer merely passive as was the purple flower in Painting 29 (on a level with her head and which she was only looking at). It is now actively at work in her in the form of the purple snake issuing from her roots. This downward movement of what was indicated by the colour purple reintroduces that other expansion of Mary's psyche already seen in several paintings, notably Paintings 19 and 23. It is the "up and down" dimension which is also equivalent to "outer and inner".

Mary's previously unrecognised Tree–Selves

It is this double dichotomy of "right and left" and "up and down" that gives rise to the fourfold structure of this, Mary's Tree-Self, divided as it is into four distinct quarters. Each has a different characteristic. The gradual development of the four parts appear upon examination of Mary's centrally significant trees.

Consider Painting 4: the standard rose tree (or Tree of Life) onto which Mary was being grafted early in her analysis. As has Mary's tree-self in the present fantasy it had a right and a left side. But there was no indication as to what was happening to the tree's roots. At that time the grafting process was associated in her mind almost exclusively with the analyst, who featured as one of the human-headed buds. What was there depicted as happening above the ground referred to what was happening in the sphere of Mary's external relationships at the time of painting it.

But Painting 5 showed something very different. The greater part of her attention was concentrated on what was happening to the tree's roots which, through successive layers of earth and water, were drawing their sustenance from the father's corpse. Then she also identified herself with the corpse with regard to its white ribs associated with her own tuberculosis. That period had included her near-death experience and her intense incest awareness. Painting 5 was, therefore, imagery *in depth* referring to the most intimate secrets of her past inner life, being readmitted at that moment into consciousness.

Mary's reluctance to face up to the stultifying aspects of these father-incest fantasies and her consequent ambivalence was graphically expressed in Painting 15: the Tree Trying to Root Itself. It was uncertain in its mind: to become rooted in the earth or to be drawn up into the purple cloud. Mary painted the cloud in the top right hand quarter of the picture. Its position "up in the air" and to the right is most significant: it was in the quarter diametrically opposite to that now occupied by the purple snake of Mary's Tree-Self. The change in the position of the images depicted in her fantasies (in this case the position of the colour purple and what it signifies) indicates a shifting of awareness from one part of the psyche to another.

The psychic movement has been first from right to left, from the purple cloud of Painting 15 to the purple flower of the vine in Painting 29, then downwards to the purple snake growing from Mary's tree-roots. In each case the image has gained in the amount of psychic awareness that was invested in it, being at first (Painting 15) a cloud, then (Painting 29) a flower, and now (Painting 30) a snake. Her psychic awareness had now evolved to the feeling of one-ness with which Mary now paints her whole Tree-Self purple too. Painting 15 was a crucial one for another reason also, that of the reversibility of the World Tree it symbolised: its roots can become the branches and the branches can become the roots. For it was at that critical point in the analysis that what had been directed outwardly by Mary in the form of her father-incest fantasies was beginning to be directed inwardly, in such a way that the whole tree of her life began to be turned "upside down".

Barrier of "black earth"

But Mary is still in conflict. For though she says, *"The red snake growing from my head wants to make friends with the purple snake growing from my roots"*. She adds, *"They can't reach each other, and pull me between them so that I flap around in ineffectual anger"*. This she expresses by the flapping arms which she adds to the tree.

What is the factor still keeping them apart? This is the familiar layer of "black earth" which we have met with in so many of her fantasies, particularly Paintings 19 and 23. It separates her ego consciousness from the archetypal figures (mostly dragons and snakes) of her psychic consciousness. It is this layer of black earth which transforms the present fantasy of Mary's Tree-Self from being only a twofold one with differentiated "right and left' sides into a fourfold one differentiated as well into "up and down". This being the first tree which Mary has fully acknowledged as symbolising herself, it represents a notable advance in the expansion of her personality.

THE ORDER OF PAINTING

Mary's description of the finished painting gives us no indication of how this came about. This we can understand only by following her account of how she painted it, that is to say, the order in which its various features came into her

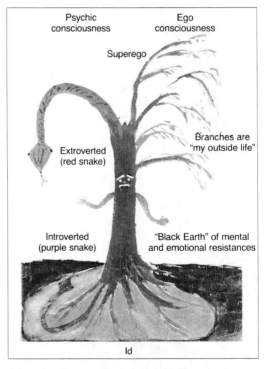

Figure 39. Diagram for Painting 30

234

mind. These show the emotional processes that were at work in her during the act of painting.

Red snake

After the brown trunk *"the red snake grew"*, thus replacing the innocent red roses of Painting 4 with something much more real and powerful. The red snake was first encountered in Paintings 8 and 9 when it became luminous. It was the same snake which in Painting 26 was struggling upwards so as to rescue the small green tree symbolising her basic personality and which the double-headed dragon was trying to devour within her brain. This rescuing operation was accomplished during a burst of anger in Painting 27: her Divided Head. For the first time Mary became conscious of her dual personality. This snake was *"very wise"* and was a hero in his rage. It was the release of this rage, partly directed against the analyst (and accepted by him), which had thus brought about that expansion of her personality.

The red snake also symbolised one-pointedness, promoting the unity of Mary's personality, as seen in the three red snakes "all of one mind" of Painting 29. The huge red snake in the present fantasy symbolises Mary's desire and rage combined in their extremest form. Rage always conceals desire. We have seen in the accounts of what had recently been happening how Mary's furies had often been quite unrelated to external facts. The analyst's counterattacks had then re-directed them towards the real enemy, which lay not outside but within. The progress of Mary's new knowledge was reflected by the red snake springing from her head and growing upward "into the air"—into unrelated fantasy and vain regret and ineffectual hostilities. But it became so lonely that it could but change its direction and be attracted downwards towards the earth of her own inner psyche. The real problem lay there.

The "hard" black earth

So Mary's psychic consciousness now prompts her to paint in *"the ground, which I made black as it is very hard and will be difficult for the snake to get through"*. This was the familiar "black earth" of her resistances.

It was this change in direction on the part of the red snake (as the carrier of her conscious personal emotions) that helped to introduce into the fantasy, in addition to the former factor of "right and left", the one of "up and down". This is a great advance on Painting 29 of her Split Self, where her red feeling side had had its back to her black side. This had symbolised, as we there learnt, the element of "pride" in these her "black" resistances, a blackness which she then for the first time described in Painting 30 as *"hard"*. So now the red snake is *facing* the black earth and recognises for the first time what a barrier it is.

It is a new gain in Mary's consciousness, expressed also in the fact that the gap in the black earth, which appeared in Painting 19 and again in Painting 23, is now filled by the trunk of Mary's own Tree-Self, with branches above and roots below.

Water

But the black earth still acts as a barrier of which Mary is now conscious as being something within herself. So what does psychic consciousness then bring to her mind? She tells us, *"Then I painted the water"*.

What then is the connection between the water and "black earth"? This water is not sea water, which as a mother-symbol has already been discussed. It is more like spring water or the "well of life"—a symbol of the male. In Painting 24, in which Mary first began to recognise her dragon-like nature and the need to extricate herself from it, this water first appeared as a small pool at the foot of the good "mothering tree" as a symbol for the fertilising father–principle. We know moreover that the blackness of the "black earth", which had come to symbolise Mary's frustrated father-incest fantasies, is also archetypally symbolic of the warm darkness of the womb and of a good mother-child relationship. It was only because Mary had experienced her mother as being so "hard" that the transference had taken place in her life from the mother to the father. This had resulted in her confused values, including the lack of a creative father-principle, now being re-born in her in the analysis. It is this principle which is here symbolised by where the tree's roots are. But Mary truly remarks that the water by itself is *"not a very firm foundation"*. This is because, in terms of Mary's fantasy, the water and the earth are separated—not appropriate for anchoring and infiltration: the earth is too "hard" and the water too "fluid". Earth being archetypally female and spring water male, this is symbolic of a lack of unity between the parents in her external life and consequently of her own inner disunity.

236

But one of the functions of the water might be to soften the hard earth or moisten it so that the roots can penetrate and draw more sustaining nourishment from it.

Painting herself (the tree) purple

But how is this to come about? Her psychic consciousness provides the answer by the dramatic revelation of the *"purple snake"* now growing from her roots, having the water as its element, whereon, as she describes, *"while I was painting the purple snake I knew that I was the tree, so* **then I painted the tree purple too and put in the arms and face**". If we examine the painting closely we shall see how this was done. The trunk and branches and the roots, which had all formerly been brown, having been all repainted purple, the same colour as the purple snake, symbolised her own new-found independent femininity.

This repainting was like a "blush". In clothed communities we usually see a blush only on the face. But when under strong emotion we speak of our whole body sometimes as "burning hot". Among primitive peoples with brown skins and with a minimum of clothing, the sudden access of strong passion may be seen in a blush extending over the whole body turning the brown to something nearer black. When the emotion is one of anger it is a terrifying sight, a warning to enemies. When Mary painted her brown tree-self with the darker colour of purple it was not with anger, but with this strong emotional realisation of her femininity—something no longer projected incestuously but as her very own.

There is thus the strongest possible contrast between this repainting of Mary's Tree-Self purple and the purple painting of the "unknown girl" and of the thistle in Painting 2 (over six years before). This former fantasy had been entirely unlinked up with her conscious life. But now the two factors are joined. She paints the tree purple and says, *"I am the tree"*.

The fierceness of her snakes

Mary was still psychically virginal. The hard black earth persisted in her fantasy, symbolising the combined self-delusive pride and fear which were so deeply ingrained in her psyche. It is for this reason too that Mary thinks of all

237

her snakes as being "fierce" as well as "wise". But as she says, *"I think the purple snake is the less fierce of the two, but he would grow if he came out into the daylight and could control the red snake".*

The fierceness of both snakes is due to their separation and to their consequent longing to unite. In Freudian terms we may think of the purple snake as being a function of instinct or the id and of the red snake as symbolising an aspect of the superego. A glance at the way in which Mary has painted these two snakes will show how each mirrors the other in that, while the red snake grows first upwards and then curves downward toward the purple snake, in the same way but in the opposite direction the purple snake grows downwards and then bends upward toward the red snake. Their separation is the cause of their ferocity, for one ferocity calls forth another one, since if superego has been too fiercely repressive of instinct, instinct becomes fierce also in trying to assert itself. The red snake appears to be more full of anger than the purple snake, reflecting Mary's growing consciousness of the repressed anger that has so debilitated her. But she has now reached a stage in her analysis in which she realises this, and at the same time the possibility of love replacing anger. This includes the realisation that the potential power for solving her problems now lies less with the red snake growing from her head than with the much wiser and more humble purple snake which is already nosing its way at the black earth from underneath—that is to say from within her. It means also that the more Mary could become aware of her own inner worth, the less would her conscious frustrations be.

Red, black, purple

This concept of the red and purple elements separated by the black earth has already been met with in Painting 25, in which the big black stone is interposed between the red booted foot above the pregnant purple dragon, and in Painting 26, in which the black skull acts as a barrier between the red hammer and the purple double-headed dragon resisting it. The present fantasy brings this problem nearer to a solution owing to the movement of the purple snake now active from within. It has enough "darkness" in it to understand the blackness of the black earth and is therefore able to relate to it.

238

The leaves

The revelation of the purple snake leading to the purple Tree-Self is as if the snake caused a new kind of sap to flow through the tree, changing Mary's personality from a primitive to a more complex human one. It led to a yet further development. The stunted branches which symbolised her *"outside life"* now sprouted leaves for, as she said, *"The leaves came last"*. This means that as her inner life begins to stir her outer life also responds with some small sign of personal burgeoning. It will be noted that these leaves are in the diagonally opposite corner of the painting from that occupied by the snake which is psychically "feeding" them.

Comparatively empty fourth quarter

The same does not apply however to the opposite diagonal. For the roots on the right-hand side of her Tree-Self are featureless because the huge red snake, which symbolises the force of her resentment against life, has sucked up all their energy. This stresses the fact that although Mary's outside life finds its expression in her work in the mental hospital, the few friendships she has made there and elsewhere are superficial ones, not yet rooted in real mutual regard.

This is why Mary says that *"the tree branches"* which represent her outside life *"are stunted because the snakes take so much energy"*.

The four quarters

We are now in a position to appreciate the fourfold structure of Mary's psyche as seen in the four quarters of her Tree-Self, divided as it is into both right and left sides and above and below the layer of black earth. For, as in Paintings 27 and 29, the right-hand side symbolises ego consciousness while the left side contains the elements of psychic consciousness, symbolised by the snakes. But there is a complication here: the same creative opposition is expressed in what is above and what below the layer of black earth. The difference between these two pairs of opposites, as has already been partly explained, is that the contrast between "right and left" above the ground refers to Mary's relationship with the outside world (both as a mental nurse and with the analyst), while "up and down" refers not to the outer world but to her relationship with her own inner life, symbolised by the purple snake.

OPPOSITE MEANINGS CONTAINED IN THE SYMBOL

One of the most impressive features of this analysis has been the demonstration of the fact that any symbol can have two opposite meanings. Part of the healing process is an increasing awareness of this fact, leading to a greater subtlety of perception and the ability to allow the more negative features of any complex to be transformed into more positive ones. Thus through the acceptance of the bad, the good may be achieved. The transformation process with regard to the colour purple has been no simple one but has passed through many phases. It is not finished yet, as we shall see in its two opposite meanings in Painting 31. We have seen a similar variety of meanings with regard to the colour red, ranging from love to hate, from heroism to despair. In the same way the colour black, which has often appeared so negative, has its positive value too, as will be seen in the next painting, 31.

PAINTING 31 (ANGRY SPLASHING) 14 NOVEMBER 1958

The Black Square

After the self-realisation that had come to her when she re-painted the brown tree purple, Mary was naturally concerned about the hard layer of black earth. This still prevented the meeting of her red and purple snakes, and she felt that this blockage in her fantasy painting corresponded somehow with her own "black moods". So I suggested that she should try, if possible, to paint these moods.

She said she had no visual fantasy representing them, and that no sheet of paper of the size she had so far used could possibly contain the amount of frustration she felt. Following up this line of thought I said, "Well, why not get some larger ones?" Apart from some of her earlier paintings on sheets measuring only 11" by 8", most of those painted up till now had been 14" by 10". But she now bought herself a block of sheets measuring 26" by 20", and on the first of these she set to work, splashing on the paints. The result was what at first appeared to be a messy jumble of colours with, in the center, a large black square which, as she said, finally "forced itself" on her. As usual, however, her description of the order in which she had smeared the different colours on was the illuminating factor, showing the sequence of her changing moods while painting it.

Black downward streak (anger) and flames of satisfied release

She said, *"I started by painting some black downward streaks"* which may be seen in the top left-hand corner of the painting, symbolising both the frustration that she felt and a certain phallic (upright) violence that went with it.

"Then I almost covered them with the curved splashes of red and yellow. These felt like flames and I enjoyed painting them."

This is a tribute to the success of the analyst's attacks upon her secret complexes. His method was based on the hope that in so doing her real passion might be aroused and come into the open and in this way she could enjoy the feeling of release and power which its acceptance brought to her. The warmth generated in their relationship was also becoming much more real and down to earth than formerly, when the analyst had felt he must be careful not to awake hostility so deep that she would not be able to cope with it.

The yellow oily streak that "nothing could get through"

But this in turn aroused her latent fears of what would happen if she really did let herself go—not so much in anger as in hidden desire. For, as she said, *"Then I felt more disturbed and painted the patch of yellow at the bottom of the paper. This seemed thick and oily, as if nothing could get through it"*. It was the same yellow that she had used together with the red to paint the flames that had been such a release, so that the analyst found it difficult to understand why what at first had been such joy to paint had now become what she described as such an "oily" barrier. Nor could she explain it herself. But a review of some of her past fantasy paintings helped to provide the clue. She had always used yellow with red to give the energy to flames (see Paintings 12, 27, 28), that is to say, the feeling of libido that they indicate. But this libido when externalised had always had in it the element of fear, particularly in Paintings 12 (the double-headed serpent threatening her) and 28 (the Flaming Dragon Man). But none had given her the joy of personal release like that of the "flames" in the present fantasy.

Apart from these the use of the colour yellow had been rare in her fantasies. There had been the yellow streak in the sky of Painting 1 which seemed to indicate a kind of dawn, and the lilies also had yellow centres. This was at a time when she had not yet become aware of the ensnaring aspect of her father-incest fantasies. The problem presented itself to her, however, first in Painting 7 (The Dragon Waiting to be Born), in which she is uncertain whether the yellow-coloured luminous globe at the top of the picture to which the snakes are flying is sun or moon (male or female, the father or the mother), indicating the confusion she was in with regard to "which parent was which". Who was her real mother: the mother who had given birth to her but had spurned her, or the father who took on the mother role? In Painting 8, seven months after that, the yellow reappears not in the sky but as the light shining in the window of her underworld city, revealing the red snake (phallic emblem) of her desire, which became luminous too (Painting 9). This had happened at a time when she had struck out on her own to become a student mental nurse. It indicated the access of power derived from the active male principle thus operating in her. But this did not release her from continued father-incest fantasies as seen in Painting 16, in which she fantasied herself naked and helpless, tied by golden (yellow) chains in a black vault symbolising the "father's womb." In Painting 21 she is still similarly chained but is beginning to be freed from them by the process of dismemberment.

The colour yellow in all these paintings was *outside* her, associated with the father both as a "saviour" (from the mother) in the form of light (Paintings 1, 7), and as the possessor of the coveted semen of her incest fantasies which, unfulfilled, bound her to him with bonds that seemed at first almost unbreakable. But once Mary had realised that the problem lay within herself and not outside, her picture of herself had changed. Thus in Painting 26 the colour yellow reappeared *within* herself in the form of the three yellow swords with which the devouring monster within her own body was trying to hold back the red snake from rescuing the small tree. This tree symbolised the breast, which it does in Painting 27 as well, for this is the first nourisher of the tree of life. So we can say that here the colour yellow was connected in her mind also with the idea of milk and "giving", which in her childhood had been so dissatisfactory. For it was not the "milk of human kindness" that she had experienced but its reverse, in the form of frustrations that had "bogged her down" early in life.

This gives us some indication of what the colour yellow meant for her,

243

and why it should now form an "oily", sticky barrier that *that nothing could get through*". It stood, therefore, for her reaction to the frustrations she had suffered both "at the breast" and with regard to her milk-substitute, the inseminating fluid of the phallic principle. Both of these substances are life-giving when used as nature meant, but cloy or make a mess when spilt, misused or misapplied. Then they can be like glue and in turn coagulate, just like the "hard black earth" forming a barrier in Mary's other fantasies.

The black streak underneath symbolising herself

The juxtaposition of this yellow streak and of the subsequent black horizontal streak which Mary painted under it, shows the connection between the "oiliness" of the yellow and the "hardness" of the layer of black earth. In previous fantasies her psyche had erected the blackness as a secondary and less penetrable barrier, to save her from awareness of the primary horror connected with the yellow substances. They, however, were fluid as the "black earth" was not, and we have seen in Painting 30 (her Tree-Self) how moisture was needed to soften it. To soften means psychically to understand, especially where anger is concerned. It means withdrawing the projections so as to realise, to some extent, oneself. So it is significant in the state of fluid change that Mary now was in (exemplified in the change to purple in her Tree-Self fantasy), that as soon as she became aware of the "oily" cloying nature of the yellow streak in her (adumbrating her incest fantasies), the next psychic movement that she had was that *"The black below it came next, and I thought of it as being me"*.

She had thus reached rock bottom in her awareness that the hard layer of black earth was indeed part of herself. And by this realisation she at one stroke achieved two things. First of all the yellow element in her ("yellow" also for "jealousy", which is the unconscious factor in incest fantasies) ceased to be "oily" or cloying but turned into the illumination in Painting 33. Oil is thick or "hard" compared to fertilising water: she had now taken responsibility for her hardness of heart and thus was on the way to mollifying it. And secondly, the layer of "black earth" from now on disappeared out of her fantasies since she had come to terms with it. For the blackness of ignorance coupled with compulsive resistances based on false thinking was well on the way to being changed into the wisdom of her snakes. This will be seen also in the form of the internalised black snake of Painting 33.

Note that the black streak which she now painted in and felt to be "herself" was a horizontal one symbolising an attitude of feminine acceptance, as opposed to the first phallic upright splashes indicating anger. It became, on the contrary, a sign of blackness of the womb, recapturing that state of "unknowing" which had preceded the formation of her "yellow" jealous incest-complexes. These had been formed since birth. But it was not a primitive unknowing such as a foetus has. It was an unknowing consciously achieved through letting incest fantasies "drop off" and thus recapturing something like primitive innocence by means of conscious thought. Her old pattern was the unconscious rationalising self-deceptive processes. These we have already seen to be included in the meaning of "blackness" in an adult who, however, is still infantile. The blackness records unconscious resentment at being possessed by these processes, for they do not lead to fulfillment of life.

Black square, a symbol for the Self

This might be thought to be unwarranted speculation were it not for the next psychic movement that Mary experienced. Her act of painting had brought about a release of energy with a remarkable effect. She said:

"I still had the black paint brush in my hand when something took hold of me and I knew that there had to be a square in the middle. I was very surprised as I don't like the shape, but I felt it very real and important".

So there is now a third use of the colour black combining the vertical (phallic, self-assertive) and horizontal (feminine and accepting) motifs in this dictate from her psychic consciousness. It had forced itself through in spite of her conscious preference. She was so surprised at its square shape that she added, *"I wanted to find out more about it"*. She then did so by taking sheet after sheet and daubing them with various colours, many of which developed squares in them. Then she had dreams about square rooms and visions of black cubes, from all of which it now emerged that it was the "shape of her psyche". This meant that her former chaotic resistances and incestuous projective identifications were now getting resolved into something truly personal and individual. They had to do with the square "enclosed garden of her soul" in which she had first met the hanging boy (Painting 3), the four dismembered limbs (Painting 21), and the fourfold nature of her Tree-Self in the last painting (30).

The square (and still more the cube) is one of the well known symbols of the Self—of individuality in its most basic form. Why then, although she felt this square to be "very real and important", did she not like its shape? For the same reason evidently as she had not liked the oily yellow streak symbolising her loss of soul. For in any pair of opposites that are suspicious of one another there is a mutual revulsion and feeling of awkwardness. Just as the healthy side of her was now beginning to be wary of her old incest desires and identification with the parents (or parental images), so also it is always difficult to give up one's dependence fantasies and to begin to be one's independent self. This means to think. The opposite leanings we have seen to be included in the meaning of the colour black.

Square-headed snakes

Squareness indicates the consciousness of self and the possibility of psychic wholeness as an individual freed from compulsive identifications with or hostile reactions against parental influence. The dragon in Mary's fantasies had for the most part so far symbolised these compulsions. This principle of independent individuality has throughout these fantasies been connoted by her "wise" snakes: they have sometimes been worshipped and sometimes feared but have always been detached and unworried except when thwarted by the "blackness" of her resistances (Painting 17). These snakes are often "fierce" as well as "wise", their fierceness being due mainly to Mary's fear of being herself and thus offending the parental images. So it is not surprising that, being the spearheads of psychic consciousness, from Painting 8 onwards her snakes have all had "square" heads—a feature that had been unexplained until the present fantasy showed what all this squareness meant in terms of personal wholeness, positive animus and spirit.

Mary so disliked the square shape in ego consciousness for fear of being what she really was—an ordinary human being with normal desires and capabilities. But it turned out to have been, through these fantasies, a favourite shape assumed by psychic consciousness. It needed to break through her all-pervading mist of incest fantasies and the dragonlike compulsions which had existed due to them.

Autonomous Dragon Complex and "Wise Snake"

Not long after the intensive period of analysis that has just been described, for external reasons the treatment lapsed until about six months later. During this period much of what had been gained had had time to be consolidated.

Mary had now settled down to paint her fantasies not on the very large sheets used for daubing her black square but on medium-sized sheets measuring 20" by 14". There is room in this volume to include only two of these.

Painting 32 contrasts the functions of the destructive dragon and the healing snake, and shows the colour black in its new mediating role. It has an upper and a lower part. The upper part consists of an almost square framework supported by pillars on either side. Between them stands Mary, headless and painted black with her arms raised and fastened to what look like beams which end still further up in purple dragon's claws. From her neck protrudes another beam supporting a purple dragon's head with its mouth wide open and with a red tongue lolling out of it in a menacing but rather futile way. A kind of vine is twined around her body and around the empty space where her head might have been.

The earth on which this structure stands is brown. Beneath it in the lower part of the picture is a solid looking vault containing a red snake with a human head gazing at a purple fish. This has somehow climbed out of the water down below and is now standing on its tail, reciprocally gazing at the snake upon a grassy bank.

Mary had had no time before bringing this painting to write more than the briefest comment on it, which had to be amplified by questioning. What she wrote was:

"The black person in the middle of the picture is me. I have lost my head, which has gone underground and joined on to a snake's body. I have been used as part of a building and have been there a long time without moving. A plant has climbed up me. The head and claws of a dragon have been attached to my neck and arms".

When asked about the dragon, she said, *"This is like me. Whenever the dragon moves his claws I have to move my arms, because I am fastened to them. When he jerks, I jerk too".* This is a typical statement of one who cannot help reacting to certain hated stimuli in exactly the same way as the hated stimuli themselves. We have had ample opportunity of seeing how this autonomous complex has ruled Mary's life. In early infancy it had caused the infant, out of self-defence, unwittingly to react just as its mother had. This reaction was later reinforced by a similar reaction to the father's possessive/frustrating attitude towards her, exemplified by his saying that she "would never leave him".

This fantasy would thus have been a merely horrifying one, were it not for the fact that Mary was now for the first time fully realising the extent to which she had been "possessed". It is in fact a great advance on any previous fantasy. If we compare the strength and vigour of this fantasy despite the baffling situation it portrays, with the feebleness of the almost foetus-like Mary in Painting 24 (only dimly aware of the power that the purple dragon exerted over her), we may appreciate the greater awareness she now has of its crippling influence. She had been learning how to deal with it.

Dragon as autonomous complex. "Operators and Things"

Before, however, coming on to this contrast between the dragon and the snake, it will be well for us to understand more fully the meaning of the dragon's power over her and how it operates. The best description that I know of how such forces may grip and control a life is in a book[80] written under an assumed name by a woman who had had an acute schizophrenic attack last-

---

80. *Operators and Things: The Inner Life of a Schizophrenic,* by Barbara O'Brien, London, Elek Books Ltd., 1960.

ing six months. During this period she imagined the world to be divided into what she called "Operators" and "Things". The Things were people like herself who, having no real minds of their own, were the unwilling victims of Operators who sometimes were real people able to influence the Things without their knowing it. They might more often be hallucinated images of people who could read Things' minds and pour ideas into them. "An Operator can extend and probe into the mind of a Thing. He can tap the Thing's mind and discover what is going on there, and even feed thoughts to the Thing's mind."[81] "People lived out their lifetimes, I reflected, taking strange actions, never aware that their actions were motivated by some Operator."[82] Things of this kind had "open heads", which would be like Mary having no psychic incest barrier, and it is on account of this that the Operators can get inside. The fact that Operators can be either real people or imaginary ones who talk, corresponds to the fact that in early infancy the Operators are the parents or any others in a position to mould the child. But once their influence has been sufficiently introjected so as to become part of the apparent personality, they are "hallucinated" just like Mary's dragons in her fantasies.

Whether from without or from within, they have in any case access to what the author calls the "latticework', by which she means the habit patterns in what one of her Operators called "the outer layer of the brain". We may be reminded of Mary's Painting 26 (the double-headed purple dragon coiled inside her skull) by the following account of how one of the Operators, trying to reveal to her the methods they employed, "drew an inner circle inside the outline of the head" and said, "All of that is latticework. Sometimes, the latticework is allowed to grow in much thicker—it depends upon the number of patterns the Thing needs. What they have done in your head has been to scrape some of the latticework away on the sides. Of course, most Things depend on their habit patterns to get them through their daily activities when an Operator isn't around to stimulate them. You would be surprised at how little thinking is done by Things. Most of them just follow patterns some Operator has carefully cultivated in their heads. When latticework is scraped

---

81. Ibid., p. 41.
82. Ibid., p. 50.

away, a Thing finds that he can't think too well. But actually it's not his thinking ability that has been affected. It's just that he has depended upon habit patterns instead of upon thinking." An Operator "knows that the Thing is not responsible for anything it does. It's being controlled entirely by an Operator. A Thing's control is in its habit patterns. When it has nothing but its thinking ability left, the most feeble Operator can control it, because Things can think only to a very limited degree".

The author had many such conversations with her Operators, whom she gradually got to know with the different characteristics that they had. It was through these very conversations, that is to say her facing up to the fact that she was being thus "controlled", that she eventually recovered owing to the self-knowledge she had gained. Thus when she asked "How limited?" was the degree to which Things can think, one Operator said, "I'll tell you this.... If it weren't for Operators, Things would be still wandering in and out of caves".[83] Operators are elements of the psyche, being brought up to ego consciousness.

With deep insight about the healing possibilities of positive regression or breakdown (if it can be used to open one's eyes to one's own faults), the author says, "I had watched men skillfully tear each other to shreds" (in savage business competition) "and had been unable to face that fact in sanity without fear and distaste, and in insanity I had got another chance to see the same picture and a better opportunity to evaluate it objectively". "'Indoctrination' was one of the words I heard most frequently from the Operators. And patiently, bit by bit, the voices had made their points. I had been led from an appreciation of how Operators worked on Things to a point where I could understand...." In the final phase of her schizophrenic episode she became aware of a special Operator without a name whom she called "Something", which we may equate with the "wise snake" in Mary's fantasies. This Something helped her to look at the picture with a shrewder, more realistic eye. This was an important piece of training in "the indoctrination into Operators' techniques. It was important for me to be able to look at the Operators whole and straight, without horror and without fear".[84]

---

83. Ibid., pp. 74-75.
84. Ibid., p. 124.

"When schizophrenia had struck, my unconscious had taken over. It had guided me while my mind had been shattered, had even probably aided in the mental repair."[85] She asks, "Can the unconscious mind think?" and answers, "It appears to search and also to consider, evaluate, weigh…. It can grasp an intricate concept. The conscious mind broods over its problem, and the unconscious, listening to the brooding, grasps the problem…. The answer is rejected by the conscious mind. The conscious mind broods on the reason for the rejection and the unconscious listens, understands…." "The unconscious goes through the thinking processes, arrives at the answer and shoots it up in a geyser of 'intuition'."[86]

This is a remarkable account of how the author learnt from her Operators how they operated upon her, and thus acquired the power they had over her to use for more constructive purposes. For the Operators on the one hand destroy by depriving their victim of individuality, but on the other hand yield up their secret if they are faced squarely enough and earnestly asked how they do it. Mary did not hallucinate Operators in human form and talk to them as the authoress of *Operators and Things* had done, though in the dream illustrated in Painting 1 she had talked to the snake. She had another method of communication: through her fantasies, particularly when she painted them. This was a kind of communication with, on the one hand, the elements of psychic consciousness which came to her in this form, and on the other, with the analyst who had encouraged her to give value to them.

Thus Mary had two main groups of Operators working from within symbolised respectively by her dragons and her snakes taking on different forms. And there was one Operator active from outside in the form of the analyst, whose task it was to mediate so far as possible what the snakes and dragons and other features of her fantasies had to say. The "geyser of intuition" which the author speaks of may thus remind us of the kind of impulse that made Mary paint her Tree-Self purple (Painting 30).

The author also refers to "battlements" from which the Operators can operate. Similarly, Mary herself says of the kind of scaffolding that she was

---

85. Ibid., p. 95
86. Ibid., p. 134

fastened to by the compelling power of the dragon, *"I have been used as part of a building and have been there a long time without moving"*, by which she means moving away from it. The regressive part of her still does not want to move, for one of her constant complaints was, *"If only things never changed. If only I knew that they would always be the same, then I could manage my life accordingly, and there would be no more bother"*. The "building" was that of the parental complexes which she had been imprisoned in or crucified upon. But by the same token she had clung to it with all the fidelity of her love and hatred combined, without until recently having any idea of it. The building has two sides to it, both equally dangerous. Consider the dragon's two claws symbolising the double danger Mary was in: one from the mother's hatred and secret pride (see dragon's claws in Painting 29) and the other from the father's dependent and possessive love. She emphasises the duration of her imprisonment and her fixedness to it by saying that *"A plant has climbed up me"*, which is a symbol in the Krishna myth for a woman clinging to a man and binding him to her. In her private symbolism the vine stood for the "clinging" sentimental kind of love she said she hated most (but indulged in herself).

Vault as the womb of psychic consciousness

But there is much more to this fantasy than this somewhat artificial-looking structure above the ground. There is a dynamic movement in it quite unlike the destructive autonomous complex shown by the dragon's power to manipulate. This she expresses tersely by saying, *"I have lost my head, which has gone underground and joined on to a snake's body"*.

To lose one's head may be to gain one's soul. This means that with the objective realisation of the power that the dragon has had over her she is succeeding in disentangling herself from it. This she does by identifying herself by contrast with the red snake, who with a human head on him is now less fierce and has always been "wise" and able to observe, to be detached and not to be compelled.

This new freedom that Mary has acquired is the direct result of the experience that she had had, while "letting herself go" in Painting 31, of finding that she herself was black. Through becoming conscious of this, the character of the blackness itself had changed from being negative as in Painting 30 (the hard "black earth") and in so many other of her fantasies, such as the angry smears in the beginning of Painting 31. In the form of the black square the fantasy was now positive, symbolising her more self-knowledgeable personality.

This square later acquired a "body" and became a cube, and in the present fantasy (Painting 32) has grown more human still. For just as in Painting 30 her Tree-Self had been suffused with purple, so now her whole clothed body is painted black in a much more formed and conscious way than she has ever painted it before. It is the central figure in the fantasy. This is no longer black in ignorance but, on the contrary, in the knowledge of past ignorance and slavery to the compulsive movements which the dragon had imposed on her. She now openly acknowledges this and is already separated from it: the dragon itself no longer has a body but only head and claws, the body being hers and hers alone. It is already separate from the dragon although still influenced by it.

For, once again, the knowledge of evil is its cure. Thus we have seen in Painting 29 of her Split Self that one component of her "blackness" had been "pride"—the pride of being dragon-like and of being thus superior to common clay. Another feature of her blackness which we had noted had been the negative thinking that had grown up within the void of her frustrated life.

But now her head representing her thinking faculty has fallen off onto the body of the wise snake below. Since she herself is black, that is, is realising her own ignorance and the futility of some of her past ways of thinking, the earth she stands on is no longer black, but brown as earth should be. And underneath this earth there are no longer the shapeless caverns she had had in former fantasies, but there is a solid vault with yet another level of earth beneath, from which the green grass grows with water moistening its roots. This vault symbolises the solid achievement of the analysis, giving her a foundation which she had not had before. It provides adequate protection from the crazy dragon-world above. And, being underground, it is also a container for the archetypal elements of psychic consciousness, and at the same time protects them. But the fact that there is another layer of earth in it, on which grass grows, in contrast to the layer up above that is sterile (except for the clinging, binding plant that grew from it), indicates that it is this deeper level that is the true basis of her potentially individuated personality. The dragon of her still-existing infantile identifications with the parental complexes has been superimposed onto the upper level.

This raises the problem of prenatal life within the womb and of the womb-like situation reproduced in the analysis, in preparation for rebirth out of "the male". Physical birth is out of the maternal womb. Rebirth is always out of the male principle, in this case mediated by the analyst. It introduces or re-introduces into the psyche of the one undergoing such rebirth those elements which, for some reason or other, have been either lost or lacking, either in the womb or in earliest infancy. What had been lacking in her parents' marriage was the principle of effective masculinity. The vault here is triangular, which is symbolically male. It is in this that the healing archetypes appear: the red snake and the purple fish. And her head has fallen down so as to become one with the body of the snake. This may remind us here of how the head of Orpheus, after he had been torn to pieces by the women, sang on, his name meaning "on the river bank". We may associate this expression with the water in the present fantasy symbolising also the father principle.

As a rebirth symbol the large size of the foetus-like head recalls also that of Mary's head surrounded by purple mist in Painting 24. But Mary is now no longer in the purple mist. Her head on the body of the wise red snake, which stands for the saving element of effective masculinity (positive animus), is in communion with the purple fish. This through its association with the purple snake in Painting 30, represents her own essential femininity. Mary, when asked about this confrontation, spoke of it as the *"snake talking to the fish"*. This may recall also the large fish in Painting 23, which was the only one of the three fishes in that fantasy which was not afraid of the dragon caught by its tail (Leviathan) but was facing up to it.

The dual meaning of "purple"

The purple fish is in the same quarter in this fantasy as was the purple snake at the root of Mary's Tree-Self (Painting 30). Now that Mary has recognised the blackness as being her own there is no longer the black barrier between the red snake and the purple fish.

So now, for the first time, the two opposite meanings of the colour purple are present in one fantasy. There is on the one hand the autonomous complex manipulating her in the form of the purple dragon overhead. Up till now she has been unable to resist it because she has been tied to it. It is all "up in the air", as a superego complex which was imposed on her from the outside. On the other hand within the womb of her own psyche, which she is now getting more familiar with, there is the fish, no longer in the water but on dry land. She is facing it and having intimate communion with it without being interfered with by the dragon because of the protection afforded by the arched vault. This is no longer a "hard shell" having to be crushed or broken through but is symbolic of a strong individuality.

The red tongue of the dragon is the same colour as the red snake, emphasising the paradox that every complex contains its own potential opposite.

PAINTING 33 (Fantasy) 1 July 1959

Internalised Black Snake

This is the last painting connected with this phase of Mary's analysis. It is in a sense the simplest of them all owing to the fact that she was by now so much more conscious of her complexes and less secretive than she had been. She was indeed in conflict about whether to carry on with the intensive analysis that she had now been having for several months or to go back to work. The fact that this conflict was now a clear issue may have been the reason for her using only the two main colours, red and black, apart from the purple mist surrounding the black snake and the yellow shafts of "lightning or bright sunshine" impinging on her head.

"This was painted because I felt tense and unhappy about going back to work and in the hope that painting would make me sleepy. (It didn't.)

"The picture started with the outline of my head painted consciously, because I had a headache. Then the black snake came by itself and was surrounded by purple mist, then the yellow, which may be either flashes of lightning or bright sunshine.

"I felt that more would happen if I was not anxious and tense, but I couldn't let myself go into the darkness properly. The scattered pieces of a body came out of the dark to meet me. I don't know what they are about but wondered if they had anything to do with my chest getting better. As I painted them I had the feeling that it might get well by itself. It's almost the first time I have really believed this.

"The snake is trying to push its way out of the head, but the claws hinder it. When it gets out it may be the root of some rare tree, but it will still be a snake, so the tree will be living in a human or rather animal way (it may have little snakes on it instead of fruit) and it will be a tree of healing rooted in my head.

"The yellow light is very bright. It may be drawing the snake out but at the same time being painful to the head."

Headache. The snake's square head. The yellow light.

As usual, the headache Mary mentions is due to the conflict she is in; the reason for it is much more conscious and more related to an actual decision she has to make than had been formerly the case. Her conflict when producing Painting 26 was due to the opposition between the double-headed dragon and the hammer-blows delivered outside. The analyst's attacks had in the main now done their work; they had been accepted by Mary as healing things.

In this regard we can again recapitulate her use of some of the colours red and black. This appears first in Painting 4 of her being grafted onto the tree of life. In Painting 25 the crushing boot is red and the stone black. In Painting 26 the colours of the hammer were also red and black, the feeling and the love, opposed by the critical faculty trying to "knock sense" into her head. In Painting 27 there were the three "friendly arrows" which were the "feeling" colour red. Painting 29 depicts her own Split Self, the black symbolising her negative feelings of superiority (the dragon's claw impinging as a warning to that black side of her). In the present fantasy, in contrast to the

258

black colour of her head with the red snake inside it (Paintings 26 and 27), her head is red with the black snake inside. This means that it is now the feeling side of her that is presented to the analyst and to the world, with the black critical faculty internalized—not projected as a hostile defence.

We are now in a position to appreciate still more the meaning of the snake's "square head" (Painting 31). It is the spearhead of psychic consciousness, now trying to penetrate her skull from the inside to meet the yellow shafts of light. But there is a great contrast between the yellow shafts, here representing light, and the yellow oily streak (Painting 31) symbolising the cloying nature of incestuous desire. In the present fantasy the lights are the opposite of sticky and cloying and symbolise illumination. Her habitual ambivalence, however, still makes her doubtful whether they are "flashes of lightning" suggesting fear, or "bright sunshine". So the cause of her headache is now no longer fear of external hostility but probably fear of creative relationship. At the same time it is fear of her most secret thoughts being exposed: *"The yellow light is very bright. It may be drawing the snake out but at the same time being painful to the head".*

"The snake is trying to push its way out of the head, but the claws hinder it". These are the dragon's claws, so often met with associated with the pain in the neck, the catching of the throat or the "stiffneckedness" (Painting 26). Mary says of the black snake that it may be the root of some rare tree, but it may have little snakes on it instead of fruit and will be a tree of healing rooted in her head.

The Kundalini Snake

In our discussion about the snake and tree in Paintings 26 and 27 it had been suggested that the snake symbolised the spinal column, and the small green tree the brain-stem with the primitive hind brain springing out of it. So when Mary makes her statements about the developing snake/tree we cannot but be reminded of the Kundalini snake of Hindu mysticism lying at the root of Yoga practices, which are both physical and at the same time psychic.

This Kundalini snake is said to have lain curled up asleep for countless ages at the base of the spinal cord, humming with potential energy like a hive of bees. Mystically, the spinal cord or regions near it has a number of chakras

259

or psychic centres which to begin with are closed, that is, the individual is not aware that they exist. They may be opened with the increase of what is here called psychic consciousness. The lower ones have more to do with instinct, and the upper ones with the transformation of instinct into psychic power.

As these begin to open from the bottom upwards, the Kundalini snake uncoils, and pierces through the lower ones towards the higher ones. As each chakra opens up it becomes available to consciousness. When it has reached the skull the whole body is thereby suffused with psychic consciousness. When it bursts through the skull is the moment of illumination and it is said a flame arises out of the hole thus pierced.

The rise of the practice of Buddhism had Hinduism as a background. Siddhartha Gautama, Buddhism's founder, after years of religious study, discerned understanding at last by sitting under the Bo tree. Here he was contemplating his navel—a metaphor for pondering his origin—joining the highly mental (spiritual) activity with deep earthy reality, and thus achieving illumination or enlightenment. Similarly Islam (literally, "submission to the will of Allah [God]") enjoins its followers to connect with the spiritual principles of eternity, omniscience, omnipotence and infinity five times daily through prayer. Its founder, Mohammed, described himself as a messenger of Allah; he is generally revered as a prophet. All of these practices when seriously and genuinely carried out lead to the joining of "the highest" and "the lowest" in humanity—the merging of instinct and spirituality, or the growth of consciousness of the unconscious. No one is suggesting that Mary has achieved this divine state, but she has the ability to meditate in terms of her fantasies which once she disclaimed as having anything to do with her. This is the foundation of her newly expanding life and of her ability to carry on the exacting nursing work she does.

In widespread symbolism the black snake is the snake of magic healing, the soter snake [87]. This may be associated with the fact that in some Yoga systems there are three aspects of the virile organ in its mystical meaning. The

---

87. Jacobi, Jolande, *The Psychology of C. G. Jung*, London, Kegan Paul, Trench, Trubner and Co., 1942, p. 93, note 52.

natural penis is symbolically "black", meaning that it represents purely instinctive desire, as unconscious as it is autonomous—outside conscious control. There is another symbolic phallic influence in the region of the heart, and this is "red". This means instinctive desire realised in the form of love. And finally there is a third one which is golden, the colour of light or certain kinds of flame, and it is this which in this system is said to issue from the head when the adept is in a state of self-realisation.

It is thus worth noting that at the crucial point in this painting where the black snake reaches her skull there are the three colours concerned: the black snake (the new kind of inner strength), the red (feeling), and the yellow (a greater awareness of potential).

Darkness and Light

Mary of course knew nothing about such worldwide archetypal symbols other than those experienced through her own dreams and fantasies. It is therefore remarkable that she should by now appreciate the value of "darkness" meaning that psychic level of unknowing out of which the healing symbols of the archetypes arise. She said, "*I felt that more would happen if I was not anxious and tense, but I couldn't let myself go into the darkness properly*". Nevertheless the darkness came to her, with yet another message which it wanted to convey. For as she says, "*The scattered pieces of a body came out of the dark to meet me. I don't know what they are about but wondered if they had anything to do with my chest getting better*". This refers to the unhealed lesion at the bottom of her lung resulting from the tuberculosis she had had shortly before her father died. It will be noted that these fragments of a "body" including two hands, two feet, a chest and abdomen (all painted black) are in the region of her chest. Why she should use these fragments as symbols for the pathological condition of her chest I do not know. She said however, "*As I painted them I had the feeling that it*" (her chest) "*might get well by itself. It's almost the first time I have really believed this*". The analysis had possibly prevented it from getting worse. The general atmosphere of hope was a healing factor in her psychological development, but the patch in the chest itself has not in fact been healed. In the severe London smog of the winter of 1962-3 it flared up again, but otherwise has been under control..

261

Coming from such a deep psychic level, it is just possible that this internalised black may have arisen out of the hitherto fourth quarter (the bottom right-hand one) of Mary's Tree-Self, Painting 30, as counterweight to the uneasy huge red snake of her then frustrated desire.

As for yellow in the form of "light", it seems almost always to be associated with the snake, as it was when Mary saw her first red snake in the lighted window (Painting 8). As we have seen, like everything in Mary's fantasies the colour yellow may have two opposite meanings. It had a negative meaning in the case of the golden chains with which Mary was bound (Paintings 16 and 21), the golden swords inhibiting the rescuing action of the snake in Painting 26, and the sticky yellow mass in Painting 31. What yellow symbolised for her was thus fatal when it bound her to the parental complexes. But it signified freedom when she could recognise these complexes as being her own, so that she could begin to deal with them.

MARY'S SUBSEQUENT DEVELOPMENT ·

This brings to an end the series of Mary's fantasy paintings that have been selected for this book. There were subsequently many more as Mary gradually found her feet in the external world, carrying on the work necessary to become a State Registered Nurse. She pursued this with the intention of returning to mental nursing with that extra qualification. Although still somewhat of a lone hand, Mary eventually became matron [head nurse] of a ward in a psychiatric hospital. She now has friends and has resumed religious interests. She is devoted to her work which she enjoys, and has less difficulty with "authorities". She reads a lot of poetry, sometimes out loud to herself, as well as books on meditation connected with her personal problems. But her great gift is the deep personal sympathy she has with certain kinds of patients who trust her and rely on her.

Interesting Notes

1. Foreword

[A longer one written earlier by Dr. Layard has been used as the official Introduction or Foreword in this edition. Ed.]

The writer of this book does not believe that the object of psychotherapy is to produce "normal" people. The "normal" are apt to be conservative. If they were not so, they would not form the backbone of society. But how desirable is it that society should remain static? Up to a point it must, or there would be no law and order, no framework in which the individual could function as a human being, a living person born into an environment he did not make but has to some extent to serve.

But he has something else to serve: himself, herself, some might say as a child of God, others as a child of nature. How reconcile these two? How is it that, as history shows, societies change, rising and falling according to what laws or for what purposes? How is it that societies so differing in social organization, in customs and beliefs, exist side by side, as diverse as China and the Middle West, as London and Little Puddleton, pygmy or plutocrat, Puritan or Polynesian? What is the purpose of all this? And why, in civilized Britain, have we now half a million people shut away in mental hospitals or in most urgent need of psychotherapy, if the backbone of our society is so good and praiseworthy that it should be held up as "normal", and such normality a thing to strive for (or maybe to warp ourselves for)?

Our religion teaches us that the ideal human being was part man and part God, was in fact both at the same time. Are we to better him? Are we not also part animal and part divine, composed of body, soul and spirit, with the emotions and instincts of animals, half, quarter or three-quarter changed into something different, for bettor or for worse? And, not infrequently, for worse? For it is well known that the worst sins are spiritual ones; that pride is more harmful than weakness.

The one is hard, the other soft. Let me present a conundrum to you. Soft things are malleable, and "God is weak". How else could he have allowed himself to be crucified "for our sakes", this being described as "unto the Jews a stumbling block, and unto the Greeks foolishness" (1 Cor. 1:23)? For are we not *all* "Jews and Greeks" in that we are divided in our thoughts, over-hidebound or over-free or over-intellectualized, lacking in varying degree that middle thing, a sentient soul, wherein such opposite extremes may be reconciled?

263

What is this soul, with which we might perceive? Psychologically, it is called the anima in the man or the animus in the woman. The anima is a word not newly coined but well known in times when men cared about such things. It is an organ of perception able to transmit to ego consciousness at least the suspicion that "the foolishness of God" may be "wiser than men; and the weakness of God is stronger than men" (I Cor. 1:25). For it is said in the same passage that there are "not *many* wise men after the flesh, not *many* mighty" nor even many "*noble*" (my italics), who understand the paradox that "God hath chosen the foolish things of the world to confound the wise", and even "base things of the world, and things which are despised, hath God chosen, yea, and things which are not, to bring to naught things that are...." (*ibid.* 26-28)

I have not chosen these words because they are in the Bible as though the Bible were the only authority, for "the devil quotes the Bible" too. I am quoting them because they happen to coincide with present-day experience. Furthermore, they give us the experience of the writer of the epistle almost two thousand years ago who says, "I am debtor both to the Greeks and to the Barbarians: both to the wise, and to the unwise". Speaking not only of others but of himself as well, he tells of those who "professing themselves to be wise, they became fools", "who changed the truth of God into a lie, and worshipped and served the creature more than the Creator...." (Rom. 1: 14, 22, 25). Knowing such things, and having suffered in himself enough to pierce through to the joy of self-realization as a human being freed from Pharisaical illusion, the apostle further writes of his own experience: "I was with you in weakness, and in fear, and in much trembling...." (1 Cor. 2: 3)

I hope the reader will not mistake me if I call attention to these words as describing the feelings of those of us who today approach the problems of human life with awe, an awe not of fake "mystery" but arising out of an understanding of life's complexity.

This book describes the case of Mary who was, when I met her first, apparently a mental defective. But what *appears* as mental defect is often quite a different condition. Its origin may be found in psychic barriers built up instinctively by the infant as necessary defences against an unsatisfactory or dangerous environment. They are barriers built up for a very good purpose — self preservation. They may go back to a pre-verbal stage and the perilous helplessness of infancy.

We all have some such barriers, which do not as a rule hamper us too much. But if they are strong, having been rendered necessary by some extreme need for self-preservation, and have been formed very early in the infant's life, these protective measures take on the quality of instincts, which are psychologically blind. Being thus blind, the child fails to notice, as it grows up, that conditions have changed. So the self-protective defences continue to operate automatically against all outside influence, even if the environment may have by then ceased to be harmful and may have become potentially beneficial to the individual's welfare, could he or she but notice it.

Seen from this angle, the defences, so necessary at first, now turn into autonomous complexes, keeping out good influences as autonomously as they formerly kept out bad ones. Their effect is to prevent the child, now grown physically but not psychically into an adult, from experiencing life in many aspects, both good and bad. What small fragments of ego consciousness the individual may by now have acquired cannot be brought to bear on them for the formation of any kind of rational judgment. They remain "in the air" (Painting 2) or relatively imprisoned (Painting 3).

Such insight into the problem is, however, by no means enough, if we are to understand it fully and to appreciate its more positive meaning. For, in terms of the visual imagery which Mary later developed, her apparent mental defect was but a "shell" guarding the treasure of an archetypal wisdom in a pure state. It functioned as a "Virgin Mother" (in the sense of a container of unfalsified potential) which, if the shell could but be pierced, would yield up treasure beyond price.

The weapons with which to prise the complex open were the same as those used symbolically by the princely lover in any fairy tale, freeing the bewitched maiden. These are the joint forces of love and faith, including attack and defence against the *lack* of love and faith which the original defences produced. And, above all, patience. This is not so much a virtue as a necessity. It is, however, dynamically exciting since patience is itself part of faith and is sustained by it.

The weapons include the abilities to listen and perceive, to woo the patient's confidence by "feeling with", thus opening up the channels of free association that have been so secretively repressed. This gives them validity through comparison with worldwide archetypal and historical parallels. The latter are, often in the form of images or figures, introduced only as an accompaniment to the basic operations of the therapist's non-possessive love and faith. Such love understands and can challenge too, making up for the *lack* of love and faith which evoked the original defences and has since been perpetuated by those defences.

The following account does its inevitably incomplete best to explain how this works, or has worked in one instance, to produce results. It does not claim to be the only way. But it may at least show a way by which unconscious psychic contents can be released not only of one patient, but of the analyst also (who has been so much rewarded); and of others too, for whom this account may perhaps prove meaningful.

2. "To become as a little child"

To "become as a little child" therefore is not to become "innocent". It is to become less innocent in the sense of less ignorant. Therefore, the same writer goes on "my speech was not with enticing words or men's wisdom, but in the demonstration of the spirit and of power: ... even the hidden wisdom, which God ordained before the world".(1 Cor. 2: 3-7).

"Before the world" does not, for us, mean ten thousand years ago, or ten million. It means here and now, that stage in the life of everyone before each individual ego is formed, in the continuous creation of each new foetus, and thus of what each one of us is equipped with at birth. The "base things" are the *basic* things, which are so frequently and wrongly despised. "The things which are not" and the "things which are" refer to a mystery not in the bogus sense of not being ultimately understandable, but to a mystery in the true sense as derived from the Greek μυστνς [Oxford English Dictionary: transliteration and English: mystes] meaning "one who is initiated" into mysteries. This in turn is derived from μυειν meaning "to close the eyes": in sum, "to initiate into mysteries" and therefore not be free to speak of what one has learned. [OED: "to close the lips and eyes". Greek secret religious ceremonies were allowed to be witnessed only by the initiated.] In other words, it signifies to keep inside, to "look inside" to see "the other truth" which may be so different from the apparent one.

There is, Skeat alleges, what he calls an interesting philological "confusion" of this word "mystery" and "mistery", also sometimes spelt "mystery" (cf. French *métier*) meaning a "trade", occupation or handicraft. This is in turn related to the Spanish *menester* meaning "want, need", and thus its satisfaction in "employment or trade". Both are at the same time allied to our "minister" which means "servant", connected with the Latin *ministerium*, "service". Philologically "mystery" and "mistery" are said to come from different roots but such alleged confusions often have a psychological basis, which is in this case the suspicion that individual man may have something other than only himself to serve, if he is to live life to the full.

This is what in this book will be called "psychic consciousness", a term which will be more fully defined later, indicating awareness of "the other side" of everything without losing sight of either side. Thus it involves "double thinking", of which the ordinary mild form is reflection (being able to think over things and weigh two conscious thoughts); a stronger one is "unusual perceptiveness", while a yet stronger one manifests itself in symbolic visions. Even in the most ordinary person the "other truth" is constantly trying to break through nightly in dreams when ego consciousness has least power to interfere.

A stage which we can term intermediate is day dreaming, which may be of two kinds, both being wish fulfilments. For in this scheme of things the psyche may be seen to have "two wills". The one wishes to fulfil, as if by magic, all ego's fantasies of ease, ambition and so on, the other being directed on the contrary by psychic consciousness towards fulfilment in a quite different sphere based on reality, first internal and then external, beginning with self-knowledge. Truth always has its opposite which is also true, and the only effective truth is that which combines them both.

3. The colour purple

The other matter to be noted is in connection with the dream accompanying Painting 13, in which the "big black swelling" on the left hand of the desired schoolgirl turned into the snake and thus transformed this psychically incestuous desire into an object of potential internal strength. A similar transformatory and internalising process is evident if we compare the purple colour in the various paintings. There is the vivid purple of the dragon in Painting 14, the purple background in Painting 13 of the confrontation with the snake, the purple colour of the brew in Painting 12, the purple dragon pushing up the coffin and of the rotting flesh in 11, the purple "great fish" in 10, the purple dragonfly snake in 7, the purple garment of the hanging boy in 3, and finally the purple image of Mary's fantasy-ego in Painting 2 sitting on the purple-flowered "thistle of matriarchal unconsciousness", fascinated by the same fantasy tree held in that painting in her hand which is now seen in the dragon's belly.

If purple means incest, these are all incest elements in Mary's uncon-

267

scious. The difference between the first and last of these fantasy paintings (which also goes right through the dream paintings and covers a span of six years in her development) is that in the first instance the fantasy was project- ed wholly outwards, whereas in the present instance it has been internalised. This shows a great advance, whatever may happen when it at last gets born into full consciousness. Difference may also be seen in that in the first instance (Painting 2) Mary is herself identified with "sweet innocence", whereas in the present Painting 14 she is identified with the dragon. That shows considerably more self-knowledge, and corresponds with many remarks she now began to make about it being "her own fault" and not always that of others that her life seemed so difficult.

4. Goethe's theory of colours

The place taken by purple in Goethe's "Theory of Colours" (written in opposition to Newton's theory that colour is split-up white light) is further suggestive as its symbolic meaning. Goethe's experiments proved to his satis- faction that colour is formed by a mingling of darkness and light, both equally necessary for the production of colour. The sky is pure black or dark- ness but, modified by the small amount of light reflected by the atmospheric particles surrounding the earth as seen as blue. The pure white or light of the sun modified by the small amount of darkness present in the same "imper- fectly transparent" medium is seen as yellow. The thicker the atmosphere, the more the two original states of light and darkness are modified by each other: the yellow passes through orange, and the blue through purple, to the red that is midway between light and darkness.

5. Faith

By faith is meant not faith in any dogma or dogmatic creed, but faith in the force of life freed from the shackles of secretive shame and thus made "not alone". For the basis of all neurosis can from one point of view be thought of as sheer *loneliness*. Deprived of a good mother-figure, the child goes lonely on its way, filling with fantasy the void left by this lack of primitive relationship, which may give rise to every kind of speculation and paranoid deduction which may be true or false. What is basically needed is a friend or a com- panion with whom to re-explore these desert places of the mind, filled with such frightening objects owing to the split between desire and experience.

The companion must him/herself have had some such basic terrors in order that he may understand and share the patient's own experience.

Faith is the quality which perceives such terror but can change it into awe. For terror separates, but awe unites. This is the "fear of God" that is the beginning of wisdom, an initiation into the mysteries of transformation from panic into the ability to love and to have more self-confidence. To be initiated one must first be weak, that is, acknowledge one's need in face of powers clearly greater than oneself. This applies not only to the patient but as well to the analyst. Her or his approach to the problems of psychological analysis may well be expressed in the words, "I was with you in weakness, and in fear, and in much trembling" (1Cor. 2: 3). The trembling implies alert awareness of his own fallibility in putting forward interpretations that may be right or wrong and which depend for their verification or otherwise on the patient's response.

6. Diagram: fourfold factors leading to the apparition of Mary's Ghost Man

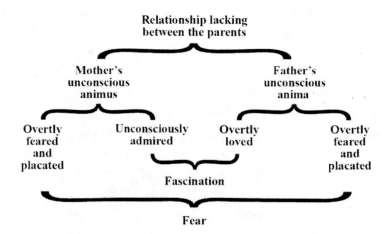

Basic Jungian Terms

Compiled with special reference to definitions as found in Frieda Fordham's "An Introduction to Jung's Psychology", Penguin, 1991, pp. 146-7, "C.G. Jung: Word and Image" edited by Jolande Jacobi, Princeton University Press, 1979, and other sources.

Anima and Animus: An unconscious image which is "an hereditary factor of primordial origin engraved in the living organic systems of an individual." "This psychological bisexuality is a reflection of the biological fact that it is the larger number of [either male or female] genes which is the decisive factor in the determination of sex. The smaller number of contrasexual genes seems to produce a corresponding contrasexual character, which usually remains unconscious." (Jacobi, p. 226) It behaves like a sub-personality.

Anima: the unconscious feminine side of a man. It is basically an imprint (archetype) of all the impressions made by womankind throughout pre-historical and historical time. It is personified in art, for example, by the representation of a woman or of nature; in personal life it manifests itself in dreams by similar representations. The anima is allied to the earth (matter) and operates like a sub-personality. It best functions as a mediator between the individual's unconscious and his consciousness.

Animus: the unconscious masculine side of a woman. It is basically an imprint (archetype) of all the impressions made by males throughout pre-historical and historical time. It is personified in art, for example, by a man or a group of men or by a spiritual image; in personal life it manifests itself in dreams by similar representations. The animus is allied to the spirit and behaves like a sub-personality. It best functions as a mediator between the individual's unconscious and her consciousness.

Archetype: a content of the collective unconscious (and the psychological counterpart of instinct). It can indicate its presence internally or externally through an image or symbol. Archetypes can be termed systems of readiness for action. They seem to be part of the inherited structure of the psyche. An archetype is autonomous and its energy is behind each complex, displaying strong feeling (paralleling the instinctual drive of the body).

270

Complex: an affectively toned group of associated ideas (Fordham, p. 146). An impelling energy with a nodal point which exerts its pressure on an individual. If not understood by or integrated into the person's consciousness it can wreak havoc. It operates like a split-off segment of personality.

Consciousness: human psychic contents are of a universal nature, and each individual can continually become aware of them. Unrecognized contents are termed "unconscious" (i.e. to a specific individual)), recognized ones have been made "conscious". The term "collective unconscious" is a blanket term for such psychic contents because they are not always given a place in an individual's awareness of her- or himself. If the ego is unconnected with these contents, that person can be termed unconscious.

A distinction should be made between what we are aware of in the external world and that in our internal life. Jungian psychology stresses the importance of the inner life while noting that we have responsibilities to fulfill in the outer world.

Dream: an image which by-passes consciousness or the ego, representing a content coming from the unconscious. It emanates from an unrecognized area of an individual's being—sometimes referred to as the soul—and displays information that, once interpreted, can be integrated into consciousness.

Ego: the centre of the conscious mind (Fordham, p. 146).

Enantiodromia: the process of something becoming its opposite, like the ocean tides; the natural movement of libido throughout life is both forwards and backwards (cf. Heraclitus).

Eros: the female principle, often indicating the forces of feeling, harmony and living connectedness.

Extraversion: libido, or psychic energy, which is concerned with or stimulated by outer objects.

Individuation: the process of becoming an individual, including integration of previously unconscious contents.

Introversion: libido, or psychic energy, which is concerned with or stimulated by internal components.

Libido: a general term meaning the life-force, used here specifically to mean its psychological manifestations.

Logos: the male principle, often representing rationality; the spiritual force, or taking things apart for examination.

Negative: in Jungian psychology it can be used to denote, for example, an aspect of a situation (or perhaps an ego interpretation) which is not in accord with the best awareness that an individual could be considering (utilizing). It can also be used to indicate the detrimental aspects of a position of judgment; of, say, a complex's energy on a person's life; of one area of a person's life compared to another, as concerns individuation; and so on. See "Opposite" and "Positive".

Opposite: the antithesis of an entity. The human mind is capable of observing polarities. Concentrating on or identifying with only one polarity can imbalance the human psyche.

Persona: "the facet of personality which is turned to the world and by which a relationship with the environment is made" (Fordham, p. 146). Those attitudes, habits, thoughts and actions which characterize an individual in everyday life.

Personal unconscious: repressed memories, wishes, emotion, etc. and subliminal perceptions of a personal nature. (Fordham, p. 146)

Positive: in Jungian psychology it can be used to denote, for example, an aspect of a situation (or perhaps an interpretation) which is in full accord with an individual's considered attitude. It can refer to the beneficial aspect of an archetype or complex.

It can indicate that something is unprofitable for ego consciousness but is actually valuable for the emergence of unconscious contents. See "Opposite" and "Negative".

Projection: a process whereby ideas, impulses, or emotions are seen as belonging to another person or object, especially undesirable ones but also positive ones.

Psyche: the conscious and unconscious of an individual; the modern (sometimes technical) word for soul, mind, or spirit.

Self: the center of the totality of consciousness and unconsciousness; the source of libido, which exerts a corrective influence on an individual; the archetype of wholeness of the psyche. It is often equated with soul.

Shadow: The inferior part of the personality; sum of all personal and collective psychic elements which, because of their incompatibility with the chosen conscious attitude, are denied expression in life and therefore coalesce into a relatively autonomous "splinter personality" with contrary tendencies in the unconscious. The shadow behaves compensatorily to consciousness; hence its effects can be positive as well as negative. In dreams, the shadow figure is always of the same sex as the dreamer. (Jacobi, pp. 228-9)

Symbol: "an expression of something relatively unknown which cannot be conveyed in any other way" (Fordham, p. 147).

Unconscious: Those impulses, facts, habits, complexes, etc. about ourselves and others of which our ego does not (yet) have information. Also refers, for example, to what we call our personal shadow, as well as being used in a general sense about any matters outside our awareness.

Bibliography

Archer, W.G., *The Loves of Krishna*. London, Allen and Unwin, 1957

Baynes, H.G., *Mythology of the Soul*. London, Bailliere, Tyndal and Cox, 1940

Bible, The, King James Version.

Blake, William, *Illustrations for the Book of Job*. New York, Dover Publications, 1995

Branston, Brian, *Gods of the North*. London, Thames and Hudson, 1955

Codex lat. Monacensis 14933. Munich, Staatsbibliothek

Codrington, R.H., *The Melanesians: Studies in their Anthropology and Folklore*. Oxford, Clarendon Press, 1891

Deacon, *Melanesia*: see Margaret Gardiner, *Footprints on Malekula: a Memoir of Bernard Deacon*. Edinburgh, Salamander Press, 1984.

Donnington, Robert, *The Instruments of Music*. London, Methuen, 1962

Eastlake, Charles Locke, tr., *Goethe's Theory of Colours* [*Farbenlehre*]. London, John Murray, 1840.

Eisler, Robert, *Orpheus the Fisher*. London, J.M. Watkins, 1921

Fordham, Michael, *The Objective Psyche*. London, Routledge & Kegan Paul, 1958

Freud, Sigmund, *Totem and Taboo*. London, Kegan Paul [1950?]

— *Three Essays on the Theory of Sexuality*. London, Imago Publishing, 1949

Graves, Robert, *The Greek Myths*. Harmondsworth, Penguin, 1955, Vol. I

Jacobi, Jolande, *The Psychology of C.G. Jung*. London, Kegan Paul, Trench, Trubner, 1942

Jaffe, Aniela, ed., *C.G. Jung, Word and Image*. Bollingen Series XCVII: 2, Princeton University Press, 1979

James, M.R., ed. & tr., *The Apocryphal New Testament*. Oxford, 1924.

Jung, C.G., *Alchemical Studies*. Princeton, Bollingen, 1967

— *Memories, Dreams, Reflections*. New York, Pantheon, 1961

— *Practice of Psychotherapy, The*. Princeton, Bollingen, 1954

— *Psychology and Alchemy*. Princeton, Bollingen, 1953

— *Structures and Dynamics of the Psyche*. Princeton, Bollingen, 1960

— *Symbols of Transformation*. Princeton, Bollingen, 1949

— *Von den Wurzeln des Bewusstseins*. Zurich, Raschev, 1954 [Essays in English in Collected Works 8, 9i, 11 & 13]

Kenton, Edna, *The Book of Earths*. New York, William Morrow, 1928

Kerenyi, Karl, *The Gods of the Greeks*. London, Thames & Hudson, 1951

— *Asklepios: Archetypal image of the Physician's Existence*. London, Thames & Hudson, 1960

Kesten, Herman, *Copernicus and his World*. London, Secker and Warburg, 1945

Layard, John, *Stone Men of Malekula*. London, Chatto & Windus, 1942

— "The Incest Taboo and the Virgin Archetype", *Eranos-Jahrbuch*. Zurich, Rhein-Verlag 1945 [Also *The Virgin Archetype*, Spring Publications, Zurich, 1972]

— "The Making of Man in Malekula", *Eranos-Jahrbuch*. Zurich, Rhein-Verlag, 1949

Martin, R.R., *The History of the Church of St. Michael at the Northgate*, pub. by Author, 1939

Muirhead-Gould, John, *The Kama Sutra*. Panther Books, 1963

Neumann, Erich, *The Great Mother: An Analysis of the Archetype*. London, Routledge & Kegan Paul, 1955

O'Brien, Barbara, *Operators and Things: The Inner Life of a Schizophrenic*. Copyright Arlington Books, Inc., 1958; London, Elek Books, 1960

Tolstoy, Leo, *Hadji Murat: A Tale of the Caucasus*, tr. W.G. Carey. London, Heinemann, 1962

Warner, W. Lloyd, *A Black Civilisation*. New York and London, 1937

References

Cruden, Alexander, *Complete Concordance to the Holy Scriptures of the Old and New Testament*, 1737

Partridge, Eric, *Origins*, London, Routledge & Kegan Paul, 1958

Index

f = figure

attitudes, 68, 195, 197, 216, 220, 225
authority, 155, 262
autonomous complexes. See complexes, autonomous
awakening, 78, 147, 153, 172
awareness, 16, 18, 72, 77, 113, 128-9, 161, 200, 233, 244, 249, 261
awe, 264, 269

Balarama, 109-10
barrier, 220, 236, 242, 244, 250, 255, 264
  See also black, stone; fence; resistances; wall
bats, 24, 40, 157-8
Baynes, H.G., 65
Behemoth, 143-5, 178-9
birds, 51f, 105, 121, 158, 189, 222
birth, 147, 211, 255
bisexuality, 30, 270
  See also hermaphrodite
black, 60-1, 107, 109, 116-19, 196
  barrier, 220, 255
  bird, 105, 121, 158
  branches, 163, 166, 194
  cauldron, 132, 154
  chains, 193, 220
  coffin, 55, 124-5, 133, 172, 194
  corpse, 73-5, 182, 254
  earth, 4, 155, 161, 178, 183, 189, 194, 231, 234-9, 241, 244, 254
  figures, 123, 225
  line, 210-11
  scales, 141, 143
  self, 13, 163, 167-8, 171, 178, 193-4, 248-9, 253-4
  side of self, 224-7, 235, 238, 240
  sky, 31-2
  square, 241, 245-6, 248, 254
  stone, 3, 154-5, 163, 183, 193-5, 200, 238
  streaks, 242, 244-5
  swelling, 136, 138-9, 267
  vault, 167, 243

See also snake, black
black-grey, 193-4
Blake, William, 144-5
bliss, 65, 80, 96, 215
blue, xvi, 29-30, 32, 107, 141, 151, 154, 165, 167, 184, 225, 268
boat, 119, 172
body, pieces, 151, 258
body imagery, 5, 205
   See also archetypal imagery
boot, 191, 193-4, 196
branches, 163, 166, 174, 194, 239
Branston, Brian, 149-50
bread, 16, 66, 90
bread and butter, 82, 88-90, 228
breakdown, 27, 251
breast, 37-40, 59, 76, 90, 96, 114, 174, 214
brown, 165, 248

caduceus, 198
cauldron, 131-3, 136, 154
cave, 39, 160-1, 167, 170, 172
chains, 151, 167, 193, 220
chakras, 259-60
character, 9, 57-8, 83, 88, 97, 115, 161, 179, 186, 195
   See also personality
chest, 258
childhood, 44, 46, 91-3, 98, 111
Christ, 40, 51-2, 54, 99-100, 108, 111, 179f, 222-3, 227-8
   See also sacrifice; saviour figures
circle, 46-9, 108, 143, 181, 218-19
claw, 224, 248-9, 258-9
cleanliness, 16-17, 83, 117
cloud, 3, 146, 148, 233
   See also incest-mist
coffin, 55, 120, 124-5, 127, 133, 172, 194
collective unconscious, 9, 271
colours, 13, 22, 27-33, 60-1, 101, 184, 268

communion, 89-90, 256
compensation, 4, 21, 66, 86, 137, 153, 225, 227, 273
complexes, 8, 68, 87, 170, 194, 218, 240, 262, 270-2
   autonomous, 24-5, 28, 37, 43, 47f, 48-9, 253, 256, 265
   deep, 70, 76
   dragon, 248-50, 253-6
   forgetfulness, 43, 48
   hysterical, 88, 484
   incest-, 27-8, 245
   infantile, 84
   inhibiting, 4
   Oedipus, 10
   parental, 104, 253, 255, 262
   secret, 185, 242
   See also compulsions
compulsions, 8-9, 11, 179, 182-3, 225, 245, 254
   See also complexes
confidence, 135, 139, 265, 269
conflict, 174, 192, 204, 207, 210, 257-8
confusion, 81, 157-9, 184, 215, 228, 236, 243
consciousness, xiii, 139, 147-8, 178-81, 196-7, 208-10, 225, 245, 271
   See also ego consciousness; psychic consciousness
corpse, 63-4, 68, 70, 72-5, 95, 124, 128, 182, 254
corruption. See rot/rotting
cosmic tree. See World Tree
Crab, 163-6, 170-1
Crab Woman, 171
critical faculty, 195-6, 200, 258-9
cross, 51f, 53-4, 72, 137, 232
Crowned Hermaphrodite, 229
crucifixion, 10f, 29, 50f, 51, 61, 100, 149, 179f
   See also sacrifice
Cruden, 17
cube, 245-6, 254
curse/cursing, 85-7

Daphne, 147

280

dragon complex. *See* complexes, dragon
Dragon Man, 101, 219.50, 220-3, 225-6, 242
dream ego, 38, 140
dream life, 39, 48, 82, 138, 140
dream mother, 82-3, 85, 89, 91, 95
dream-ego, 117, 138
dreams, 20, 43, 57, 82-3, 94-5, 130-40, 169, 172-3, 188, 217-18, 245, 252, 271
drives, 8-11, 208
drop-through, 90-1, 95
Dual Mother, 10, 82-3, 127
duality, 10, 110, 140, 197, 208-9, 227-8
  See also two
duck, 157-8, 222

ear, 38, 208, 212, 215, 226
Earth, 144
earth, 54, 77, 134, 148, 154, 156, 162, 165, 248
  See also black, earth
earth mother, 83-4, 88, 188, 198
ego, 9, 11-12, 65-6, 83, 90, 271
ego consciousness, 7-13, 23, 65-71, 80-1, 160-4, 212, 234, 239, 264-7
  See also consciousness
emotions, 104, 118, 132, 134-5, 137, 157-8, 161-3, 177, 205
  See also feelings
enemy, 82-3, 161
Epimetheus, 202
Eros, xii, 50, 52, 105
Eros figure, 126
escapism, 121, 157-9, 192, 216, 220
Eve, 35-6, 61
external world, 46, 146, 262, 271
  See also outside world
extraversion, 103, 109, 271
eyes, 147, 164, 208, 223f

face, xvi, 29, 82-4, 88, 140, 224, 231, 237

of self-knowledge, 18, 131-2, 138
of sex, 16, 145, 237, 242
of womanhood, 136-7, 228
feelings, 142, 148, 175, 195, 205, 258-9, 260-2
See also emotions
feminine principle, 6, 197
femininity, 7, 30, 205-6, 227-8, 237, 255
fence, 219-21
See also barrier
fierceness, 237, 245
fire/flames, 100-1, 132-3, 141-3, 154-7, 171, 202, 207-13, 219-23, 242, 261
fish, 120, 122.123, 125, 164, 178, 183, 248, 255
fixation, 38, 148, 194, 196
flower. See purple, flower
flute, 106f, 107-8
foetus, 141, 143, 169, 174, 188, 245, 249, 255, 266
foot, 191, 193, 196, 224
Fordham, Michael, 65
forest, 90-1, 95, 106
fountain, 73, 174, 185, 189
See also spring; well
four, 47, 171
fourfold structure, 232-4, 239, 246, 269
four-ness, 236
freedom, 11, 253, 262
Freud, Sigmund, 9-10, 101
fruit, 52, 61, 63, 68, 185, 189, 258
frustration, 76, 212, 241-2
Furtmeyer, Berthold, 61
fury, 128, 142, 207

garden, 35, 43-4, 58
Garden of Eden, 1-2
garden of the soul, 21, 46-9, 246
gardener, 58-60
ghost man, xvi, 16, 50, 94-6, 99, 102-3, 109-10, 210, 217, 269

giant, 149, 219, 221
girl, 24-5, 27, 151, 160-1, 167
God, 179, 221
gods, 52-3, 102, 104, 110, 147, 168
Goethe, Johann Wolfgang von, 31-2, 268
golden, 151, 167, 261
   See also yellow
Golgotha, 53, 72
Grace (Aunt), xv, 30, 68, 82, 84, 88, 155
graft/grafting, 57, 98
grass, 67-8, 69f, 77, 177, 254
grassy bank, 177-8, 248
Graves, Robert, 103n32
Great Mother, 163, 165, 170
green, 107, 114, 154, 167, 170, 205-6
   See also dirty green; dragon, green; grass; snake, green; tree, green
grey, 22-3, 68
grey-white, 211
guilt, 16, 90, 93, 117, 175, 196
gypsy, 82, 85-6, 228

habit patterns, 18, 90, 94, 145, 216, 250-1
hammer, 199-202, 204, 220, 231, 258
hands, 13, 15-17, 19, 26, 57-8, 60, 98, 136, 140, 193, 224-5
hanging boy, 43, 46-7, 49-51, 54-5, 58, 61, 73-4, 151, 219
hanging god, 52-3
hate, 59, 83, 214, 253
head, 155, 199, 201-2, 207-8, 212, 224, 245, 248-9, 253, 257-8, 261
headache, 200-1, 204, 208, 210, 212, 257-8
healing, 70-1, 118, 204, 240, 248, 251, 260
heart, 222f-223f, 261
hell, 54, 72, 175, 180, 217, 221
Hephaestos, 202, 210
hermaphrodite, 102, 166, 229
Hermes, 102
hero. *See* saviour
hierosgamos, 31

Holy Ghost, 144, 228
homosexual, 38, 104
hope, 154, 156, 165, 261
hortus inclusus, 46
hospital, 80, 116-17
hostility, 158, 207
house, 18, 116, 224-5
human fruit, 52-3f, 58
husbandman. *See* gardener
Hygieia, 118
hysteria/hysterical. *See* complexes, hysterical

id, 9, 87, 238
identification, 33, 59, 76, 81, 84, 86, 253, 255
ignorance, 244, 266
illumination, 244, 259-60
impulses, 8, 45, 171, 252, 272-3
incest, 28-9, 31, 54-5, 76, 79, 87, 171, 267
    See also psychological incest
incest-bonds, 75, 121, 133, 243
incest-complex, 27-8, 245
incest-death, 129
incest desire, 33, 36, 57-8, 69f, 114, 168, 185
incest-mist, 184-5, 187
    See also cloud; purple, mist
incest taboo, 7, 10, 17, 21, 140, 208-9
incest wish, 87, 136-7
individuality, 246, 256
individuation, 5, 13, 81, 117, 120, 204, 271
infantility, 4-5, 66, 90, 195
infection, 82, 88-9, 214, 245, 255
inhibition, 8, 23, 58, 176, 200, 204
Initiating Goddess, 170-1
Initiating Mother, 164, 170
initiation, 96-7, 123, 134, 164, 266, 269
inner life, 45, 232, 239-40
inner strength, 232, 261, 267

left side, 24, 59, 61-2, 98, 208, 212, 231-2, 234, 239
lesbian, 38, 105, 137
Lesbos, 105
Leviathan, 143-5, 178-80
libido, 37, 39, 71, 138, 166, 209, 242, 271
  See also life force
life force, 25, 45, 84, 95, 168, 173, 203
  See also libido
light, 31-2, 46, 62f, 107, 141, 257, 261-2, 268
lightning, 258
Lockhart, Russell Arthur, xi-xiii
loneliness, 44-5, 120, 124, 153, 164, 193, 268
Longinus, 51f
love, 26
  analyst's, xiii, 195-6, 201, 220, 265-6
  for aunt, 84, 88
  father-, 37, 189, 225
  for father, 19, 21, 37, 39, 80-1, 125, 195
  father's, 7, 40, 197
  of God, 221
  impulse, 45, 88, 269
  -life, 50, 58
  mother-, 189, 214, 225
  physical, 79, 106
  possessive, 31, 253
  for self, 90
  sentimental, 253

Magdeburger, Hieronymus, 50f
male mother, 92-3
male principle, 137, 165, 243, 255
Malekula, 170
man, 124, 178, 180
mandala, 46, 108
mandragora. See mandrake
mandrake, 130-3
Marduk, 73

3, 209
mythology, personal, 5, 11-12

Osiris, 73, 168
outside world, 37, 78, 199, 213, 239
    See also external world

painful, 258
Pan, 102-3
Pandora, 76, 202
paranoid (n.), 88, 161, 175
parthenogenesis, 6
passions, 11, 151, 175, 183, 210, 213
penis, 260-1
Persephone, 76
persona, 272
personal unconscious, xiv, 9, 272
personality, 71, 139-40, 142, 209, 235, 239, 254-5
    See also character
phallus, 36, 39, 150, 214
pillar, 167-8, 172, 175, 194, 248
Piper, 98, 101-3, 218
plant, 23, 26, 52f, 113-14, 130, 174-6, 189, 214, 228, 249, 253, 255
poetry, 262
possession, 76, 249
possessiveness, 30-1, 37, 62, 76-7, 253
potential, 261
power, 29, 225, 266
pregnancy, 196-7
    See also dragon, pregnant
pride, 17-18, 29, 31, 180, 188, 215, 236-7, 253-4, 263
prima materia, 34-5f, 36, 74, 84, 133
principle of division. *See* division
principle of individuation. *See* individuation
projection (v.), 38, 60, 85, 146, 158, 161, 169, 181, 198, 217, 225, 272
projections, 5, 46, 58, 75, 140, 161, 169, 218, 231-2
Prometheus, 202
Psyche, 76
psyche, 66, 135, 138, 148, 153, 161, 210, 245, 272
psychic awareness. *See* awareness

psychic consciousness, 6-16, 20-1, 25-6, 40-2, 47-50, 58, 66-71, 111, 158-9, 234-7, 245-7, 252-4, 260-1, 267
  See also consciousness
psychic force, 4, 48, 107, 156
psychic life, 11, 50, 73, 117, 128, 154-5, 204
psychic movement, 69f, 70-2, 233, 244-5
psychic power, 117, 138-9, 154-5, 260-1
psychic pregnancy, 142, 199
psychic structure, 19-22, 83, 239
psychic womb, 132, 156, 170
psychological incest, 28-9, 75-9, 128-9
psychosis, 27, 32, 184
psychosomatic disease, 78-9, 82
psychosomatic expression, 12, 84, 205
psychosomatic self, 75-8
psychotherapy, 50, 75-6, 263
purple, 27-33, 54, 151, 161, 184, 186, 223, 232, 238, 240, 255-6, 261-2
  atmosphere, 161, 223, 227
  claws, 248-9, 258-9
  cloud, 3, 146, 148, 233
  fish, 120, 123, 125, 248, 255
  flesh, 74, 124-5
  flower, 26, 28, 227-9, 231-3, 255
  girl, 27, 237
  mist, 4, 141, 148, 184, 187-8, 203, 212-13, 220, 258
  self, 237, 239, 244, 252, 254
  thistle, 26-9, 33, 237-8
  water, 132-3, 136, 154
  See also dragon, purple; snake, purple; tree, purple

rage, 139, 235
  See also anger
realisation, 237-8, 244, 253
reality, 147-8, 216
rebirth, 40, 104, 126, 167, 171-2, 255
recognition, 79, 92, 115, 123, 126, 133, 135, 137, 213
reconciliation of opposites, 4, 9, 87, 90, 181, 198, 263

schizophrenia/schizophrenic, xi, xvi, xvii, 39, 198, 208-10, 249-52
scythe, 24, 28, 41-2
sea, 120, 122, 144, 157, 165-6
sea of life, 163
seed, 34, 38, 40, 54, 68, 193
  See also acorn
Self, 11, 60, 76, 147-8, 171, 245-6, 272
  See also black, self; black, side of self; purple, self; red, self; red, side of
self
self-contradiction, 90, 157-8
self-deception, 148, 237, 245
self-knowledge. *See* knowledge, self-
self-persecution, 175, 177
self-realisation, 241, 264
self-sacrifice. *See* sacrifice
self-satisfaction, 17-18, 45, 60
separation. *See* split
serpent, 36, 50f, 51, 60-1, 109-10, 131-3, 135, 211
  See also snake
Sesha, 109
seven, 3, 62, 98, 146, 148, 179f, 205
sexual desire, 44, 75, 145
sexuality, 31, 127-8, 137, 175
shadow, 5, 17, 272-3
shadow figures, 83, 273
shell, 54, 164, 191-2, 195-6, 200, 256, 265
Shiva, 223
Siddhartha Gautama, 260
Sitwell, Sacheverell, 105
six, 62, 98
Skeat, Walter William, 78, 266
skull, 36, 61, 201, 203-4, 238
sleep, 118, 123, 129, 172
sleeper, 124, 126, 128
small tree, 24, 26-7, 33-4, 36-7, 41-2, 52, 141-2, 145, 197, 200, 202-4,
213-14
snake, 4-6, 73, 87, 127, 156-8, 160, 163, 174, 191-2, 196, 224

swaying, 137-8, 153
swords. *See* yellow, swords
symbolic imagery, 12, 17, 39, 104, 170, 181, 205
  See also archetypal imagery
symbolism, 2-4, 12-13, 22-3, 232, 260
symbols, 73, 123, 134-5, 155, 195, 201, 217, 240, 245-6, 261, 273
  See also specific symbols
sympathy, 262
Syrinx, 102

tail, arrow-headed, 6, 113, 132, 142, 174, 178, 248
tail, forked, 141, 144
temenos, 58
terror, 121, 123, 269
Things, 249-53
thinking, 137, 195, 200, 205, 215, 220, 227, 246, 250-2, 254
thistle, 24-9, 33, 37, 48, 113-14, 237-8
thought, 209, 212
three, 25-6, 28, 82-3, 149, 178, 200, 204, 224, 228-9
  See also Trinity
three-ness, 235
throat, 199-200, 205, 259
Tiamat, 73
Tolstoy, Leo, 28
tombstone, 126-7
tongue, 93, 96, 123, 143, 156, 178, 248, 256
transference, 37, 39, 57-8, 103, 138, 180-1, 204, 236
transformation, 51, 55, 61, 77, 89, 95, 104-5, 136, 155, 168, 240, 260, 267, 269
tree, 4-5, 72, 104, 127, 136-8, 163, 185
  black, 3, 143, 156
  dead, 24, 34, 36-7, 40
  fantasy, 39, 47, 134, 141-3, 145, 147, 178, 199, 267
  fruit, 15, 19-21, 63-5, 70, 189, 193
  gallows, 53
  green, 2, 205-6, 212-15, 226, 235, 259, 293
  of healing, 258-9

of knowledge, 54, 77
mother-, 189-90, 206
of new life, 42, 69f
philosopher's, 13, 34-5f, 51, 60
purple, 3, 230-2, 237, 241
uprooted, 3-6, 12, 146-8, 150-1, 199
See also World Tree; Yggdrasill
Tree Mother, 189
tree of life, 22, 39, 48, 70, 194, 221, 232
Tree of Life and Death, 52-3, 55, 57-8, 60-2
Tree-Self, 232-7, 239, 244, 246, 252, 254-5, 262
Trinity, 4, 23, 83, 105, 226-8
trust, 262
tuberculosis, 73, 75-6, 78-9, 258, 261
twelve, 107, 168
two, 113-15, 119, 127, 131-3, 136-8, 160, 178, 191-2, 196, 201-2, 210-12, 224, 226, 229
See also duality

Ulysses, 172
unconscious, 8, 131-2, 150, 166, 217, 273
unconsciousness, 7, 29, 31-2, 80, 131, 143, 179-81
underground, 120, 132, 153-4, 160-1, 168, 178, 183, 249, 253-4
union of opposites, 6, 106, 201-2, 214
unity, 4-5, 21, 76, 215, 227-8, 235
unknowing, 118, 200, 245, 261
unknown man, 74, 125-7, 129, 131, 172, 181, 194
up in the air, 24-5, 41, 44, 47, 121, 151, 153, 160, 167, 233, 256

vagina, 38, 144
vagina dentata, 26
van Gogh, Vincent, 121
vase. *See* jar
vault, 167, 243, 248, 253-4
victim, 177-8, 182, 192, 209
vine, 224, 227-8, 248, 253
Virgin Mother, 36, 51f, 61, 91, 265

Vishnu, 105-6, 109

wall, 15, 20, 44, 46-50, 58, 125, 195
  See also barrier
water, 68, 95, 100, 106, 131, 160, 178, 189, 230-1, 236, 248
  See also purple, water; spring; well
weakness, 263-4
well, 73, 119, 149-50, 236
  See also fountain; spring
white, 16, 31-2, 73, 75, 80, 81.102.181, 109, 233, 268
wholeness, 91, 196
window, 80-1, 117, 262
wisdom, 53-4, 82, 85, 87-9, 143, 269
woman in the moon, 34
womb, 55, 76, 102, 125-6, 141, 164, 245, 253
Word, 50, 145
World Tree, 175f-176f
  See also tree, purple; Yggdrasill
worms, 21, 26, 149, 218

yellow, 32, 107, 243-5, 258, 261-2, 268
  light, 32, 243, 257-9, 262
  streak, 242, 244, 246, 259
  swords, 200, 204-5, 226, 243, 262
Yggdrasill, 53, 149-50, 233
Yoga, 259-60

Zeus, 210

Editor's Acknowledgments

My first thanks are to Professor Lord Richard Layard, John Layard's son, for bestowing the manuscript on me, thereby showing his confidence that I could carry the project through to conclusion. And it was Roger Woolger, as former secretary to Dr. Layard, who had introduced me to Dr. Layard in the first place.

In 1976 a New Zealand friend expertly and economically photographed the paintings (since lost), thus preserving them for posterity.

Since 1990, I have been unfailingly supported in this publication endeavour by John A.B. Allan, Ph.D., IAAP, Professor Emeritus, Department of Counselling Psychology, Faculty of Education, University of British Columbia. As author and activist in diverse enterprises he continues to propagate Dr. Jung's psychology.

I am indebted to two young typists, Zhang Liping and Jiang Lin, who could neither speak or write English, nor understand the written language, but who patiently transformed a photocopy of Dr. Layard's typed pages, over-written by my copyediting, into fair copy; this was the winter of 2000-2001. For these services I thank Winnie and Joseph Wu, proprietors of Henrose Language School, Dalian, People's Republic of China.

Dr. Ladson Hinton, of the International Association for Analytical Psychology, Seattle, had been enthusiastic upon receiving a first CD of this early typescript.

I wish to acknowledge the services of Linda Claassen and her staff of the Mandeville Collection, University of California at San Diego, for their help in my accessing material in the John Layard Archives. My research there confirmed the completeness of my typescript, and a few comments from the Archives have been incorporated into this book.

Cameron R. Hood of Vancouver provided early digital imaging, mainly of black and white illustrations; ABC Photocolour prepared the 35 mm slides of Mary's paintings for print reproduction; and Shirley Chen competently supplied sketches, diagrams, and a cover in colour. I thank Harold Hockley who kindly executed the black and white illustration of Mary's found snake. Neall Calvert was generous with copyediting tips and Mel Tobias has been most helpful and supportive from the beginning of the enterprise. John William rescued the whole in a time of crisis.

The work of Ken White and Norm Hurst, U&I type, Vancouver, who respectively designed and wrestled the mass of material into book form, is greatly appreciated. Murray W. Stein, IAAP, Zurich, kindly vetted the early book form, and Daryl sharp, IAAP, Toronto, has been helpful concerning indexing. Anthony Stadlen in London and Terry McBride, IAAP, in Sydney (a longtime Layard aficionado), also provided encouragement. Russell A. Lockhart of Everett, Washington State, has been most gracious in producing an original and glowing Foreword.

In the last stage, while Dianne Tiefensee assembled the index, Patty Osborne and Steven Osborne of Vancouver Desktop Publishing Centre smoothly eased the whole into final production.

Further indebtedness and thanks go to Dr. Christian E. Loeben, Egyptologist, the August Kestner Museum, Hannover; the British Museum, London; the Church of St. Michael at the Northgate, Oxford; Allen and Unwin, London; Thames and Hudson, London; Art Resource, New York; Dover Publications, New York; Bayerische Staatsbibliothek, Munich, and especially Dr. Wolfgang-Valentin Ikas, Abteilung f'ur Handschriften und alte Drucke; Ami Tohnberg, ARAS Picture Archives, New York; M. Hautmann, "Kunst" 1929, Plate 32; Edouard von der Heydt Donation, Rietberg Museum, Zurich; Hedi Hardmeier, Zurich; William Morrow Pub'g, New York; Niedeck Linder Agency, Zurich; and Klett-Cotta Buchhandluung, Stuttgart.

Dr Layard also expressed his gratitude to Professor C.G. Jung, Erich Neumann, Karl Kerenyi and others for permission to reproduce many images incorporated in amplification of his text.

Every effort has been made to obtain permission from copyright holders. If, regrettably, any omissions have been made, we shall be pleased to make suitable corrections in any reprint.

299

Anne S. Bosch
Studied at the C.G. Jung Institute in Zurich and analysed with Dr. M-L von Franz, Dr. Richard Pope and Dr. Gotthilf Isler. She is a member of the International Association of Jungian Studies, the International Arthurian Association and is a therapist in her native Vancouver. Anne also edited Layard's *A Celtic Quest* (Spring Publications). She has lived in six countries, taught in Switzerland and at a University in China, and is well travelled.

What do you think?

The editor would very much appreciate your input on this work. Please respond to as many questions as you wish. Thank you.

Have you read a book with references to Carl Jung before?

Did you find the intercultural comparisons interesting/appropriate?

Do you find the idea that everything, from a universal point of view, has a negative as well as a positive side?

Are you aware of Goethe's theory of colours which differs from Newton's (the one we are normally taught in school)? Are you interested in it?

Have you read other books by John Layard or Carl Jung? Which ones?

Thank you for taking the time to share your thoughts.
If you need more space for your comments, please feel free to use the back of this sheet or anything else.
Please email them to: abosch@layardsmary.com
or send by post: Carisbrooke Press, 207 Carisbrooke Crescent, North Vancouver, BC, V7N2S2, Canada